Open Rhodes
Around Britain

Open Rhodes
Around Britain

Gary Rhodes

Photographs by Anthony Blake

BBC Books

Acknowledgements

I would like to thank Nicky Copeland, Khadija Manjlai, Jacqueline Korn, Borra Garson, Anthony Blake and Joy Skipper, Clare Adkins, Petra Hurst and, in particular, Gabrielle Jackson for making the television trilogy so exciting; my kitchen team and chef friends, Stuart Busby, Wayne Tapsfield and Jane Huffer for all their time and help in putting these dishes together; the teachers and pupils of Crofton Junior School; and friends of the family Trish Mckenzie and her son Gavin, who both appear in photos in this book. I would also like to thank my wife Jennie and my two sons Sam and George for providing me with endless cups of tea, and much more! A special thank you to Alex Ferguson for building the greatest team in British football history!

This book is published to accompany the television series *Open Rhodes Around Britain*, which was first broadcast in 1996. The series was produced by BBC Education for Adults.
Executive Producer: Fiona Pitcher
Producer: Gabrielle Jackson

Published by BBC Books, an imprint of BBC Worldwide Publishing,
BBC Worldwide Limited, Woodlands, 80 Wood Lane,
London W12 0TT

First published 1996
© Gary Rhodes 1996
The moral right of the author has been asserted.

ISBN 0 563 38747 5

The recipes on pages 24, 28, 58 and 198 have previously appeared in *BBC Good Food Magazine*.

Edited by Wendy Hobson
Recipes tested by Orla Broderick
Designed by Isobel Gillan
Illustrations by Kate Simunek
Photographs by Anthony Blake
Styling by Anthony Blake and Joy Skipper
Food prepared by Gary Rhodes
Cutlery and crockery provided by Villeroy & Boch
Props and kitchen utensils from The Kitchenware Company, Richmond
Children's aprons provided by Denny's

Set in Ellington and Erhardt
Printed and bound in Great Britain by Butler & Tanner Ltd, Frome and London
Colour separations by Radstock Reproductions Ltd, Midsomer Norton
Jacket printed by Lawrence Allen Ltd, Weston-super-Mare

BACK COVER *Open Leek Tart with Warm Poached Egg*
PRECEDING PAGES (*Clockwise from top*): *Dark Chocolate Mousse, White and Dark Chocolate Mousse, White Chocolate Mousse, individual portion of White Chocolate Mousse (all on p.208), Chocolate and Prune Soufflé Cake (p.171) and Chocolate Truffle Cake (p.196).*

Contents

Introduction

Well, here we are on Rhodes Around Britain III! I would like to think that three books and television series predominantly featuring British dishes (and I'm sure we could do many more!) are proof that the British love good cooking and eating.

When my first book, *Rhodes Around Britain*, was being produced, the catering industry was only just starting to recognize British cooking. Restaurants and brasseries were featuring some of the old classics all finished with a new twist. I would like to think that now we can hold our heads high amongst chefs, cooks and all other countries as far as food is concerned.

Now the British have restaurateurs with restaurants in Paris, Australia, the United States, and many more countries, all with that Great British theme.

I often dream of running a chain of British restaurants with sites in many of the world's capital cities, showing everybody what the British can do with food. I would love to change the international feeling about British cooking. Knowing that people could visit one of these restaurants and try our faggots, stews, pies and, of course, bread and butter pudding any day of the week would be fantastic! But what am I going to call this chain: 'Planet Rhodes', 'Kentucky Fried Rhodes' or maybe 'McRhodes'? I can see them queuing up now and asking for two smoked McHaddocks with double rarebit! Somehow I'm not sure 'Planet Rhodes' would work though. Can you imagine the decor in the restaurant? Instead of film stars' motorbikes, suits, jackets and boots, you'd have chefs' hats, whisks, knives and clogs! Probably enough to put you off your food!

But seriously, it would be so exciting to be able to promote British cooking across the world. This would change our long-lasting bad reputation for food and hopefully inspire more and more people to come and see what we have to offer. I'd like to think that London (and it's spreading around the rest of the UK) is leading the way with restaurants of all varieties, and we don't seem to be running out of customers!

Good food and good company – a perfect lunch.

Which brings me on to the next point, what are customers looking for? Well, obviously a good standard of eating and service with, hopefully, a value for money price. But what sort of food? I've mentioned that I feel we have many old and more than plenty of new restaurants happening all over the UK, but let's not forget all the 'others' – and by 'others' I mean the Indian, Chinese, Thai and many more.

Every high street has at least one Indian and one Chinese restaurant or takeaway. Why do we have so many? Is it because we just like to have the convenience of eating out or takeaway food, or is it because we just love a good variety of eating? I suspect it's a combination of both. It's very handy to just be able to lift up the phone and order (and sometimes even have it delivered!), or go out with friends for a meal and try something different. But I don't think that these international cuisines are new to us any more. We take all of these varieties of cooking and foods for granted. They have become almost part of our own culinary tradition.

Shopping has become a whole new experience for me. Visiting either a megastore or, for that matter, the small market stalls in Soho, opens your eyes to new flavours and tastes. Some I've never even heard of or seen before. Such items first started to appear on one small stall or shelf and were featured as 'specialities'. Now these specialities have become part of our daily diet.

The pastry chef's idea sounds good – and tastes even better.

In 1979 I started my first job at the Amsterdam Hilton and I shall never forget my first day. I was shown into the kitchen by one of the sous-chefs and introduced to the chef-de-partie in charge of all the cold starters. As I was being introduced, he was trimming up some green, slightly furry fruits – you've guessed it, they were kiwi fruit. At the time, I was nineteen years old, I had just finished a three-year catering course and had never even heard of, let alone seen, a kiwi fruit! Now they are just another common fruit, one that we all know and enjoy. That is just a small example of how our eating habits and knowledge have changed over the years. The range of spices and herbs used in our daily cooking is quite unbelievable. Coriander has become a classic flavouring that every chef is using (including me!)

Well, I'll be honest with you. Should I? Okay I will. I'm now, as this book is being written, 36 years of age. Yes, you're right – I'm young! I often try and remember my eating habits of thirty years ago. One thing I do remember is my parents offering a peeled prawn to try. I was just terrified at the look of it; it seemed almost prehistoric looking and there was no chance at all of even thinking about eating it. I wouldn't eat sprouts, parsnips, cauliflower and certainly not those prawns! Adventurous eating 30 years ago was a tinned Fray Bentos steak and kidney pie (and those I did enjoy)!

So eating habits have changed almost like fashions, but with the wider variety of eating experiences available, I believe that children and young people will be more adventurous and enjoy eating these new dishes. I can't remember the first time I even tried a pizza but it probably wasn't until I was starting my teenage years, whereas my young children, Samuel and George, have so many more choices and are not afraid to try anything – and that's certainly not because I am a chef. It seems to be the same in most children. Some of their favourites amaze me. They eat slice after slice of spicy salami. They love curry, whereas as a child I wouldn't even smell it! There's also kabanos sausages, chicken or pork satay sticks, Italian pastas, pizzas, and as for Chinese dishes, they just can't get enough, from spicy seaweed, prawns and sesame on toast to spicy spare ribs and crispy squid.

Even in the last few years, chefs have been learning and becoming more adventurous with spices and flavours, trying to create new dishes with a different finish. Bok choi has become a fashionable vegetable, usually finished with some form of soy dressing. Chillies have become an almost natural seasoning and lemon grass and lime leaves can be found everywhere.

I'm all for discovering new tastes and flavours but also believe that you first have to learn about the flavour itself before you can think of using it. All of these spices and tastes will give you a new twist and approach to your dishes. It makes them sound very trendy and different but do they always work? Soy sauce has been around for a long time and has a very powerful flavour. I wonder how many times an ingredient like that is misused and the real fullness of a dish is not achieved.

I always tell young people who wish to come and work with me that the beauty of cooking is the never-ending variety of dishes, ideas and flavours you can create. You just can't stop learning and I have always said that since my first day at catering college when I started my course, that course has never stopped and I hope never will.

I have also said that good cooking does not always have to consist of new dishes, even with all the 'new' flavours we are finding now. Remember, cook what you believe in and what you enjoy.

Spicy flavours are popular in the late 90s just as nouvelle cuisine was the vogue in the 70s, and every chef wants to be part of it, but in so many cases we tend to run before we can walk. Elizabeth David was a communicator about foods and the understanding and cooking of them. I still find that reading her books inspires me. There is a paragraph from Elizabeth's *French Provincial Cooking* that mirrors exactly how I feel cooking should be. It's talking specifically about French cookery, but the concept really applies to all forms and styles.

'But there is one mistake we nearly all make when first attempting French cookery. We make it too complicated. A galaxy of seasonings, oceans of wine and cream, thick sauces and a mass of garnishes are alien to the whole spirit of French cookery. Does a Paris milliner put lace trimmings on a fur hat?'

This ties up perfectly with the advice of Auguste Escoffier, one of those extremely rare great chefs whose work is respected everywhere, particularly in his native France, although he spent most of his working life in other countries. Two of the most valuable words he ever wrote were these: '*Faites simple*'. By that he does not mean skimping the work or the basic ingredients; throwing together a dish anyhow and hoping for the best. That is the crude rather than the simple approach. What I think he does mean is that we should avoid unnecessary complication and elaboration. To prove the point, try simplifying a recipe, which calls for rather a lot of ingredients, down to the barest essentials. You may well find that the dish is more pleasing in its primitive form and then you will know that your original recipe was too fanciful. If, on the other hand, the simplified dish seems to lack flavour, to be a little bleak or insipid, start building it up again. By the end of this process you will have discovered what is essential to that dish, what are the extras which enhance it, and at what point it is spoilt by over-elaboration. This system is also useful in teaching one how to judge a recipe for oneself instead of following it blindly from a cookery book.

So now that I've expressed to you feeling about foods and flavours, what about this book? The reason I have included styles from different cuisines is because I do feel they have become a very strong part of British eating. The ones I have included are simple to prepare and of course very tasty to eat.

This is the third of my books, giving us a trilogy full of recipes which provide you with more variations than ever in your eating and cooking. I work on the principle of giving you as many options as possible; but if you don't have the time to cook the 'main' recipe then why not have a go at the simpler variations. Almost every recipe has its own introduction, some giving you finer details of the ingredients used (especially unusual ones) as well as the simple variations. I do hope you are going to enjoy reading the book and, even more, cooking from it.

There's another line from Escoffier, the master of classic French chefs who was at the Savoy in London and who introduced the classics to us, which sums up his philosophy of cooking – and mine.

'*La bonne cuisine est la base du véritable bonheur.*'

I think you can translate it in the way that feels right for you, and for me it reads, 'good cooking is the base to good living'. I do hope you feel the same way.

GARY RHODES

Notes on the Recipes

1 Follow one set of measurements only; do not mix metric and imperial.

2 Eggs are size 2.

3 Wash fresh produce before preparation.

4 Spoon measurements are level.

5 A tablespoon is 15 ml; a teaspoon is 5 ml.

6 If you substitute dried for fresh herbs, use only half the amount specified.

7 Mixed herb tea bags are readily available and can be used as an alternative to bouquets garnis.

8 Unless otherwise stated, 'season' or 'seasoning' simple means seasoning with salt and pepper.

9 I recommend Bournville chocolate where recipes call for 'good quality plain chocolate'.

10 When blind-baking pastry cases, it is best to leave the excess pastry hanging over the rim. Once the pastry is cooked, simply trim off the edges to give a neat even finish.

11 Gas guns can be used to give a crispy sugar glaze to many desserts. It is important to be fully aware of how to operate and use the gun as this is not a conventional kitchen utensil. And, obviously, gas guns should not be used by children.

12 Oven temperatures and cooking times are flexible and may vary according to the equipment and ingredients used.

13 Butter and cream may be reduced, if not excluded, in most savoury recipes.

14 Ingredients are listed with the most important ingredient(s) first, followed by the other ingredients in order of use.

Soups, Starters and More!

I f you are wondering what or where the 'more' is, well remember, this book is part of a trilogy and my previous two had 'soups, starters and snacks' and 'soups, starters and main courses', so I just couldn't leave this one out. What the 'more' actually means is both of those extras. Many of these dishes can be turned into snacks – try the omelettes, scrambled eggs and salads. As for main courses, well I think that just about every dish can be turned into one.

ABOVE *Open Leek Tart with Warm Poached Egg*
(see p.28).
LEFT *Red Mullet Broth (see p.20).*

Order of the day: buying ingredients while the boys cook.

A lot of the starters that are featured here can be bought already made, in particular the pork and chicken satay sticks. However, once you've made these yourselves I doubt you'll buy them again. They are so simple to make and, with your own peanut sauce, eat so well.

One of my favourites from this chapter is the Griddled Scallops with Cabbage and Smoked Salmon (see p.30). The flavour of the scallops is beautifully tender with the seared edges giving you an almost caramel tinge. The cabbage and smoked salmon could stand as a complete dish on their own. The flavour of the Mustard Dressing (see p.271) biting into the cabbage and warm smoked salmon is sensational. Salmon and mustard is a classic combination so you can imagine just how well it works. I've also eaten it with a warm poached egg on top. Once the yolk is broken into and trickles and mingles into the dressing and is eaten with the cabbage and smoked salmon … I don't think I need to tell you any more!

Most of these dishes also have a very British feel about them. There are also scallops with bacon, mackerel with red cabbage, crab dumplings, kippers on toast, scrambled eggs, black pudding and fried sandwiches.

So all you have to do is cook them and eat them!

Simple Salad

This salad is as simple as its title. It eats very well as a vegetarian main course, starter, or goes with so many other dishes, such as Blackened Chicken (see p.81). The chicken can be cooked on an open barbecue, then served sitting on this salad. A great dish all year round but especially good in the summer.

These are not strict measures for the ingredients, but give you an idea how to balance the flavours. It's really a handful of each mixed with salad leaves – Little Gems, rocket and baby spinach work very well. The artichoke hearts are to be found in delicatessens or large supermarkets. These are sold loose and are usually marinated in olive oil and herb dressing. If the salad is going to be a starter, then work on approximately half a choke per portion; for a main course use one choke per portion. Adjust the quantity of salad leaves according to how you are serving the salad.

SERVES 4

175–225 g (6–8 oz) fine French beans
4 artichoke hearts preserved in oil
Mixed salad leaves such as Little Gem, rocket and baby spinach
25 g (1 oz) black olives, stoned and halved
2 spring onions, shredded

2 plum or salad tomatoes, cut into 8 wedges
½ small red pepper, seeded and cut into wafer-thin strips
6 tablespoons Spicy Tomato Dressing (see p.269)

The French beans must be topped and tailed, blanched for 1 minute in boiling salted water, then refreshed in cold running water to retain their rich colour and bite. All you need to do with the artichoke hearts is quarter them lengthways, including the stalk. Mix all the ingredients together in a bowl, spoon in the dressing and toss together gently so that it coats all the ingredients. The salad is ready to eat.

Variations

Other flavours that can be added to the salad or sprinkled on top are: chopped fresh herbs such as basil, tarragon or parsley; fried bread croûtons or toasts; freshly grated Parmesan.

Pistou Salad

'Pistou' is really a Provençal soup made in a similar way to minestrone, but much simpler and without the dried haricots or butter beans. It's usually made with potatoes, French beans, onions and tomatoes, then finished with garlic, basil and Gruyère.

Well, I decided to take some of those flavours and treat this dish almost like a pistou/minestrone – no strict rules but containing the bare essentials. All these flavours except the salad leaves can be made into a soup with the addition of some vegetable stock.

SERVES 6–8

3–4 Pickled Red Onions (see p.98)
8–12 small new potatoes, cooked and
    kept warm
Salt and freshly ground black pepper
Juice of $\frac{1}{2}$ lemon
225 g (8 oz) fine French beans
4 tablespoons Pesto Sauce (see p.281)
4–6 small globe artichokes preserved in
    olive oil, quartered

$\frac{1}{2}$ bunch of spring onions, shredded
2–3 plum or salad tomatoes, cut into
    8 wedges
A few black olives, stoned and halved
50 g (2 oz) salad leaves such as baby
    spinach, rocket
Parmesan flakes

Prepare the red onions, reserving the marinating liquor for the dressing. The new potatoes, should be halved, then seasoned before you squeeze the lemon over them. Blanch the French beans in boiling salted water for 1 minute, then drain well and refresh in iced water.

To make the dressing, mix the pesto sauce with 3–4 tablespoons of the red onion liquor to give you a richer and looser pesto dressing.

I prefer to keep just the potatoes and onions warm and mix and season with the other ingredients, adding the salad leaves at the last minute, then dressing carefully on plates. Finish with some Parmesan flakes and good crusty bread.

Variation

To make the same recipe into a soup, just cook the onions in a little olive oil, add some cooked new potatoes, tomatoes, black olives and artichokes and cook for a few minutes. Top with some Vegetable Stock (see p.259) and cook for 8–10 minutes. To finish, add the spring onions, French beans and pesto sauce. Serve the soup with Parmesan flakes and good crusty bread.

TOP *Pistou Soup.*
BOTTOM *Pistou Salad.*

Watercress, Spinach and Parmesan Salad with Cider Vinegar and Mustard Dressing

This is a great vegetarian starter, main course or side salad recipe; it really can be any of these. Its simple ingredients are complemented by a good sweet dressing that has a bite. The recipe makes about 350 ml (12 fl oz) of dressing; any left over will keep well, chilled, for a few days.

This is a very basic recipe that can have so many combinations: spring onions, garlic croûtons, French beans and lots more tastes can be added. The cider dressing can also be used in salads of your choice. I sometimes use it to season and flavour spinach to go with pork dishes.

SERVES 6–8 as a starter

2–3 bunches of watercress, about 100 g (4 oz)
100 g (4 oz) baby spinach leaves (*pousses épinards*)

100 g (4 oz) Parmesan, flaked, or 50 g (2 oz) Parmesan, freshly grated

For the Cider Dressing

1½ tablespoons cider vinegar
1 heaped teaspoon caster sugar
1 egg
1 egg yolk

2 teaspoons Dijon mustard
300 ml (10 fl oz) groundnut oil
Salt and freshly ground black pepper

To make the dressing, warm the cider vinegar with the sugar, then allow to cool. Mix the egg and egg yolk with the mustard and add the sugared vinegar. Whisk the ingredients together, then gradually add the groundnut oil a drop at a time, whisking continuously, as you would when making mayonnaise. Season with salt and pepper.

Sprinkle the dressing over the mixed salad leaves and Parmesan, then divide between individual plates or serve in a large bowl for everybody to help themselves.

Kipper Rarebit on Toast

Kippers simply cooked in milk with butter or just grilled eat really well. The wonderful, silky soft texture of the flakes work in salads, risottos and now with my cheese on toast!

Of course, this dish doesn't have to be just a snack, it eats well as a starter or main course. I sometimes like to serve the poached flakes of kipper on spinach topped with some rarebit and glazed until golden, then finished with a warm poached egg. When you break the egg and eat it with the rarebit, kipper and spinach – well, it's a dream.

Here's the recipe for 'kipper cheese on toast'! I have included the rarebit recipe but of course you may already have it from Rhodes Around Britain. *It also eats well if tomatoes have been sliced and laid on the toast first.*

MAKES 6 slices

2 kippers	A knob of unsalted butter
150–300 ml (5–10 fl oz) milk	6 thick slices of bread

For the Rarebit

225 g (8 oz) Cheddar	1 tablespoon fresh white breadcrumbs
2 tablespoons milk	1 teaspoon English mustard powder
1 small garlic clove, crushed	A few shakes of Worcestershire sauce
Fine pinch of paprika	Freshly ground black pepper
1 tablespoon plain flour	1 egg, beaten

Place the kippers in a pan and cover with milk and butter. Bring to the boil, remove from the heat and leave to stand for 5–6 minutes. Lift the kippers from the pan and trim off all skin and bones. You should have 225 g (8 oz) of flesh.

To make the rarebit, melt together the Cheddar and milk with the garlic and paprika. When the mixture becomes smooth, add the flour, breadcrumbs and mustard powder and cook for a few minutes until the mixture comes away from the sides of the pan. Add the Worcestershire sauce and season with pepper. Leave to cool slightly. While just warm, beat in the egg. The mix is now ready.

Pre-heat the grill. At this stage, the kipper should be broken into flakes. Now add enough of the rarebit to the kipper to bind together. Toast the bread. Spoon and spread the kipper rarebit on the toast and place under the grill until golden. The dish is ready to eat.

Note

The remaining rarebit mix will keep for up to a week refrigerated, or it can be frozen.

Red Mullet Broth

This soup can be a broth or have a bisque-like consistency. If you'd prefer a thicker soup without the grilled fish fillets, then simply follow the recipe, blitz and push through a sieve and the soup is made. That recipe was featured in Rhodes Around Britain. *This one has a totally different taste and texture. It's just a question of making a good stock and then garnishing it. I've also included, as an optional extra, some slices of crispy Bayonne or Parma ham. I like the edge they give the dish. A good quality streaky or back bacon can also be crisped and served for a bit of extra taste.*

MAKES 1.2 litres (2 pints) to serve 4

For the Stock

350 g (12 oz) red mullet, fresh or frozen
1 onion, cut into rough 1 cm ($\frac{1}{2}$ in) dice
1 carrot, cut into rough 1 cm ($\frac{1}{2}$ in) dice
1 leek, cut into rough 1 cm ($\frac{1}{2}$ in) dice
2–3 celery sticks, cut into rough 1 cm
    ($\frac{1}{2}$ in) dice
1 fennel bulb, cut into rough 1 cm
    ($\frac{1}{2}$ in) dice
1 garlic clove, crushed
$\frac{1}{2}$ bunch of fresh tarragon or a few dried
    tarragon leaves

A pinch of saffron (optional)
1 star anise (optional)
A knob of unsalted butter
4 tomatoes, quartered
2 glasses white wine, about 300 ml
    (10 fl oz)
1.2 litres (2 pints) Fish Stock (see
    p.260) or water with an extra 100g
    (4 oz) of red mullet to improve the
    finished taste

For the Fish and Soup

4 small red mullet fillets (1 per portion)
1 tablespoon olive oil
1 large carrot, cut into 5 mm ($\frac{1}{4}$ in) dice
1 large onion, cut into 5 mm ($\frac{1}{4}$ in) dice
2 celery sticks, cut into 5 mm ($\frac{1}{4}$ in) dice
1 small fennel bulb, cut into 5 mm
    ($\frac{1}{4}$ in) dice (optional)

Red mullet stock from above
Salt and freshly ground black pepper
12–16 × 1 cm ($\frac{1}{2}$ in) strips of Bayonne or
    Parma ham
2 tomatoes, skinned and diced
25 g (1 oz) unsalted butter
A few fresh tarragon leaves, chopped

To make the stock, cook the vegetables with the garlic, herbs, saffron and star anise, if using, in the knob of butter for a few minutes until beginning to soften. Add the tomatoes and continue to cook. Chop through the red mullet, including head and bones. Add the fish and cook for another 2–3 minutes. If you are using water rather than stock, add the additional fish as well. Now add the white wine, bring to the boil to reduce by three-quarters. Add the fish stock or water and bring to a simmer. This can now be cooked for 20–30 minutes, allowing the stock to reduce a little as it cooks to increase the flavour. The stock can now be strained through a sieve. You will have a loose red mullet stock ready to make into soup.

Pre-heat the grill.

To make the soup, warm the olive oil in a pan and add the diced vegetables. Cook without colour for 6–8 minutes until softened. Add the red mullet stock and bring to a simmer and cook for 10 minutes. While the soup is cooking, butter a tray and sit the seasoned red mullet fillets on top. These can now be cooked under the grill and will only take between 3–4 minutes. Grill the Bayonne or Parma ham until golden and crispy.

Add the tomato dice and butter to the soup and season with salt and pepper. Add the tarragon. The soup can now be served in soup plates with a grilled red mullet fillet sitting on top. The ham can be sprinkled on top. The broth is now ready to eat and enjoy.

Variation

As you can see from the picture if you are including bacon or ham, you can use sage leaves instead of tarragon. Then it's best to flour them lightly and fry in a deep-fat fryer at 180°C/350°F or in hot oil at least 1 cm (½ in) deep, for 1–2 minutes until crispy.

Red Mullet Broth.

Chilled Tomato Soup

This is almost like a puréed gazpacho. It's a lovely soup for a hot summer day when you've got the whole family to feed. Just some good bread and this soup will do for lunch. This recipe gives you good quantity and keeps very well chilled. If the tomatoes are not quite as ripe as you would like, adding 2 teaspoons of caster sugar to the tomatoes will add a little sweetness to the flavour.

MAKES 1.5 litres (2½ pints) to serve 6–8

4 tablespoons red wine vinegar
1 garlic clove
150 ml (5 fl oz) olive oil

1 teaspoon caster sugar (optional)
Salt and freshly ground black pepper

For the Stock

675 g (1½ lb) plum or salad tomatoes,
   blanched, skinned and seeded
400 g (14 oz) tinned red pimentos
½ Ogen or Charentais melon, skinned
   and seeds removed
½ cucumber, peeled and seeded

10–12 fresh basil leaves
250 ml (8 fl oz) Vegetable Stock
   (see p.259)
100 g (4 oz) good quality fresh white
   breadcrumbs

First blitz the stock ingredients to a purée in a food processor or liquidizer. Now blitz the wine vinegar, garlic, olive oil and sugar, then mix the two together and push through a sieve. The soup is now made and should be checked for seasoning with salt and pepper, before eating and enjoying.

Mulligatawny Soup

This is a wonderful winter soup. When it's freezing cold outside, just sit and eat a bowl of this to warm you through and through. This recipe has two varieties: chicken or vegetarian. Both work equally well.

The list of ingredients does look a bit daunting, but all these flavours work and give you a very tasty soup. However, not all are essential, in particular the soy, teriyaki and Worcestershire sauces. These are flavours that I have added that I've found help release other tastes. The soup can be garnished with plain boiled rice and, if it's not vegetarian, poached strips of chicken. Plenty of choice and even more taste!

MAKES 1.2 litres (2 pints) to serve 4–6

1 potato, chopped into 1 cm ($\frac{1}{2}$ in) dice
1 large carrot, chopped into 1 cm ($\frac{1}{2}$ in) dice
1 large onion, chopped into 1 cm ($\frac{1}{2}$ in) dice
1 leek, chopped into 1 cm ($\frac{1}{2}$ in) dice
2 celery sticks, chopped into 1 cm ($\frac{1}{2}$ in) dice
1 garlic clove, crushed
1 teaspoon crushed fresh ginger root
$\frac{1}{2}$ teaspoon chopped fresh thyme
1 teaspoon ground turmeric
1 teaspoon cayenne pepper
1 teaspoon paprika
$\frac{1}{4}$ teaspoon dried chopped chillies
$\frac{1}{4}$ teaspoon cumin seeds
1 star anise
1 bay leaf
$\frac{1}{2}$ teaspoon mixed spice
2 tomatoes, quartered
3 tablespoons soy sauce (optional)
3 tablespoons teriyaki sauce (optional)
1 tablespoon Worcestershire sauce (optional)
1.2 litres (2 pints) Chicken Stock (see p.258) or Vegetable Stock (see p.259)
A knob of unsalted butter
Salt

Melt the butter in a pan, stir in the chopped vegetables, then add all the other ingredients except the stock. Stir and cook over a moderate heat for a few minutes. Cover with a lid and allow the vegetables to soften, stirring occasionally. Add the stock and bring to a simmer. The soup should now cook for 45 minutes.

Once cooked, blitz in a food processor or liquidizer, then push through a sieve. This will give you a good thick curried soup. Check for seasoning with salt. Add the chicken and boiled rice, if using, just before serving.

Variations

Another flavour that can be added is a squeeze of fresh lemon juice, which enhances all the tastes. Or if you would like it slightly sweeter, then add a tablespoon of honey. Chopped apple can also be cooked in the soup for a fruity taste.

Six Oyster and Leek Soup

Oyster soup is a lovely way to eat oysters. Each portion of the soup is finished by adding six fresh oysters and all their juices. I normally make the soup with an oyster fish stock. This is made by adding some defrosted frozen oysters (12 oysters to 600 ml (1 pint) of stock) to a home-made or ready-made basic fish stock to give a good oyster taste. After the stock has been made, the remaining ingredients for the soup are very simple: shallots, leeks and, of course, fresh oysters.

MAKES 1.2 litres (2 pints) to serve 4

2 leeks, thinly sliced
24 fresh oysters, opened and kept in oyster juices
2 teaspoons olive oil
50 g (2 oz) unsalted butter
4 large shallots or 2 onions, sliced

1–2 glasses of Champagne or sparkling wine, about 150–300 ml (5–10 fl oz) (optional)
900 ml ($1\frac{1}{2}$ pints) Fish Stock (see p.260) or oyster stock (see above)
1 teaspoon chopped fresh tarragon
Salt and freshly ground black pepper

Warm the olive oil and 15 g ($\frac{1}{2}$ oz) of the butter in a pan, add the sliced shallots or onions and cook without colouring until they begin to soften. It's also good to add 1 or 2 glasses of Champagne as an extra and then boil to reduce until almost dry. We all know how well oysters and Champagne taste together. Add the stock and bring to a simmer. The soup only needs to simmer for 10 minutes before being ready to finish.

To finish, bring the soup to the boil and add the sliced leeks. The leeks will only take 1–2 minutes to become tender. The remaining butter can now be added and stirred in. Add the chopped tarragon and the fresh oysters with any remaining juices. Check for seasoning with salt and pepper and the soup is ready. Once the soup is complete and the oysters have been added, do not re-boil as this will overcook them. The soup should only be brought back to a soft simmer, then removed from the heat.

To serve, divide the oysters into bowls, then finish with remaining soup and garnish.

How to Open Oysters

Keep the fresh oysters chilled until you are ready to finish the soup. Protect your hand with a cloth, and lay the oyster rounded-side down in your hand so that you can catch the juices as you open it. Insert an oyster knife between the shells near the hinge and lever the shells apart. Pour any juices into a bowl through a fine sieve and add to the soup as described above. Gently loosen the oyster from the bottom shell with a sharp knife. They are now ready to use.

Crab Bisque

Try this with my Crab Dumplings (see p.34) – the flavours obviously work so well together, it's delicious! This soup, which also works as a sauce, can take on some garnishes: perhaps add some chopped tomatoes, leeks and basil to finish it or even the whitemeat from the crab? You can also keep the whitemeat for a good crab salad.

MAKES 900 ml (1½ pints) to serve 4

1 cooked crab shell, broken into small pieces
2 tablespoons cooking oil
1 medium carrot, roughly chopped into 1 cm (½ in) pieces
1 onion, roughly chopped into 1 cm (½ in) pieces
½ leek, roughly chopped into 1 cm (½ in) pieces
1 2 celery sticks, roughly chopped into 1 cm (½ in) pieces
1 garlic clove, crushed

1 small fennel bulb, chopped, or 1 star anise (optional)
A few fresh tarragon leaves
1 few strands of fresh saffron (optional)
4–6 tomatoes, quartered
1 glass of brandy, about 50 ml (2 fl oz)
1 glass of dry white wine, about 150 ml (5 fl oz)
2 teaspoons tomato purée
900 ml (1½ pints) fish stock, crab cooking liquor or water
40 g (1½ oz) unsalted butter (optional)

Heat the oil in a large pan and add the chopped vegetables, garlic, fennel or star anise, tarragon and saffron. Add the crab shell, cover with a lid and cook for 10–15 minutes to soften the vegetables. Add the tomatoes and continue to cook for a further 5–6 minutes. Add the brandy and boil to reduce by two-thirds, then add the white wine and boil to reduce by two-thirds again. Add the tomato purée and stock and bring to a simmer. Leave to simmer gently for 30 minutes. Blitz the soup in a food processor or liquidizer, then push through a sieve to give a thicker consistency. The bisque will now be packed with crab flavour. If it's too thick, then simply loosen with more stock or water.

Note

The crab cooking liquor listed in the ingredients can be made simply by cooking the crab shells in fish stock or water first. This will give you a good crab stock, maximising the taste. The bisque can be used as a sauce, which eats very well if finished with a dot of cream and a squeeze of lemon.

Chicken or Pork Satay Sticks

Here's a quick and easy marinade for chicken or pork (fish can also be used) that lifts the whole flavour of the complete dish, rather than the sauce trying to do that on its own.

For the meat to really take on the taste it's best to make at least 8 hours in advance and for a really strong flavour, 24 hours.

This recipe will give you approximately 16 half-filled 15 cm (6 in) bamboo skewers (a starter portion will need 3–4 sticks). If you prefer pork I always use loin or pork fillet; both are very tender when cooked.

SERVES 2–4

4 chicken breasts or 450–675 g (1–1½ lb)
     pork loin or fillet

For the Marinade

6 tablespoons soy sauce
6 tablespoons teriyaki sauce/marinade
1 large garlic clove, crushed

1 teaspoon finely chopped fresh root
     ginger
1 teaspoon chopped fresh coriander

For the Peanut Sauce

225 g (8 oz) crunchy peanut butter
3 garlic cloves, crushed
15 fresh coriander leaves
50 ml (2 fl oz) soy sauce

2 tablespoons Japanese sake
¼–½ teaspoon chilli oil
120 ml (4 fl oz) coconut milk
Water

TOP LEFT *Prawns and Sesame on Toast (see p.32).*
TOP RIGHT *Soy sauce.*
BOTTOM *Chicken and Pork Satay Sticks.*

Cut the chicken or pork into a small dice no bigger than 1 cm (½ in). These cubes can now be pushed on to soaked 15 cm (6 in) bamboo skewers, only covering half of each skewer with the meat.

Mix together all the marinade ingredients. The kebabs can now be placed in the marinade, covered with clingfilm and chilled for a minimum of 8 hours to achieve a good taste. If you can leave them for 24 hours you really will have the maximum taste. The quantity of marinade should be enough to cover all the meat. If all is not covered, then simply turn every 2 hours.

To make the sauce, blend the peanut butter with the garlic and coriander in a food processor or liquidizer. In a separate jug, mix the soy sauce, sake, chilli oil and coconut milk. With the motor running, pour the mixture slowly into the processor until all the liquid has blended in. The sauce should be thick but not set like peanut butter. If the sauce is too thick, just loosen it by adding a tablespoon of water at a time.

The kebabs are now ready to cook. The cooking process is really now up to you. These can be brushed in oil or butter and then fried, grilled or barbecued, taking 6–8 minutes. Meanwhile, warm the sauce in a pan, or serve it cold if you prefer (either eats very well).

Open Leek Tart with Warm Poached Egg

This is a dish that has few ingredients but many flavours. Leeks themselves hold many tastes, giving different strengths from the white to the green. If thin pencil leeks cannot be found, then simply buy standard leeks and split them lengthways. The crispy pastry base has a good texture, and sitting the warm poached egg on top and tasting the yolk mix with all the other flavours is sensational. On top of all that, it's also a wonderful vegetarian starter or main course dish.

SERVES 4

½ quantity Shortcrust Pastry (see p.251)
8 thin pencil leeks, about 1 cm (½ in) thick
4 eggs
A knob of unsalted butter
Salt and freshly ground black pepper

About 4 tablespoons Red Wine Dressing (see p.274)
4 teaspoons walnut oil
2 teaspoons roughly chopped fresh flatleaf parsley

Pre-heat the oven to 200°C/400°F/gas 6. Line a baking tray with greaseproof paper. Roll out the pastry 1–2 mm thick and cut into 4 × 10 cm (4 in) discs. Rest the pastry discs on the lined baking tray, then cook the pre-heated oven for 8–10 minutes until golden and crispy. To keep them flat, cover with another sheet of greaseproof paper and a light ovenproof baking tray.

The leeks should be trimmed and washed, leaving them whole. Bring a large pan of salted water to the boil and add the leeks. Cook for 1–3 minutes, depending on the size of the leeks. Drain, then refresh in iced water. Lightly squeeze the leeks to remove excess water, then cut into 6 cm (2½ in) sticks.

To poach the eggs, fill a small pan with a mixture of two-thirds water and one-third malt vinegar; the high quantity of vinegar will immediately hold the egg white around the yolk. Bring to the boil, then break in the eggs and poach for 3–3½ minutes. If you wish to cook these early, then simply refresh in iced water, then re-heat later in boiling water for about 1 minute.

To finish the dish, melt a knob of butter in a pan, add the leeks, season with salt and pepper and heat through for 2–3 minutes. Sit the pastry discs in shallow soup bowls or on plates and spoon some of the red wine dressing around. Add the remaining dressing to the leeks, then divide them between the discs and sit the warm poached eggs on top. To finish, mix the walnut oil mixed with the chopped parsley and trickle over the top.

Seared Scallops and Watercress Salad with Smoked Bacon and Parsley

This recipe uses two dressings that are featured in other dishes in the book but, when all is put together, you have a completely different finished result in texture and taste. This is one of the beauties of cooking, being able to turn flavours to each other and get different results with maximum flavour. The smokiness of the bacon working with the sweet-bitter flavour of seared scallops is sensational!

I have listed 1–2 bunches of watercress because bunches come in various sizes! A handful of sprigs will be enough per portion.

SERVES 4

12 large scallops, cleaned and trimmed
1–2 bunches of watercress
2 tomatoes, blanched and skinned
4 rashers smoked streaky bacon
Oil for frying
A knob of unsalted butter

8 tablespoons Mustard Dressing
  (see p.271)
1 tablespoon chopped fresh flatleaf
  parsley
Salt and freshly ground black pepper
3–4 tablespoons Cider Dressing
  (see p.18)

The watercress should be picked into sprigs, removing only the coarse base of the stalks. Cut the skinned tomatoes into quarters, then into 5 mm ($\frac{1}{4}$ in) dice. Cut the rashers of bacon into thin strips. These can now be fried in a hot pan, literally just brushed with oil, as the fat content in the bacon strips will melt in the pan. The bacon will take 5–6 minutes to fry and become very crispy, almost a crackling texture.

The scallops can now be cooked in a very hot pan or griddle, also just brushed with oil and with a knob of butter added. The scallops will only take a few minutes to cook, giving an almost crisp edge and very succulent centre.

To serve, warm the mustard dressing, adding the bacon, tomato and chopped parsley and seasoning with salt and pepper. Dress the watercress sprigs with the cider dressing. Spoon some of the finished mustard dressing on to the plates and sit 3 scallops per portion on top. Finish the dish with a handful of the watercress sprigs in the centre. It is now ready to eat and enjoy.

Griddled Scallops with Cabbage and Smoked Salmon

Scallops must be one of almost every chef's favourite ingredients. Fresh from the shell and cooked a minute later, you can't get much fresher.

One of the most important things to remember with scallops, as with most fish, is not to mask their delicate sweet flavour, only enhance it. With this dish I feel we're doing just that. It works and eats so well – all the tastes helping each other.

SERVES 4

12 large scallops, cleaned and trimmed
½ small Savoy cabbage, about 175 g
   (6 oz)
100 g (4 oz) smoked salmon
Oil for frying

2–3 tablespoons water
A knob of unsalted butter
Salt and freshly ground black pepper
3–4 tablespoons Mustard Dressing
   (see p.271)

Remove the dark outside leaves from the cabbage and cut the rest into quarters. The cabbage can now be cut into 1 cm (½ in) strips. The slices of smoked salmon can now also be cut into similar-sized pieces or thinner julienne strips. The dish is now ready to finish.

Heat a frying-pan or griddle plate and trickle with a little oil. Place the scallops in the hot frying-pan or on the griddle. It is very important to cook scallops in a hot pan to seal in all the juices and not create a stewing effect. The scallops should be turned when half-cooked and seasoned with salt and pepper. Cook for no more than 1–2 minutes in total.

At the same time, heat a pan and add the water and butter. Once the water and butter are boiling, add the cabbage. Season with salt and pepper and keep turning in the pan. The cabbage will only take 1–2 minutes and it's best eaten when just becoming tender but still has some texture. Add the smoked salmon to the cabbage, check for seasoning and add the mustard dressing. This will mix with the cooking liquor which balances the mustard taste.

To serve, simply spoon the cabbage and smoked salmon at the top of the plates and finish with some of the mustard dressing liquor and griddled scallops sitting in front.

Variations

A drop of fresh lemon juice will fire up the liquor even more.

If you don't like mustard, then either leave it out altogether – the dish still eats well – or add a little grated fresh horseradish and snipped fresh chives. Both flavours work well with the cabbage and scallops.

If you can't find good fresh scallops, then simply use another fresh fish, such as monkfish, to go with the cabbage and smoked salmon.

Griddled Scallops with Cabbage and Smoked Salmon.

Prawns and Sesame on Toast

Whenever I eat at a Chinese/Szechuan restaurant Ha To Sie *are always my first choice. They have become regular favourites. I've always wanted to know exactly how the dish is made, so you can imagine how happy I was to get hold of this recipe. I'm sure there are endless different recipes for this dish, but as I have always said, that's one of the beauties of cooking.*

This recipe is also easy to make. It's more or less just blitzed in a food processor, spread on toast and sprinkled with sesame seeds. Then just fry the toast. The bread is best when 1–2 days old. This allows it to dry slightly and move on from the doughy texture.

You can eat the toasts as starters, snacks or canapés. I like to eat them with just a squeeze of lemon but they also eat very well with Peanut Sauce (see p.26).

SERVES 4–6

275 g (10 oz) raw prawns	2 tablespoons chopped fresh coriander
2 tablespoons chopped spring onions	½ green chilli, finely chopped
2 tablespoons chopped water chestnuts	A pinch of salt
2 teaspoons grated fresh root ginger	6 slices of bread
1 teaspoon cornflour	2 tablespoons sesame seeds
1 egg white	Oil for deep- or shallow-frying

Place all the ingredients except the bread and sesame seeds in a food processor or liquidizer and blitz till all are combined. The mix is now ready to spread on to the bread. Once the mix is on the bread, sprinkle a teaspoon or two of sesame seeds over each slice and cut off the crusts. The prawns on toast are now ready to cook. Another plus with this dish is how well it keeps, and it can be prepared several hours in advance then just chilled until needed.

Pre-heat the oil to 180°C/350°F. Fry the toasts for about 1–1½ minutes on each side or until golden, then cut each slice into 8 triangles or fingers before serving.

Note

The raw prawns listed in the ingredients does mean raw and not the normal pink cooked prawns. This gives you a better paste texture to spread on the toasts. A good prawn to use is a raw frozen white king prawn. These come from Thailand and have a very thin, soft shell. They also come with the heads already removed. With the soft shell there is no need to peel them first. Simply blitz and the shell breaks down.

Basic pink peeled prawns can be used and will work, but you may find you will need an extra egg white to help hold the mix together.

Smoked Eel Pâté

As you know by now, I love having as many variations as possible with all my recipes. Well, this recipe is no exception: its variations are plenty. I made this recipe in a limousine driving along Fifth Avenue in New York for my Christmas Special television show in 1995. I think that tells you just how easy this recipe must be.

Smoked eel is a fish we don't see and taste enough of. It has a very meaty texture and is succulent to eat. Although, of course, if you don't have smoked eel, you can use any smoked fish for this pâté and it will taste equally delicious: smoked salmon, mackerel or trout will work just as well.

You can serve the pâté in many different ways. It can simply be set in a bowl and eaten immediately, or firmed in the fridge (if you're making it well in advance, then top it with the thinnest layer of melted butter). It can be rolled in clingfilm and chilled, then sliced into rounds, or set in a small or individual terrine moulds. It's a great dish to have as a starter, snack, canapé, or perhaps as a salad or part of your buffet. I also use it as part of a main course dish. Just some good fillet of fresh fish grilled, then topped with a slice of the pâté melting over. It looks really good and tastes even better.

SERVES 4

100 g (4 oz) smoked eel or other smoked
    fish fillet, chopped
50 g (2 oz) unsalted butter

3 tablespoons Crème Fraîche (see p.275)
Salt and freshly ground black pepper

The quickest way to make this is to blitz the smoked eel or fish in a food processor or liquidizer until puréed. Add the butter and blitz again. All you have to do now is add the crème fraîche and season with salt and pepper. If you are adding extra flavours (see Variations), work them in at the same time. Your pâté is now ready – it takes just minutes to make!

If you have used a food processor, the pâté will be of a smooth consistency. If you'd prefer a coarser texture, then simply dice the fish quite small and just work in the butter and crème fraîche with a spoon.

Variations

Any or all these flavours can be mixed in to sharpen and fire the taste of your pâté: a squeeze of fresh lemon juice; a pinch of cayenne pepper; 1 teaspoon English or Dijon mustard; 1 teaspoon snipped fresh chives; 1 teaspoon chopped spring onions.

Crab Dumplings

Here's another dish that has come from one recipe, had a small change and become something completely different. The dumpling recipe started in More Rhodes Around Britain *made with bone marrow. It's also featured in this book made with horseradish to go with tuna (see p.68). These dumplings will go so well with the Red Mullet Broth (see p.20), Mulligatawny Soup (see p.23), home-made Crab Bisque (see p.25) or even just tinned bisque. Or perhaps you could feature these as a fish starter using a tin of bisque finished with a squeeze of fresh lemon juice and dot of cream or Crème Fraîche (see p.275) as your sauce. They also eat very well with the Spinach with Soured Lime Cream and Spicy Curry Dressing from the halibut recipe on p.64.*

MAKES 4 large or 8 small dumplings

100 g (4 oz) white crab meat
100 g (4 oz) fresh white breadcrumbs
2 tablespoons double cream
3 egg yolks

Salt and freshly ground black pepper
Freshly grated nutmeg
600 ml (1 pint) Fish Stock (see p.260)
    or water for poaching

Place the breadcrumbs, double cream and egg yolks in a food processor or liquidizer and season with salt, pepper and nutmeg. Blitz until thoroughly mixed. Before adding the crab meat, make sure it has been checked for any shell. Fold the crab into the mix, then chill for 1 hour before cooking.

Once set, heat the fish stock or water to simmering point. The dumplings can now be shaped between two serving spoons or rolled into balls by hand and dropped into the liquor. Bring back to a simmer and cook large dumplings for 8–10 minutes and small for 5–6 minutes. Remove from the stock with a slotted spoon and serve immediately.

Variation

The dumplings also work very well shallow-fried for about 5 minutes.

Devilled Herring Fingers

Devilled whitebait must be one of the first dishes you're taught at catering college. It's a real classic and a dish that I still enjoy. However, eating fish heads, tails and so on is not to everyone's taste! So something that I do from time to time is replace the whitebait with herring fillets. These just need to be cut into fingers, dipped in milk and flour and fried.

Whitebait is often served as a starter with just a squeeze of lemon, but the herring fingers can be the dish of your choice: perhaps a crispy fried herring salad or with a barbecue dip. The herrings also work very well as a garnish for another fish dish, such as roasted salmon with spicy crisp herrings.

I like to eat the fingers as appetizers. They really get the taste buds going when served in a bowl with a good lemon mayonnaise or soured cream dip.

SERVES 4

4–6 large herring fillets, trimmed and cleaned	4 tablespoons milk
4 heaped tablespoons plain flour	Oil for deep-frying
2 teaspoons cayenne pepper	Salt

Cut the herring fillets diagonally across into 5 mm ($\frac{1}{4}$ in) strips.

Mix the flour with the cayenne pepper. Dip the 'fingers' through the milk, then into the flour, shaking off any excess. The herring is now ready to be dropped into hot oil and deep-fried for about 1 minute until golden and crispy. Remove from the oil, drain on kitchen paper and sprinkle with salt. It really is as easy as that. Now all you have to do is eat them!

Tuna Carpaccio

Fresh tuna fish must be one of the most versatile fish to cook with. It has a fillet steak texture and eats so well when cooked medium rare to medium.

Carpaccio is most commonly known using beef. It's simply raw beef sliced very thinly and then served with a tasty dressing. Well, this dish is going to be very similar, but instead of serving the tuna completely 'raw' I almost cure it, as you would when making gravadlax. This really helps the flavour of the tuna, giving you the strong flavours of salt, sugar and fresh dill.

As a garnish for this dish, giving you more texture, a green salad will work; or how about trying the Crispy Spinach (see p.163)? I prefer to serve the spinach. This does give you two totally different textures, with the 'raw' tuna and crispy spinach. I normally serve just a small pile of the spinach at the top of the plate.

This dish can also become a sort of canapé by rolling some of the spinach in the tuna. Biting through the very tender succulent fish into the crispy spinach is wonderful.

Serves 6–8

450 g (1 lb) tuna fillet
25 g (1 oz) coarse sea salt
50 g (2 oz) demerara sugar
1 heaped teaspoon pink peppercorns, chopped or crushed

2 teaspoons chopped fresh dill, plus more for dressing (optional)
Finely grated zest of $\frac{1}{2}$ lemon
A pinch of freshly ground black pepper
150 ml (5 fl oz) olive oil

Trim the tuna of all skin, leaving just pure tuna meat. Mix together the sea salt, sugar, pink peppercorns, dill, lemon zest and pepper, and spread over the fish, then pour over the olive oil. Cover and chill, turning occasionally, for 48 hours. During this time the salt and sugar will dissolve and cure the fish. Lift the fish from the oil. It is now ready to serve or can be wrapped in clingfilm and frozen until needed.

Pour the oil into a pan and bring to the boil. Pour it through a sieve and leave to cool. This will leave you with a strong flavoured dressing. When using the dressing, some more chopped dill can be added to lift the flavour.

To serve, slice the tuna *very* thinly, allowing 3–4 slices per portion. If you have frozen the fillet, it's best to slice on a machine and then arrange and allow to thaw on the serving plates. To finish, spoon the marinade dressing over and serve with a spoonful of crispy spinach.

TOP *Tuna Carpaccio.* BOTTOM *Grilled Mackerel with Pickled Red Cabbage and Creamy Anchovy Sauce (see p.42).*

Seared Tuna with Garlic and Almond Cream

I like to eat tuna just like a steak, medium rare, keeping the moist and succulent meat with a good texture and taste. Searing the fillet in a good hot pan will give me just that – it's virtually in and out. If you prefer the tuna well done, then just pan-fry the fish for a little longer on both sides. The garlic and almond cream spread on top and glazed gives an even better taste.

If you can't get tuna, this recipe will work with most other fish. They will, however, need to be properly pan-fried and not just seared.

For a good finish to this dish, I sit the hot, grilled tuna on top of a French Bean and Sesame Salad (see p.158).

SERVES 4

4 × 175 g (6 oz) tuna fillet steaks

For the Garlic and Almond Cream

3 garlic cloves, crushed
A pinch of salt
2 medium slices of white bread, soaked
    in water
2 teaspoons white wine vinegar

2 egg yolks
150 ml (5 fl oz) olive oil
65 g (2½ oz) ground almonds
1–2 drops of soy sauce (optional)

To make the garlic and almond cream, crush the garlic with the salt. Squeeze the excess water from the bread, then blitz it in a food processor or liquidizer with the garlic. Whisk the white wine vinegar with the egg yolks, then gradually whisk in the oil a drop at a time as you would when making mayonnaise. Mix the garlic and bread mixture with the mayonnaise and blitz in the ground almonds. Enhance the flavour with the soy sauce, if liked.

Pre-heat the grill.

The tuna should now be seared on both sides in a hot pan. Spread the cream on top, being fairly generous. All you need to do now is glaze the cream under the hot grill and the fish is ready to sit on top of the prepared salad.

Grilled Trout Fillets on Almond Toasts or Trout and Almond Toasts

This recipe is taking a classic combination of flavours – trout and almonds – and giving you two different ways of eating them.

The first alternative is to toast the almond cream on toast, and then sit the grilled fillet on top. The other alternative is to steam the trout lightly and then, once cold, break it down and add it to the cream. Both work very well. The fillet of fish gives you a coarser texture and the steamed version gives you many options for eating it as a starter, snack or on small toast canapés.

SERVES 4

4 × 100 g (4 oz) trout fillets, with skin left on

½ quantity Garlic and Almond Cream (see opposite), made without garlic or with just ½ clove

8 × 1 cm (½ in) slices of good quality bread

A knob of unsalted butter

Salt and freshly ground black pepper

4 tablespoons olive oil

Juice of ½ lemon

½ teaspoon chopped fresh parsley (optional)

2 teaspoons of broken flaked almonds, toasted (optional)

Salad leaves for garnish (optional)

Pre-heat the grill.

First prepare the almond cream. Once ready to eat and serve, toast the bread. Butter the trout fillets and season with salt and pepper. These can now be placed under the grill and cooked for 4–6 minutes until cooked and crispy. While the fish is cooking, generously spread some almond cream on to the toasts and glaze under the grill.

Whisk together the olive oil and lemon juice and season with salt and pepper. The chopped parsley and toasted almond flakes can also be added to create an interesting texture.

Sit the golden toasts on plates and top each with a fillet of trout. Garnish the plate with a few salad leaves, if liked, and then spoon some dressing over the salad and fish.

Variation

For the steamed version, simply steam the seasoned fillets on butter paper over boiling water for 3–4 minutes. Once cooked, allow the fillets to cool before removing the skin. Then simply break them down into flakes and mix with the almond cream. Spoon and spread on the toasts and finish under the grill. The same garnishes can be used on this method.

Seared Salmons on Soured Baked Potato

Fresh or smoked salmon, or even both, can be used with this dish. I like to use smoked salmon as its smoky flavour, half cooked, works so well with the sharp, tangy, sour taste.

SERVES 4

4 × 5 mm (¼ in) slices of smoked salmon,
    each about 75–100 g (3–4 oz)
½ quantity Soured Baked Potatoes
    (see p.152)

1 tablespoon olive oil
A squeeze of fresh lemon juice
1 tablespoon chopped fresh parsley or
    snipped fresh chives

Make the soured baked potatoes, filling all four of the half-skins so you have a smaller quantity than you would for a main course. All you then have to do is sear the salmon in a hot pan on one side only to cook just half-way through and give a golden edge to the fish. Sit a soured baked potato on a plate and arrange the salmon on top. Trickle with some olive oil, lemon juice, parsley or chives and you have a finished dish.

The salmon slices also work very well with the julienne used in the Griddled Scallops recipe on p.30.

Smoked Eel, Trout or Salmon with Potato Salad and Mustard Oil

This recipe has very different tastes from a basic potato salad. With this one I'm using horseradish (fresh or creamed) and red onions as flavours. It also doesn't have a mayonnaise base but instead the Mustard Dressing is being used. However, this can be made an awful lot quicker and still be very tasty by using a good quality jar of mayonnaise mixed with creamed horseradish and a dot of mustard. So you can see cooking doesn't have to be too much of a chore! There are always alternatives.

SERVES 4

225–350 g (8–12 oz) smoked eel,
smoked salmon or smoked trout fillets

For the Mustard Oil

50 g (2 oz) dried mustard seeds
1 tablespoon water
1 teaspoon English mustard powder

5 tablespoons grapeseed oil
1 teaspoon ground turmeric
A pinch of salt

For the Potato Salad

450 g (1 lb) cooked warm, small new
   potatoes
1 teaspoon finely grated horseradish or
   horseradish sauce
1 red onion, finely chopped
1 tablespoon olive oil

A squeeze of fresh lemon juice
Salt and freshly ground black pepper
4–6 tablespoons Mustard Dressing
   (see p.271) or mayonnaise
1 teaspoon chopped fresh parsley
Salad leaves to serve (optional)

To make the mustard oil, the mustard seeds must first be roasted in a dry frying-pan over a moderate heat for a few minutes until golden. Allow to cool. Mix the water with the mustard powder, then blend all the ingredients together. The mix should now be left for 24 hours to infuse the flavours. After this time, pass through a muslin cloth or very fine sieve. You will now have a clear mustard oil.

Now make the potato salad. As soon as the potatoes are cooked, cut them in half and add the horseradish, red onion, olive oil, lemon juice and season with salt and pepper. To finish, simply add the mustard dressing, or mayonnaise and chopped parsley.

To serve the dish, sit the potato salad on plates and top with the smoked fish, or serve at the side. Finish the dish with a trickle of the mustard oil. Salad leaves can also be used, if liked, dressed with a little mustard oil.

Grilled Mackerel with Pickled Red Cabbage and Creamy Anchovy Sauce

There are so many ways of pickling foods. In this recipe, the ingredients are prepared in the morning and will be ready to eat in the evening. Many other recipes have to be planned well in advance: ingredients steeped in cold vinegar with spices can take up to six weeks to mature. The vinegar used can be natural or sweetened. Also the strength of the pickle can be determined by the spices and quantity of dried chillies used.

There's also hot and cold pickling. Cold pickling is probably best if you're using onions or cabbage to be eaten at a later date, as this will keep them crisper. A hot method is better for pickling fruits.

In this recipe, I'm using the hot technique so the cabbage will be ready within hours. You can leave out the muslin bag of pickling spices if you prefer. Also, I prefer to leave this recipe unsweetened, but if you like sweeter pickles, then simply add 15–25 g ($\frac{1}{2}$–1 oz) of white sugar to the vinegar before boiling.

The cabbage and dressing work very well together, but so do just the mackerel and the cabbage on their own! Or you could try Mustard Dressing (see p.271) or Cider Dressing (see p.18).

SERVES 4

4 mackerel fillets
A knob of unsalted butter

Salt and freshly ground black pepper

For the Pickled Red Cabbage

$\frac{1}{2}$ red cabbage, approximately 225–350 g
(8–12 oz)
A pinch of salt

50 ml (5 fl oz) red wine vinegar
1 teaspoon dried pickling spices tied in muslin

For the Dressing

2 egg yolks or 1 hard-boiled egg
25 g (1 oz) anchovy fillets, drained and chopped
2 teaspoons capers
2 teaspoons Worcestershire sauce
1 teaspoon Dijon mustard
A dash of Tabasco sauce

Juice of $\frac{1}{2}$ lemon
1 small garlic clove, crushed
2 tablespoons finely grated Parmesan (optional)
Freshly ground black pepper
150 ml (5 fl oz) olive oil

The cabbage must be made several hours in advance. Cut the cabbage into 3 and remove the core and stalk. Shred the cabbage very finely and add a pinch of salt. Bring the red wine vinegar to the boil with the pickling spices. Once boiling, pour on top of the cabbage, stirring to make sure the cabbage is covered. Place a lid on top, remove from the heat and leave to steep for several hours. When the cabbage is ready to use, remove and squeeze the muslin bag to release all the flavours. Warm just to room temperature.

Pre-heat the grill.

The dressing can be made very quickly in a food processor or liquidizer. Blitz the egg yolks or hard-boiled egg with all other ingredients except the olive oil. The oil can then be added slowly as the mix is blending. Once all oil has been added, just push the dressing through a sieve to give a creamy consistency. You should have about 300 ml (10 fl oz) of dressing.

To cook the mackerel, lightly butter and season the fillets before sitting under the pre-heated grill. The fillets will take between 4–6 minutes, leaving the skin crispy.

To serve, spoon some pickled red cabbage on to the centre of the plates and pour the creamy dressing around before sitting the crispy hot grilled mackerel on top.

Red Wine Vinegar

A lot of the basic red wine vinegars available in most supermarkets and food stores are thin and not very red-wine flavoured. They will work but will not give you the fullest of flavours. Good red wine vinegar is now available at most large superstores and delicatessens. The way to check is to look for the hallmarks of a good wine. For instance, a red Bordeaux vinegar is made from Appellation Contrôlée Bordeaux wines. Of course, these are more expensive and could also become too strong and powerful. I always find it best to use two-thirds basic red wine vinegar and one-third strong red wine vinegar. So if you see some, do try it – you will not be disappointed with the results.

Cooking the 'Perfect' Omelette

I'm sure we could all argue over this subject. What is the perfect omelette? Is it the one that's beautifully golden brown? Is it flat or round? Is it totally colourless? Is it firm? Is it slightly runny?

Well, I suppose the easiest answer is the most perfect is the way you like to eat it. Well why not? However, for me, the perfect omelette hasn't been eaten by many people. Making an omelette is really just a dish that involves the setting of eggs with the added flavour of your choice: crispy bacon; black pudding; cheese and onion; tomato and chive; smoked salmon; spring onion and chilli; button or wild mushrooms; mixed herbs; sweet peppers; spinach; potato; garlic, it's up to you! It's not really a cooking process, more of a 'warming' to thicken the egg, giving you a set scrambled effect with a complete soft and light finish with no colour.

Here's the recipe for a plain omelette as a main course.

SERVES 1–2

4 fresh eggs   A small knob of unsalted butter
Salt and freshly ground black pepper

It is very important to have a good non-stick, 15–20 cm (6–8 in) omelette pan.

Warm the pan on the stove. While the pan is warming, crack the eggs into a bowl and whisk with a fork. It's very important not to season the eggs until the omelette is about to be made. If eggs are salted too early they break down and become thin, runny and slightly discoloured, giving a dull look.

The omelette pan should now be hot enough to add the knob of butter. As the butter melts and becomes bubbly, season the eggs and pour them into the pan. This will now only take between 3–4 minutes to cook. To keep them light, keep the eggs moving by shaking the pan and stirring the eggs with a fork. This prevents them from sticking and colouring. You will soon have a scrambled look to the eggs. Now cheese can be added or any other flavour. Allow the eggs to set on the base for 5–10 seconds. The eggs will still be moist and not completely set in the centre. Holding the pan at an angle (down), slide and tap the omelette towards the edge, folding it over as you do so.

This can now be turned out on to a plate and shaped under a cloth to give a cigar shape. The omelette is now ready. It will have no colour but be filled with an almost soufflé texture. This makes it a dream to eat with every mouthful melting.

Spicy Scrambled Eggs

This is a great quick snack dish that also holds well as a starter or canapé. The quantities of garlic and ginger may seem a lot for just a 3-egg omelette, but mixed together and cooked they do balance the strength of both flavours.

SERVES 1–2

3 eggs, beaten
A knob of unsalted butter
½ heaped teaspoon crushed garlic
½ heaped teaspoon crushed fresh
    ginger root
1 tablespoon finely chopped onion

½ teaspoon chopped red chilli
½ teaspoon ground turmeric
1 tomato, seeded and diced
Salt and freshly ground black pepper
½ teaspoon chopped fresh coriander
    leaves (optional)

Heat a frying-pan and add the butter. Crush the garlic and ginger together to a paste. Once the butter is bubbling, add the garlic and ginger paste, the chopped onion, chilli, turmeric and tomato. Cook for a few minutes until lightly softened. Add the beaten eggs and stir over the heat until the eggs have softly scrambled. Taste and season with salt and pepper if necessary and stir in the chopped coriander, if using, and serve.

Spicy Scrambled Eggs.

Black Pudding Fritters

This isn't really a new recipe. I'm sure in many parts of the country you will find this dish in fish and chip shops! However, I thought I would include it because it's such a fun dish (and, of course, very tasty) and works so well as a snack, canapé, in finger buffets, as a starter or even as a main course with mashed potatoes and peas!

Well, these fritters do go very well with the Home-made Tomato Ketchup (see p.266) or a mayonnaise-based sauce. A good tartare sauce works very well: that's basically mayonnaise with chopped capers, gherkins, parsley and onions or shallots. The acidic flavour from the capers and gherkins almost electrify the black pudding. Other good mayonnaise flavourings are horseradish cream or purée, Dijon or grain mustard or a beetroot purée. In fact, the beetroot purée mixed with mayonnaise and then spiced with fresh or tinned horseradish is a real winner to go with this dish.

SERVES 2–4

1 × 225 g (8 oz) black pudding, peeled

For the Batter

225 g (8 oz) self-raising flour
300 ml (10 fl oz) lager
Plain flour for dusting

Oil for deep-frying
Salt

Pre-heat the oil to 180°C/350°F.

The first thing to do is prepare the black pudding. This can be cut into 12 × 2.5 cm (1 in) pieces – these are really the perfect size for snacks – or split the pudding through the middle, then cut in half to give you quarters. These are a good size for a starter or part of a main course.

The next stage is to make the batter. Sift the self-raising flour into a bowl and whisk in the lager, making sure you are left with a good thick consistency. This will increase the lightness of the finished dish, creating an almost soufflé effect. Lightly dust the black pudding with the flour and then dip in the batter. This is best done with a cocktail stick, completely covering the pudding itself while preventing your hands from becoming covered.

Providing that the oil has been heated to 180°C/350°F, the cooking time will be between 3–5 minutes until crispy and golden brown. Remove from the fryer, shaking off any excess fat. Lightly sprinkle with salt and serve, perhaps with the sauce of your choice, or why not be really traditional – and eat them with chips out of newspaper!

Mozzarella and Tomato Fried Sandwiches with Garlic Mushrooms

Egg-fried sandwiches work so well as starters or snacks. Basically they are sandwiches dipped in beaten egg, then fried in oil and butter until golden brown. The sandwich takes on a whole new texture and taste. These will give you a completely new croque monsieur, simply dip it into the egg and fry.

Of course, there are many combinations of savoury fillings, whether meat, fish or vegetarian. The recipe I'm going to give you is vegetarian, with an Italian feel.

Mozzarella is an Italian cheese that was made from water buffaloes' milk. A lot now is made from cows' milk. It is stored in its own milk and has a slightly rubbery texture. It is also used on pizzas and in Italian salads.

SERVES 2

4 × 25 g (1 oz) Mozzarella slices	2 tablespoons olive oil
4 thick slices of white or brown bread, buttered	A small knob of unsalted butter
	2 eggs, beaten
1 tomato, sliced	25 g (1 oz) Garlic Butter (see pp.134–5)
Salt and freshly ground black pepper	100 g (4 oz) button mushrooms, sliced

Lay the Mozzarella on 2 slices of bread, leaving a 5 mm ($\frac{1}{4}$ in) border clear. Sit some slices of tomato on top of the cheese and season with salt and pepper. Cover with the remaining slices of bread, pushing all around the outside to seal in the cheese and tomato. Heat a frying-pan with the olive oil and butter. Dip the sandwiches in the beaten eggs, making sure the egg has soaked in. Fry over a medium heat for a few minutes on each side to a golden brown.

While the sandwiches are cooking, heat another frying-pan and add the garlic butter. Once it is bubbling, add the sliced mushrooms. Season with salt and pepper and cook on a fast heat to prevent them from becoming too soft and wet. Instead these should take on a good colour and be ready within minutes.

To serve the dish, place the sandwiches on plates and spoon some garlic mushrooms on top, pouring over any excess juices.

Chick Pea Patties

Chick peas are a dried pulse that, once soaked to become tender, are eaten raw or cooked. They are used in many national dishes: falafel from Israel and hummus from the Middle East are two classics.

This recipe is similar to a falafel. It's basically seasoned and flavoured minced chick peas that are then rolled or moulded before being deep-fried until golden and crispy. Chick peas are also often part of couscous dishes, so to go with this dish I am serving a parsley couscous relish.

Couscous is made from fine semolina that has been rolled in flour. Most couscous available in Britain has previously been cooked, so when soaked or warmed becomes immediately edible. Couscous originally comes from northern Africa and contains the same ingredients as most pastas: semolina and flour.

The chick peas will need to be soaked for a minimum eight hours so it's best to soak them the day before; 24 hours soaking will guarantee a tender finish. It's also important to make sure they are not too old, preferably no more than 12 months. This dish needs to be eaten immediately, so simply fry and serve. These eat very well on their own with just a squeeze of lime. But to eat them at their best serve them with the couscous relish.

MAKES 16 patties

450 g (1 lb) chick peas, soaked for
  24 hours
6 spring onions
¼ bunch of fresh flatleaf parsley,
  including stalks
1 garlic clove

1–2 red chillies, seeds removed and
  very finely chopped
¼ bunch of fresh coriander
40 g (1 ½ oz) fresh root ginger
Salt and freshly ground black pepper
Oil for deep-frying

For the Parsley and Couscous Relish

2 tablespoons couscous, soaked
  overnight
1 bunch of fresh flatleaf parsley, finely
  shredded
2 plum or salad tomatoes, skinned,
  seeded and diced

4 spring onions, finely diced
Juice of 1 lemon or lime
6 mint leaves, chopped
4–6 tablespoons olive oil

Once the chick peas have been soaked, rinse and strain off. Now it's time to mince the chick peas with all the other ingredients through a fine mincer. Check for seasoning with salt and pepper. Shape the patties between 2 tablespoons.

To make the relish, mix together all the ingredients and season with salt and pepper, adding enough olive oil to give a moist consistency. You will have about 300 ml (10 fl oz).

When ready to fry, the temperature of the oil should be about 150°C/300°F. The patties will take between 4–6 minutes to deep-fry and become golden brown.

To serve the complete dish, spoon some of the relish on to plates, making a flat disc in the centre. Now simply sit the patties on top.

OPPOSITE
Chick Pea Patties.

Soy and Teriyaki Sauces

These are two seasoning sauces that I use a lot of in various recipes. They have become very much part of our larder.

Soy sauce was first brewed in Japan by the Mogi family in the early to mid 1600s. The same family still run the Kikkoman Company today. Kikkoman is the name of the soy and teriyaki sauces mostly used. In fact, it is the largest manufacturer selling soy sauce in the world. Up to 1.2 billion litres (315 million gallons) of soy sauce is consumed in Japan in one year alone; that means roughly ten one-litre bottles per person per year.

Soy sauce is made from soya beans fermented with wheat, water and salt. The mixture is then brewed for six months before the sauce is ready. Soy lends itself to many dishes: rice, pasta, marinades, sauces, fish, meat and more. It's also used as a seasoning, simply left on the table.

Teriyaki is really a form of marinade used in barbecues to lift other flavours. This is made from a brewed soy sauce, vinegar, wine and spices. It has a sweeter taste than soy and has had the other flavours added to create a piquancy associated with a classic barbecue.

The two sauces mixed together help flavour marinades and dressings.

Sautéed *Foie Gras* on Sweet Mashed Potatoes with Crispy Cabbage

Foie gras *isn't everyone's cup of tea or, for that matter, very easy to get hold of. But don't be put off by that because this recipe works very well as a starter or main course with many other flavours. Chicken livers can be used as a replacement, or even lambs' or calves' liver if the dish is served as a main course. On top of that, many fish will work very well.*

Sauternes is a classic sweet white wine to accompany foie gras, *so reducing shallots with that wine to flavour the mashed potato is very exciting. If you can't get Sauternes, then just buy another sweet white wine and increase the quantity by half again.*

SERVES 4

4 × 75–100 g (3–4 oz) slices of *foie gras*
4 tablespoons chopped shallots
300 ml (10 fl oz) Sauternes
225 g (8 oz) Mashed Potatoes (see
    p.154), finished with butter but
    without cream
Salt and freshly ground black pepper

Oil for deep-frying
6–8 large Savoy cabbage leaves, cut into
    1 cm ($\frac{1}{2}$ in) strips
2 tablespoons Veal or Beef *Jus* (see
    p.261) or alternative (see p.262)
    (optional)

Mix the chopped shallots with the Sauternes and bring to a simmer. Reduce until all the wine has been absorbed by the shallots. Mix with the mashed potatoes and season.

Heat the oil to 180°C/350°F and deep-fry the Savoy cabbage for 30 seconds–1 minute until golden-edged and crispy. As soon as the cabbage has been dropped in the oil, cover with a lid to prevent any spitting created from the cabbage water content. After the first 15–20 seconds, the lid can be lifted. Once cooked, drain and lightly salt.

All we have to do now is cook the *foie gras*. Heat a frying-pan and season the *foie gras* with salt and pepper. Place the *foie gras* in the pan. It's important to cook in a hot pan, as this will seal the *foie gras* and give a good golden colour. The *foie gras* will need just $1\frac{1}{2}$–2 minutes on each side. Quite a lot of excess fat will be left in the pan. Pour off and reserve half of this fat, leaving the rest in the pan.

To present the dish, spoon some Sauternes shallot potatoes on to plates and sit the *foie gras* on top. You can now add the *jus* or gravy, if using, to the remaining fat in the pan. This creates a sauce for the dish. It will come to the boil very quickly. Season with salt and pepper and pour a tablespoon over each portion. Now just top the dish with the crispy cabbage to finish.

The remaining *foie gras* fat can be kept chilled or frozen and used as a cooking fat for many dishes. It's very good just melted and mixed with mashed potatoes instead of butter.

Main Courses

With a lot of the main course recipes I'm keeping with the British Classics but giving all a slightly new twist. For example, the roast beef has been rolled in milled black pepper. It's roasted in the normal fashion but once cooked, rested, carved and tasted, you'll find the fiery bite of cooked pepper works so well with the sweet, succulent meat. There's also Roast Cod with Horseradish Yorkshire Pudding (see p.62), Confit of Pork Belly with Rich Sherry Lentils (see p.92), Roast Chicken with Crispy Pancetta and Lemon and Thyme Dumplings (see p.76) and more.

ABOVE *Grilled Calves' Liver Steak with Spiced Potatoes (see p.106).*
LEFT *Pan-fried Salmon with Anchovy Cream Noodles, Crispy Bayonne Ham and Parsley (see p.55).*

I've also included some recipes with Indian and Eastern flavours, all of which seem to be becoming more and more part of our daily eating. I would like to think there is something here to suit everybody's palate, from corned beef hash to haggis!

Enjoy your meal — *bon appétit.*

Fish

Cooking fish is such a pleasure. Once you've bought the fish of your choice and, of course, you know how fresh it is, watching the texture change just slightly as it steams, poaches, fries or grills, is so exciting as you start to recognize its flavours as it cooks.

In a restaurant kitchen you're always looking for new dishes and ideas, obviously to make menu changes and keep your guests guessing as to what will be on the menu next week. You do go through spells of finding it really hard work to come up with something 'new' (I'm not really sure there is!). But in this section of the main course chapter I'm more excited than ever. The variety of cooking gives you so many different results with steaming, roasting, grilling and pan-frying, and all the dishes have flavours that work together so well.

I would have liked to have had every fish dish photographed; instead all I had was a headache having to decide which ones to choose! I do hope, in a nice sort of way, that you're also going to have a headache trying to decide which one to cook first!

If it makes it any easier, all my recipes in this book are flexible, so if you fancy the tuna fish with tartare potatoes or sea bass with shrimps and gremolata mash, then have them. There should never be strict rules in cooking, only to cook well.

Pan-fried Fish with Anchovy Cream Noodles, Crispy Bayonne Ham and Parsley

The reason this is just titled pan-fried 'fish' is because there are so many you can use: sea bass, tuna, salmon, John Dory and monkfish to name but a few.

SERVES 4

4 × 175–225 g (6–8 oz) fish fillets
225–350 g (8–12 oz) fresh or dried
   noodles, cooked
A good handful of fresh parsley
Oil for deep-frying

4 slices of Bayonne or Parma ham, or
   streaky bacon if either is unavailable
Plain flour for dusting
A knob of unsalted butter
Salt and freshly ground black pepper

For the Anchovy Cream Sauce

A knob of unsalted butter
1 onion, finely chopped
½ leek, shredded
1 bay leaf
½ garlic clove
1 glass of dry white wine, about
   150 ml (5 fl oz)

300 ml (10 fl oz) Fish Stock (see p.260)
150 ml (5 fl oz) double cream
50 g (2 oz) tinned anchovies, well
   drained and chopped
A squeeze of fresh lemon juice

Pre-heat the grill.

To make the sauce, melt the butter in a pan and add the onion, leek, bay leaf and garlic. Cook over a moderate heat for a few minutes until softened. Add the white wine and boil to reduce by two-thirds. Add the fish stock and boil to reduce by half. Add the double cream and the anchovy fillets and cook for a few minutes. The sauce can now be blitzed in a food processor or liquidizer or with a hand blender, then pushed through a sieve. Check for seasoning and add just a few drops of lemon juice to lift the finished flavour.

The parsley can be cooked in a deep-fat fryer or in 1 cm (½ in) of hot fat in a frying-pan. It's important to use a lid and check all excess water is shaken off before cooking.

Cut the ham into 1 cm (½ in) strips and pan-fry for 1–2 minutes, then finish crisping under the grill. The noodles can now be re-heated in the anchovy cream sauce.

Whichever fish is being cooked can be lightly floured on the presentation side, brushed with butter and seasoned with salt and pepper. Now all you have to do is cook the fish until tender in a hot pan; the timing will, of course, depend on the type of fish you choose.

To present the dish, divide the noodles and sauce between bowls or plates. Sit the fish on top, then sprinkle with the crispy Bayonne or Parma ham and parsley.

Pan-fried Sea Bass with Spring Onions and Creamy Potatoes

There's more to the spring onions than the title of this recipe is telling you. They have been mixed with soy sauce, five-spice powder, red chillies and mirin. Mirin is a Japanese sweet rice wine which is available in major supermarkets, oriental food stores and some delicatessens. If you can't find it listed as mirin, then buy a basic rice wine or rice vinegar – the recipe will work with either.

Should sea bass be difficult to find, this dish works just as well with any other fish. For this dish I prefer to have the sea bass skinned, but I don't waste the skin – I deep-fry it to serve with the fish and call it Sea Bass Crackling! The creamy mashed potatoes should be very creamy, only just holding their shape. When you eat them with the fish they are like a thick cream sauce. You will notice that I am using whipping or single cream; basically this is because double cream would thicken the potatoes rather than loosen them to the creamy consistency I am after.

SERVES 4

4 × 175–225 g (6–8 oz) sea bass fillets, skinned and skins reserved
3 tablespoons soy sauce
3 tablespoons mirin (sweet rice wine)
A small pinch of five-spice powder
3 tablespoons olive or sesame oil
Salt and freshly ground black pepper

1 bunch of spring onions, finely shredded
1 red chilli, very finely chopped
Plain flour for dusting
A knob of unsalted butter
1–2 tablespoons oil
Oil for deep-frying

For the Creamy Mashed Potatoes

675 g (1½ lb) Mashed Potatoes (see p.154)
75 g (3 oz) unsalted butter

150–300 ml (5–10 fl oz) whipping or single cream
Freshly grated nutmeg

To make the dressing, boil the soy sauce, mirin and five-spice powder together, then remove from the heat. Mix with the olive or sesame oil and season with salt and pepper, if necessary. Mix the spring onions with the chopped chilli.

To fry the sea bass, lightly flour on the skin side and season with salt and pepper. Heat a frying-pan and add the butter. Once the butter is bubbling, cook the bass on the floured side for 2–3 minutes, then turn it over and continue to cook for a further 3 minutes. The fish could take a little longer to cook – this really depends on the thickness of the fillets.

Once the fish has been turned over, heat 2–3 tablespoons of the dressing and add the spring onions and chilli. This must be cooked on a high heat and stirred to ensure even cooking. The spring onions will take 1–2 minutes to cook.

To finish the mashed potatoes, add the butter, then 150 ml (5 fl oz) of the cream. Season with the salt, pepper and grated nutmeg. This will give you a good creamed potato mix. The remaining cream can now be added a little at a time until a loose consistency is achieved.

Dry the reserved fish skin on a cloth and cut into 2.5–5 cm (1–2 in) pieces, then lightly flour and deep-fry until golden and crisp. Drain on kitchen paper and season with salt. For safety, always use a lid when deep-frying to prevent any spitting of hot fat.

To present the dish, spoon or pipe some creamy potatoes at the top of the plate and top with a crispy skin. Sit the sea bass at the front of the plate and spoon the spring onion and chilli mix on top. The dish can now be finished with a trickle of the remaining dressing around the fish.

*Pan–fried Sea Bass with Spring Onions
and Creamy Potatoes.*

Grilled Sea Trout with Soured New Potatoes and Watercress Dressing

Sea trout is not the easiest of fish to get hold of, but do try it if you can; the flavour and texture is so good. If you can't get hold of it, then just replace it with salmon, red mullet, halibut, bass or cod – just about any fish will work. If you're choosing cod, leave the skin on and crisp it under the grill – it's delicious. I love the combination of the trout with the soured new potatoes – this recipe has so many possible variations leading to other dishes. When you take a look you'll see why.

SERVES 4

4 × 175–225 g (6–8 oz) sea trout fillet portions (from a 1.75–2.75 kg (4–6 lb) fish), trimmed of all bones, with skin left on
Salt and freshly ground black pepper

A knob of unsalted butter
¼ quantity Watercress and Herb Dressing (see p.270)
1 quantity Soured New Potatoes (see p.152)

Pre-heat the grill.

Lightly butter a baking sheet and arrange the fillets on it skin-side up. Season the skin with salt and pepper and dot with a little butter. Sit under a hot grill and cook until the skin becomes crispy. It will only take 5–6 minutes until the fish are cooked. Spoon some watercress dressing on to the centre of a plate and top with the soured new potatoes and crispy sea trout.

Roast Cod with Crispy Shrimps and Gremolata Mashed Potatoes

Starting to pan-fry cod, and then finishing by roasting in the oven, works so well, especially if you leave the skin on the fillet to give you a crispy topping to very succulent fish underneath. Leaving the skin on also protects the flesh and holds the fillet together. Small brown shrimps are the best for the crispy shrimps. They have to be picked and trimmed, just leaving the tails encased in shell. Frying them in nut-brown butter makes them even crisper and very tasty to eat with a squeeze of fresh lemon juice. If the small brown shrimps are unavailable, you can use shelled shrimps or just peeled prawns – all will work.

SERVES 4

4 × 175–225 g (6–8 oz) portions of cod fillet, with skin left on	100–175 g (4—6 oz) brown shrimps, preferably tails with shell left on
2 tablespoons plain flour	A squeeze of fresh lemon juice
50 g (2 oz) unsalted butter	Salt and freshly ground black pepper
50–100 g (2–4 oz) Gremolata (see p.278)	½ quantity Lemon Butter Sauce (see p.264), warm (optional)
450 g (1 lb) Mashed Potatoes (see p.154), made without butter	

Pre-heat the oven to 200°C/400°F/gas 6.

Lightly dust the skin side of the cod fillets with flour and brush each with a little butter. Heat an ovenproof frying-pan and add half the remaining butter. Once bubbling, sit the cod fillets in, skin-side down. Allow to fry for 2–3 minutes until the skin becomes golden and is starting to crisp. Turn the fish fillets over in the pan, leaving skin-side up, then finish in the pre-heated oven for 4–6 minutes, depending on the thickness of the fillet.

While the fish is cooking, the gremolata can be worked into the hot mashed potatoes. The quantity depends on the richness of lemon, garlic and parsley you would prefer in the potato. I like to make sure that all these flavours are quite powerful in the finished dish.

To cook the shrimps, heat a small frying-pan and add the remaining butter. Once bubbling, add the brown shrimps. Allow the shrimps to fry and crisp for approximately 1 minute. Add a squeeze of fresh lemon juice and season with salt and pepper.

To finish and serve the dish, shape the potatoes between two large serving spoons and place at the top of the plate. Sit the roasted cod at the front of the plate and spoon over the crispy shrimps. Lemon butter sauce can also be used to give a creamy finish to the dish by spooning some of the warm sauce around the fish and shrimps. The warm gremolata potatoes can also be served separately.

OPPOSITE *Roast Cod with Horseradish Yorkshire Pudding and Shrimp Gravy* (see p.62).

RIGHT *'Grill marking' halibut* (see p.72).

BELOW *Steamed Halibut on Spinach with Soured Lime Cream and Spicy Curry Dressing* (see p.64).

Roast Cod with Horseradish Yorkshire Pudding and Shrimp Gravy

Does this dish sound familiar? Well, you may have heard the idea before but the result is completely different.

Roast beef with Yorkshire pudding must be the most classic British dish. All over Europe and probably the world, whenever British cooking is mentioned, guess what? Yes, the next line always includes roast beef!

It was really Yorkshire pudding that was the starting point for this dish. Yorkshire Pudding is not just for beef. In this recipe, I've fired it up with horseradish cream to give an extra bite. The gravy is made with fish bones to give a completely different taste while retaining the body and strength of that classic sauce. Fish or chicken stock can be used: both will work, but obviously the fish stock will give you a stronger fish flavour. And, of course, there's the wonderful flavours to come through of the cod itself with crispy skin and succulent flakes.

Serves 4

4 × 175–225 g (6–8 oz) portions of cod fillet, with skin left on
Salt and freshly ground black pepper

1 tablespoon plain flour
A knob of unsalted butter
Sprigs of watercress

For the Yorkshire Puddings

½ quantity Yorkshire Pudding batter (see p.160)
Finely grated zest of 1 lemon

2 tablespoons horseradish cream, or more
A drop of oil

For the Fish Gravy

450 g (1 lb) fish bones or shrimp shells, chopped
A few parsley stalks
A drop of oil
1 glass white wine, about 150 ml (5 fl oz)
300 ml (10 fl oz) Fish Stock (see p.260) or Chicken Stock (see p.258)

150 ml (5 fl oz) Veal or Beef *Jus* (see p.261) or alternative (see p.262)
100 g (4 oz) peeled shrimps
1 tablespoon roughly chopped fresh flatleaf parsley

Pre-heat the oven to 200°C/400°F/gas 6. Heat 4 × 10 cm (4 in) moulds, 2.5 cm (1 in) deep with a teaspoon of oil in each.

To make the gravy, fry the chopped fish bones with the parsley stalks in the oil until golden. Or the bones can also be coloured in a hot oven. Add the white wine and boil to reduce until almost dry. Add the stock, bring to the boil and reduce by half. Add the *jus* or gravy and bring to a simmer. This can now be gently simmered for 20 minutes before being strained through a fine sieve. Check the consistency and seasoning of the gravy; you should have about 300 ml (10 fl oz). The sauce should not be too thick and heavy as this will overpower the cod. A looser consistency is best.

To make the puddings, add the lemon zest to the batter, with horseradish cream to taste. Two tablespoons gives it a fiery taste. At raw stage, the mix will taste stronger than at finished cooked stage. Pour the finished batter into the hot moulds and cook in the pre-heated oven for 20–25 minutes.

To cook the fish, first season with salt and pepper and lightly dust the skin side with plain flour. Brush the floured side with butter. Heat an ovenproof frying-pan or roasting tin. Trickle some cooking oil into the pan and sit the fish in on top of the stove skin-side down. The butter will melt, crisping the skin as it does. Once golden brown (this will take 2–3 minutes), turn the fish in the pan and finish by roasting in the pre-heated oven for 6–8 minutes. Don't put the fish in the oven until the Yorkshire puddings are about 8 minutes from ready.

Add the shrimps to the warm gravy. Once they are added, the gravy should not be heated past a mild simmer or this will toughen the shrimps. A squeeze of juice from the zested lemon will lift all the flavours from the gravy. Once the Yorkshire puddings and cod are cooked, sit the pudding at the top of the plate and the cod in front. Add the chopped parsley to the gravy and spoon the sauce over or around. The dish can be finished with a sprig of watercress to complete a classic garnish. The whole thing works so well, the horseradish and lemon Yorkshires helping to mop up the shrimp gravy and contrasting with crispy roast cod – sounds good to me!

Note

It is important to add the horseradish and lemon at the last minute as this will prevent the acidity from both flavours breaking down the batter consistency.

Steamed Halibut on Spinach with Soured Lime Cream and Spicy Curry Dressing

This recipe has three definite flavours that all work together very well. The fish itself is delicious to eat simply pan-fried or steamed on its own but also works well with other tastes. The spinach and soured cream could well stand up as a vegetarian dish on their own. As for the spicy dressing, this is quite powerful. It's really the flavours associated to a curry paste that have been loosened by the oils. The sharp/hot taste is quietened down by the spinach with the soured cream. Consequently, both are helping lift the halibut taste without spoiling it.

Please promise me you won't use this dressing just for this dish because it will work with so many other dishes. A good rich, spicy salad or barbecued lamb, pork or chicken are just a few to think about.

Although this recipe may appear long-winded, it is, in fact, really very simple. Once the dressing is made — before you add the tomato and coriander — it will keep up to 2 weeks in the fridge. The soured cream mix also keeps well for a few days.

Serves 4

4 × 175–225 g (6–8 oz) halibut fillets, skinned

675 g (1½ lb) spinach, picked and washed

A knob of unsalted butter

Salt and freshly ground black pepper

3–4 tablespoons Soured Cream, Lime and Mint Yoghurt (see p.276)

For the Spicy Curry Dressing

½ teaspoon chopped fresh thyme

¼ teaspoon crushed dried chillies

½ teaspoon cumin seed or ground cumin

1 star anise

6–8 shallots or 1 small onion, finely chopped

150 ml (5 fl oz) sesame oil

5 tablespoons olive oil

4 teaspoons soy sauce

4 teaspoons teriyaki sauce

2 teaspoons Worcestershire sauce

1–2 drops Tabasco sauce

¼ teaspoon finely chopped fresh ginger root

½ garlic clove, crushed

½ teaspoon ground turmeric

¼ teaspoon cayenne pepper

¼ teaspoon paprika

¼ teaspoon mixed spice

1 teaspoon clear honey

2 tomatoes, blanched and skinned

1 heaped teaspoon chopped fresh coriander

To make the dressing, tie the thyme, chillies, cumin and star anise in a piece of muslin. Then all that has to be done is mix together all the ingredients except the tomatoes and coriander and place over a low heat, bringing the dressing to a gentle simmer. This can now be left to cook for 8–10 minutes. The dressing should then be left to cool slightly and should only ever be served warm to appreciate all the flavours. Once cooled, the muslin bag can be squeezed and removed. This dressing will keep very well in the fridge for 2 weeks.

The blanched and skinned tomatoes will also be mixed with the dressing when the dish is being finished. Halve the tomatoes, removing all the seeds and water. The tomato flesh can now be cut into 5 mm ($\frac{1}{4}$ in) dice.

The spinach can be prepared in advance if you wish. To cook the spinach, simply plunge into boiling salted water for about 1 minute, and then drain and refresh under cold water. Once cold, any excess water can be lightly squeezed out.

Arrange a piece of butter paper in a steamer and season with salt and pepper. Place the halibut on top and steam over boiling water. The cooking time will vary depending on the thickness of the fillets: an average time will be approximately 5–6 minutes. While the fish is steaming, warm the spinach in a little butter and season with salt and pepper. Once hot, add the yoghurt cream. Once this has been added, just warm, do not re-boil or the yoghurt cream will thicken and become almost dry.

Add the diced tomatoes and chopped coriander to the dressing. Sit the soured lime cream spinach on to the plate with the steamed halibut on top and finish with 1–2 tablespoons of spicy dressing per portion.

Roast Skate with Mustard Seed Butter and Toasted Crumbs

Skate with black butter is the most classic of all skate dishes, and you can't get much simpler than that!

Skate can lend itself to so many different fish dishes whether they are starters or main courses, on or off the bone. Filleting skate seems to be a fairly modern idea but for this dish it's going to be on the bone. In many respects with almost all fish you will get better results if they are cooked on the bone, the fillets keeping all the flavour and juices. However, eating fish on the bone can become a chore and fiddly. Well, with skate you won't really have that problem; the fillets more or less just slide off.

SERVES 4

4 × 350 g (12 oz) skate wings on the
    bone
Salt and freshly ground black pepper
2 tablespoons plain flour
25 g (1 oz) unsalted butter

50 g (2 oz) fresh white breadcrumbs
1 glass of red wine, about 150 ml
    (5 fl oz)
1 teaspoon chopped fresh parsley

For the Mustard Seed Butter

50 g (2 oz) unsalted butter, softened

50 g (2 oz) grain mustard

Pre-heat the oven to 200°C/400°F/gas 6. Pre-heat the grill. Grease a baking tray.

Season the skate wings with salt and pepper and lightly dust with flour on the top (presentation) side. Heat a large frying-pan and add a knob of butter. Colour the presentation side first, and then turn in the pan before transferring the fish on to the baking tray. The fish can now be finished in the pre-heated oven for about 10–12 minutes.

To make the mustard seed butter, simply mix the two ingredients together. This can now be kept chilled or used immediately.

Toast the breadcrumbs under the grill to give a golden and slightly crunchy texture, turning occasionally until evenly golden.

A minute or so before the fish has finished cooking, remove it from the oven, place a tablespoon of the mustard butter on each skate wing and spread evenly, then return to the oven. Once cooked, remove from the oven and sprinkle the toasted crumbs on top.

Sit the fish on plates. Heat all the butter and juices left on the tray and add the red wine. Bring to the boil and check for seasoning. The consistency may be a little thin.

If so just add some more grain mustard butter for a smoother finish. Add the chopped parsley and spoon around the fish. The flavour of the red wine adds body and strength to the juices and butter.

Variation

A classic way to finish the dish instead of using the wine and parsley would be to just heat a frying-pan, add butter and colour to nut-brown stage with a squeeze of fresh lemon juice.

The addition of capers either to the nut-brown butter or the wine sauce also works very well.

*Roast Skate with Mustard Seed Butter
and Toasted Crumbs.*

Grilled Tuna on Greens with Horseradish Dumplings and Red Wine Dressing

Tuna is looked on as the 'meat' of fish, cooked medium-rare to medium as for a fillet steak. With this in mind, I wanted to give it the garnish of a steak and serve it almost like roast beef – the greens and dumplings obviously being the garnishes for the beef and red wine the dressing for the steak. The dumpling recipe is really the same as the bone marrow dumpling from More Rhodes Around Britain *with the addition of freshly grated horseradish. You will need this quantity of horseradish to give the real strength of the radish although, of course, you can make it even more fiery by simply adding more. If fresh horseradish is unavailable then add bottled grated horseradish, mixing and stirring until you have the right strength. This dish can also work with other fish and meats: beef steaks, chicken breasts or turbot would go well.*

The dumpling recipe should always be made 1–2 hours in advance to allow the mix to set. The mix will, in fact, keep chilled for 3–4 days, so if you have some left over, simply roll into dumplings and cook them either separately or in your stew.

SERVES 4

4 × 175–225 g (6–8 oz) tuna steaks
675 g (1½ lb) spring greens
Salt and freshly ground black pepper

25 g (1 oz) unsalted butter
8 tablespoons Red Wine Dressing
(see p.274)

For the Dumplings

100 g (4 oz) fresh bone marrow
100 g (4 oz) fresh white breadcrumbs
2 tablespoons double cream
3 egg yolks
3–4 tablespoons grated fresh
horseradish

A pinch of freshly grated nutmeg
About 600 ml (1 pint) Fish Stock
(see p.260), Chicken Stock (see
p.258) or water

To make the dumplings, break down the bone marrow in a food processor or liquidizer, then add the breadcrumbs. Add the cream and egg yolks with the grated horseradish. Season with nutmeg, salt and pepper and chill for minimum 1 hour before shaping into 8 large or 4 small dumplings. I like to shape the mix into ovals between 2 tablespoons. Drop the dumplings into simmering stock or water and poach for 10–15 minutes. Remove with a slotted spoon and drain on kitchen paper.

The greens should have any thick stalks removed and be cut down into 1 cm ($\frac{1}{2}$ in) thick strips. Blanch in boiling salted water for 1–2 minutes until the greens feel tender. Now you can either simply drain off the water, season with salt and pepper and lightly butter, providing they are to be eaten immediately, or refresh under cold water, and then toss in butter in a hot pan or microwave later.

As for the tuna, this can be cooked on a grill plate or pan-fried in a knob of butter and seasoned with salt and pepper. The tuna will only need 2–3 minutes on each side, keeping it pink and tender.

To serve the dish, sit the greens in the centre of the plate and top with the tuna and a dumpling. Spoon the red wine dressing around to finish.

Variation

The dressing can be made stronger by boiling it and adding 1 glass of red wine (about 150 ml/5 fl oz) and then reducing it by half.

Seared Salmons on Tartare Potato Cake with Warm Poached Egg

The plural 'salmons' is used for this dish because I'm using fresh and smoked salmon, both cooked. This gives a great combination of flavours that go so well with the tartare potato cake. I've named the potato cake 'Tartare' because basically I'm using some of the ingredients associated with tartare sauce: shallots or onions, capers and, with this recipe, marinated anchovy fillets. You can buy marinated anchovy fillets at delicatessens, and they are the best variety to use in this dish. Tinned anchovies can also be used but the full flavour won't quite be achieved. Of course the anchovies, capers and shallots are all optional extras, but the sharp flavour of these ingredients works so well with the salmon.

To sum the whole dish up, I can promise you that when you break the poached egg on to the salmon the richness of the yolk and smoky taste working with the fresh salmon and potatoes is very exciting and certainly not to be missed!

SERVES 4

4 × 75–100 g (3–4 oz) slices of fresh salmon, about 5 mm ($\frac{1}{4}$ in) thick
4 × 75–100 g (3–4 oz) slices of smoked salmon, about 5 mm ($\frac{1}{4}$ in) thick
3 large jacket potatoes, boiled in their skins until completely cooked
Salt and freshly ground black pepper
2 shallots or 1 small onion, finely chopped

1 tablespoon fine or chopped capers
12 marinated anchovy fillets, chopped
25 g (1 oz) unsalted butter
4 eggs
1 teaspoon chopped fresh flatleaf parsley
$\frac{1}{2}$ quantity Lemon Butter Sauce (see p.264)

Pre-heat the oven to 200°C/400°F/gas 6. Butter 4 × 10 cm (4 in) rings for the potatoes.

Peel the potatoes and slice into rounds. Sit the first layer of potatoes in the base of the rings, season with salt and pepper and sprinkle on the chopped shallots or onion, capers and anchovies. To finish simply top with another layer of potato. These potato cakes can be made up in advance and chilled.

To cook the potato cakes, melt half the butter in a frying-pan and with a spatula or fish slice lift the cakes into the pan. These can now be pan-fried for 4–5 minutes until golden on one side. Turn over the cakes and finish cooking in the pre-heated oven for approximately 15–20 minutes.

To poach the eggs, fill a small pan with a mixture of two-thirds water and one-third malt vinegar; the high quantity of vinegar will immediately hold the egg white around the yolk. Bring to the boil, then break in the eggs and poach for 3–3½ minutes. If you wish to cook these early, then simply refresh in iced water, then re-heat later in boiling water for about 1 minute.

To cook the salmons, heat a frying-pan and add the remaining butter. The fresh salmon must be the first as this will take slightly longer than the smoked. Season the fresh salmon with salt and pepper and the smoked with just pepper. Lay the fresh salmon in the pan and cook for 1–2 minutes before turning and adding the smoked salmon. The smoked salmon should be cooked on one side only for 1–2 minutes. This will also finish the cooking time for the fresh salmon.

To present the dish, add the chopped parsley to the warm lemon butter sauce and re-heat the poached eggs in boiling water. Sit the potato cakes on plates and top with a slice of each salmon and a warm poached egg. To finish, just spoon some lemon butter sauce over and serve.

Seared Salmons on Tartare Potato Cake
with Warm Poached Egg.

Smoked Haddock Tart with Grilled Halibut

This is a delicious combination – the grilled halibut with its own sauce flavoured with tomato and tarragon eats so well with the tart, I just had to include it in this recipe – but the tart can stand quite happily as a complete dish on its own. The basic tart recipe itself is an old favourite of mine because, with the taste of smoked haddock travelling through the whole tart, well, it's sensational. If you are not serving the tart with the halibut and sauce, simply cook the smoked haddock in the cream rather than the stock.

The dish can also take on so many combinations. Add mushrooms, leeks, spring onions or fresh herbs. It can also be finished by topping with Welsh or Stilton Rarebit (see p.130), both going very well with smoked haddock and giving you a golden, almost crispy, cheesy topping. If the tart is to be served on its own, then I feel it eats well with the Spicy Tomato Dressing (see p.269).

For a change, I sometimes mix half quantities of the cream sauce with Lemon Butter Sauce (see p.264). This gives a rich creamy, buttery sauce, almost velvety in consistency.

The most important thing is that you have a go at this dish – it's a must!

MAKES 4–6 × 10 cm (4 in) tarts or 1 × 25–30 cm (10–12 in) flan

For the Tart

1 quantity Shortcrust Pastry (see p.251) or Puff Pastry (see p.250)
275–350 g (10–12 oz) smoked haddock fillet
300 ml (10 fl oz) water or Fish Stock (see p.260)

A knob of butter
2 onions, sliced
2 eggs, beaten
300 ml (10 fl oz) double cream
2 tablespoons freshly grated Parmesan

For the Grilled Halibut

4 × 225 g (8 oz) halibut fillets
Plain flour

Salt and freshly ground black pepper
A knob of butter

For the Grilled Halibut Sauce

150–300 ml (5–10 fl oz) smoked haddock stock liquor (from above)
150 ml (5 fl oz) double cream
A knob of butter

A squeeze of fresh lemon juice
1–2 tomatoes, blanched, skinned, seeded and diced
1 teaspoon chopped fresh tarragon

Pre-heat the oven to 200°C/400°F/gas 6. Grease and line 4–6 × 10 cm (4 in) tart tins or 1 × 25–30 cm (10–12 in) flan tin.

Roll out the pastry and use to line the tins. Fill with greaseproof paper and baking beans or rice and bake for about 15–20 minutes. Remove the paper and beans.

Lightly poach the smoked haddock before making the tart mix. To do this, sit the haddock fillet in the water or stock and bring to a soft simmer, then cook for 2 minutes. Leave to cool, then remove the haddock. Reserve the stock for the sauce.

Melt the butter in a pan and add the sliced onions. Cook for a few minutes until softened. Beat the eggs into the cream, then add the Parmesan. The cream mix can now be added to the sliced onions. Cook this on a moderate heat for a few minutes, just to thicken. Remove from the heat.

Break the haddock into flakes and divide between the pastry cases. Top each tart with the cream and egg mix and finish in the pre-heated oven for 10–15 minutes for individual tarts or 25–30 minutes for a large tart.

The tart mix can be made in advance, mixing the fish flakes with the tart mix and then leaving to cool and chilling. If this is done, the tarts will take an extra 5–10 minutes to cook from cold in the oven.

The halibut eats very well 'grill-marked' and then cooked under the grill for a few minutes. Of course it can be just pan-fried or grilled without the markings. To 'grill-mark', lightly dust the presentation side of the fish with plain flour and season with salt and pepper. Now a thin metal skewer/kebab stick can be heated on an open gas. Once *red* hot, simply lift (using an oven cloth) and mark the fillet, re-heating the skewer or stick between each marking. The fillets can now be placed on a buttered tray, brushed with butter and cooked under a hot grill for 3–5 minutes, depending on the thickness of the fish.

To make the sauce, boil the haddock stock and add the double cream. Bring to the simmer and cook for a few minutes, stirring. Whisk in the knob of butter and check for seasoning with salt and pepper. Add a squeeze of lemon juice with the diced tomato flesh and chopped tarragon.

To serve, spoon the sauce over and around the tart before sitting the halibut on top.

Poultry and Meat

You'll find that each recipe in this section and, in fact, almost every one in the book, has its own introduction. This should give you a good idea of the dish itself and some extra information on its seasonings and flavours. Having the 'extras' helps you with alternatives and options with the dish itself.

Whenever I'm working with poultry or meats, my first thoughts are with traditions. The Roast Turkey Breast with Lemon and Herb Stuffing (see p.88) is a good example. Based on a traditional idea – turkey and stuffing – the difference is that the breast is off the bone and has been filled with the stuffing. This, of course, means that with every thick slice you have the stuffing as well.

I've also been asking myself about our daily eating habits and what can be quick and easy to prepare. Basically I don't want this to be a 'coffee table' cookery book or one that's only brought out to choose dinner party menus. Although you'll find that the dishes here are more than interesting enough to entertain with, they are equally appropriate simply for lunch, tea or supper. Take the Blackened Chicken recipe (see p.81), for example. This really does give you a completely different taste and finish to a plain chicken breast. But once you have mixed the spices, you can keep them almost indefinitely. So you only have to mix a few spices to give you a great alternative whenever you fancy it.

The same applies to the other dishes. The Peppered Roast Beef (see p.104) is sensational, just giving you a fiery bite around the succulent sweet moist beef. The Pot Roast Shoulder of Lamb (see p.100) or the Roast Chicken on Cabbage with Crispy Pancetta and Lemon and Thyme Dumplings (see p.76), would be wonderful to serve as a main course at your next dinner party. The Pork and Black Pudding Patties (see p.90) are really a burger alternative just packed with flavour.

And how about a curry? There are lots of good quality tinned or jarred flavourings available at the moment, but there isn't a better feeling than knowing you've made your own. The Chicken Balti recipe (see opposite) couldn't be easier. The results give you a good, spicy, creamy curry.

So now it's up to you, and with recipes from hash to haggis, the classic feeling is there and, just like the peppered beef, all finished with a twist!

Chicken Balti

The spices used for this recipe can be made in quantity and then kept in an airtight jar until needed.

You'll also notice this recipe is for four people but in the ingredients the chicken breasts are listed as 4–6. This is basically because you need a little extra whenever chicken breasts are diced and used in a stew or curry. As you can see, this dish is simple and easy to make, and all you need now is a good rice dish to go with it!

SERVES 4

4–6 chicken breasts, cut into 2 cm ($\frac{3}{4}$ in) dice	$\frac{1}{2}$ teaspoon ground cloves
4 tablespoons cooking oil	$\frac{1}{2}$ teaspoon turmeric
1 large onion, finely chopped	$\frac{1}{2}$ teaspoon paprika
1 garlic clove, crushed	1 teaspoon salt
2 teaspoons cardamom pods or crushed cardamom seeds	2 green chillies, chopped
2 teaspoons cumin seeds	1×400 g tin evaporated milk
2 tablespoons ground coriander	1 heaped teaspoon chopped fresh coriander
	Salt and freshly ground black pepper

Heat a non-stick pan and add the cooking oil. Add the chopped onion and garlic and cook for a few minutes, allowing them to colour. Add all the spices, salt and green chillies and continue to cook for a few minutes.

Add the diced chicken and turn in the pan until completely sealed on all sides. Now it's time to add the evaporated milk. Bring to the simmer, stirring to prevent the milk from sticking. Once simmering, reduce the heat, allowing the chicken to cook gently for 15–20 minutes until the chicken is tender and the sauce has thickened. It is important to stir this dish regularly. This will prevent the evaporated milk from catching and burning in the pan. As the curry is cooking, the sauce will take on all the flavours and also thicken. The total cooking time will be between 35–40 minutes.

To finish the dish, simply add the freshly chopped coriander and check for seasoning with salt and pepper.

Roast Chicken on Cabbage with Crispy Pancetta and Lemon and Thyme Dumplings

Roast chicken and bacon are common company, usually helped along with sausages and bread sauce, a favourite for the Great British Sunday Lunch. I wanted to take a classic like this and turn it into something more than just a Sunday Lunch.

Pancetta is an Italian cured bacon that can be found in most delicatessens. The fat that almost dissolves in the cooking gives a wonderful full flavour to the bacon. A good smoked or unsmoked streaky bacon can be used instead. You'll notice I have mentioned corn-fed chicken. Basically this has a fuller flavour than the basic battery-fed chickens that are mostly available to us. The basic chicken will, however, still work with this recipe.

SERVES 4

1 × large (1.75 kg/4 lb) corn-fed or oven-ready chicken	150 ml (5 fl oz) dry white wine
12 rashers pancetta or 8 rashers streaky bacon	300 ml (10 fl oz) Chicken Stock (see p.258)
75 g (3 oz) carrots, diced	300 ml (10 fl oz) Veal or Beef *Jus* (see p.261) or alternative (see p.262)
75 g (3 oz) onions, diced	1 medium Savoy cabbage
75 g (3 oz) celery, diced	Cooking oil
75 g (3 oz) leek, diced	A knob of unsalted butter
1 sprig of fresh thyme or a pinch of dried thyme (optional)	Salt and freshly ground black pepper

For the Dumplings

100 g (4 oz) fresh bone marrow	A pinch of grated nutmeg
100 g (4 oz) white breadcrumbs	1 heaped teaspoon chopped fresh thyme
2 tablespoons double cream	Finely grated zest and juice of 1 lemon
3 egg yolks	Chicken Stock (see p.258) or water

When you cut up the chicken, make sure you keep all the bones for stock. Remove the legs at the joint and split the drumstick from the thigh. Trim off the knuckle ends of the drumsticks and remove the bones from the thighs on the meat side, leaving the skin attached. The thighs can now be rolled or folded and held together with a cocktail stick. The breasts can now be left on the bone, removing the back bone carcass; the wings can be trimmed back to a single bone attached to the breast. This can be cleaned and trimmed, exposing the bone itself.

The carcass bones can now all be roughly chopped and either roasted or coloured in a pan with the diced carrot, onion, celery and leek – specific quantities are not too important. Also a sprig or pinch of thyme can be added. Once the chicken and vegetables are coloured, add the wine and bring to the boil, then boil to reduce until almost dry. Add the chicken stock and also boil to reduce by two-thirds. Now the *jus* or gravy can be added and brought to a simmer. Once simmering, cook for 20–30 minutes without reducing as this would make the sauce too strong. The sauce can now be strained through a sieve. You now have about 300 ml (10 fl oz) of a well flavoured chicken sauce to go with the roast.

While the sauce is cooking, make the dumpling mix. Break down the bone marrow in a food processor or mixer. Add the breadcrumbs, cream, egg yolks, nutmeg and thyme. Add the lemon zest and juice and season with salt and pepper. Once the lemon has been added, a curdled texture may appear. This should just be ignored; once cooked the dumpling will gel together and not separate. You will have about 350 g (12 oz) of mix. The mix is best left chilled for at least 2 hours before cooking. It keeps very well for 3–4 days; the lemon juice will change the colour of the mix, making it almost salmon pink, but this will disappear once cooked.

Pre-heat the oven to 200°C/400°F/gas 6.

Cut the cabbage into 2 cm (¾ in) thick strips. Rinse carefully and drain in a colander.

To roast the chicken, heat a roasting pan with a trickle of cooking oil and a small knob of butter. Season the bird with salt and pepper. Colour all the pieces golden in the pan. Remove the drumsticks and thighs, then sit the breasts on the bone in the pan and cook in the pre-heated oven for 10 minutes before adding the drumsticks and thighs and cooking for a further 10–15 minutes or until completely golden and crispy. During the cooking time, baste the chicken with its own cooking fat to keep it moist and help the colouring. Once cooked, remove from the oven and leave to rest for a few minutes.

While the chicken is cooking, cook the dumplings and cabbage. Shape the dumpling mix into 4 ovals between 2 tablespoons or roll into balls before dropping into simmering chicken stock or water and cooking for 10–15 minutes, depending on the size. Any excess dumpling mix can be left refrigerated and used for another dish.

Melt a knob of butter in a pan with 2 teaspoons of water. Once bubbling, add the cabbage and turn up the heat, stirring all the time. Once beginning to soften, season with salt and pepper. The cabbage will only take 2–3 minutes to become tender without becoming overcooked and floppy.

While the chicken is resting, grill the rashers of pancetta or bacon until crisp.

Now the breasts can be taken off the bone. Divide the cabbage between plates or bowls. Sit the rashers of pancetta or bacon on top, then the portions of chicken. Spoon the hot gravy over the chicken pieces, then finish with a lemon and thyme dumpling.

LEFT *Taking roast pigeon out of the oven.*

BELOW *Roast Chicken on Cabbage with Crispy Pancetta and Lemon and Thyme Dumplings (see p.76).*

RIGHT *Shredded Duck with Thai Noodles (see p.82).*

Spicy Fried Chicken

This chicken dish is simple to make and so easy to cook. The chicken is dry-fried. This basically means it doesn't have any sauce but the instant marinade keeps it moist to eat with lots of flavours happening. Looking at the seasoning ingredients you'd think it was going to need marinating for several hours before cooking. Well it doesn't. You literally just mix the chicken in the 'marinade' and fry. The dish will eat very well with a straightforward salad or boiled or fried basmati rice.

SERVES 4

4–6 chicken breasts
Groundnut or sesame oil for frying
A squeeze of fresh lemon juice
   (optional)

1 tablespoon chopped fresh coriander
   (optional)
A sprinkling of Garam Masala (see
   p.265) (optional)

For the Marinade

4 tablespoons natural yoghurt
3 tablespoons lime juice
$\frac{3}{4}$ teaspoon ground turmeric
$\frac{3}{4}$ teaspoon paprika

2 garlic cloves, crushed
3 cardamom pods, crushed
$\frac{1}{2}$ teaspoon salt

Mix all the marinade ingredients together. Cut the chicken into thin strips and spoon and mix the marinade on to the chicken. Heat a large frying-pan with just a drop of the cooking oil. The pan must be hot before frying the chicken. Fry, tossing the chicken to give an all-over golden brown finish. Providing that the chicken has been cut into thin strips, it will only take 4–5 minutes to cook.

To finish the taste, squeeze a trickle of lemon juice on to the chicken and add the chopped coriander. To finish the dish totally, just sprinkle with garam masala and serve. This is not essential but will give an even fuller taste.

Note

It is best to fry a handful of chicken at a time as this prevents the heat being lost from the pan and the meat stewing.

Blackened Chicken

This recipe is so called because the spice mixture used to season the meat leaves it with a black finish with plenty of spice flavours. The same spice recipe can be used on fish. Once made, the spices can be kept in an airtight jar for use another day.

Try the chicken dish with different combinations of flavours. It goes very well with Simple Salad (see p.15), especially during the summer when the chicken has been cooked on an open barbecue. It also eats well with stir-fried rice or pasta dishes. I particularly like to eat it as a topping and extra to an open BLT (bacon, lettuce, tomato) sandwich: a really good lunchtime dish.

SERVES 4

4 chicken breasts
1 tablespoon oil

A knob of unsalted butter

For the Blackened Spice Mix

1 tablespoon salt
$1\frac{1}{2}$ teaspoons garlic powder
$1\frac{1}{2}$ teaspoons freshly ground black
    pepper
1 teaspoon ground white pepper

1 teaspoon onion powder or granules
1 teaspoon ground cumin
$\frac{1}{2}$ teaspoon cayenne pepper
$\frac{1}{2}$ teaspoon paprika

Pre-heat the oven to 200°C/400°F/gas 6.

Mix all the spices together. The chicken breasts can now be either completely rolled in the spices or just coated on the skin side.

To cook the chicken, either pan-fry or grill. If you are pan-frying, then simply heat a pan and add the oil and butter. Once the butter is bubbling, add the chicken breast skin-side down and cook for a few minutes until blackened, then turn the chicken and continue to cook until blackened, if liked, on the other side. The chicken will take between 10–12 minutes to cook completely. If you are grilling, brush with oil and butter and grill until blackened on all sides and then season. Finish in the pre-heated oven for about 10 minutes until cooked through. It's now up to you how you want to serve it.

Note

I prefer just to 'blacken' and season the skin side.

Shredded Duck or Grilled Fish with Thai Noodles

This dish suits both meat and fish, in particular duck. I make a duck confit, and shred it, just before serving, over the spicy noodles. As an alternative to the duck, grilled sea bass, cod, turbot, halibut or perhaps a king prawn kebab will all work well with this dish. The noodles I normally use are fettucine. These can either be home-made, bought fresh or dried. Thai fish sauce, or Nam Pla, is a fish sauce used throughout Southeast Asia as a seasoning, similar to soy sauce, for many savoury foods. It is made from salted fish and so consequently has a salty, anchovy taste.

SERVES 4

4 × 100–225 g (4–8 oz) portions of duck or fish confit
350–450 g (12–16 oz) noodles, cooked and tossed in a little dressing

A knob of unsalted butter
Salt and freshly ground black pepper

For the Duck Confit

4 duck legs
2 teaspoons rock salt (optional)

900 g (2 lb) lard or goose fat, melted

For the Thai Sauce

5 tablespoons Champagne or white wine vinegar
3 tablespoons Thai fish sauce (Nam Pla)
120 ml (4 fl oz) olive oil
1 large garlic clove, crushed
1 teaspoon very finely chopped fresh root ginger

Juice and grated zest of $\frac{1}{2}$ small lemon
Juice and grated zest of $\frac{1}{2}$ small orange
1 small red chilli, finely chopped
1 teaspoon crushed black peppers
1 lemon grass stick, finely chopped

To Finish the Dish

1 large red onion, chopped
8–10 fresh basil leaves

8–10 fresh mint leaves
8–10 sprigs of fresh coriander

If you want to make the duck confit, it can be made well in advance, then stored in its own fat until needed. Remove any remaining feather stalks from the duck legs, salt them on the skin side and chill for 24 hours. This will draw any water from the fat and help crisp the skin when the legs are cooked. The legs can also be immediately cooked, once prepared, without salting.

Pre-heat the oven to 160°C/325°F/gas 3.

Sit the legs in a braising dish and cover with the warm melted fat (lard or goose fat). Bring to a simmer, cover with a lid and cook in the pre-heated oven for 1½–2 hours. To check the legs, remove one from the fat and push the skin side. When you feel the meat is starting to become tender and give, remove from the heat and leave to cool in the fat. Simply cover the duck legs completely with the fat and chill. They will keep almost indefinitely.

To make the Thai sauce, mix together the Champagne or wine vinegar with the fish sauce. Whisk the olive oil into this mix a drop at a time, as for a mayonnaise. Add all other ingredients, making sure anything cut is very finely chopped. This can now be kept bottled until needed. You will have about 300 ml (10 fl oz).

Pre-heat the oven to 200°C/400°F/gas 6.

To roast the duck confit, remove the duck legs from the fat. In a hot pan, colour the duck on the fat side until golden, then finish in the pre-heated oven for 15–20 minutes until crispy.

To cook the fish, you can pan-fry or grill. Most 100–225 g (4–8 oz) portions of fish fillet will only take approximately 6–8 minutes once coloured.

To finish either dish, warm the noodles in a knob of butter and season with salt and pepper. Add the red onions, herbs and Thai sauce to moisten all the pasta. This can now be spooned into bowls. If you are serving grilled fish, then simply sit the portions on top of the pasta. The duck can now be either left whole and placed on top, or shredded down with a spoon and fork (as is done in Chinese restaurants to go in pancakes) and sprinkled over the top. The flavour of the Thai sauce with the noodles, fish or duck is sensational.

Note

To guarantee a really crispy duck skin, cook the confit legs skin side down in 1 cm (½ in) oil (almost deep-frying) until golden and crispy. The legs can then be finished by cooking in the oven for 10–15 minutes.

Variations

Roast duck breasts can also be served with this dish, or chicken, pork, lamb, beef, shrimps, prawns, lobster, crab, mussels…

Roast Pigeon and Pea Tart

The wood pigeon is the most common and easily available type of pigeon and can certainly be used in this recipe. However, I prefer to use squab pigeons. Squab pigeon is a specially reared young pigeon that, when cooked, is beautiful and tender without being over-strong in taste. The breasts are very meaty and squabs are now a lot easier to get hold of. Of course, there's always one drawback and in this case it's price. A wood pigeon will be less than half the price of a squab. Whichever you choose, the recipe still works. The pea tart is made up from a cooked shortcrust 7.5 cm (3 in) diameter flan moulds and the peas are braised split peas cooked to a purée. As for the pigeon sauce, we'll be making that from the carcasses of the pigeons.

The pea purée and sauce can both be prepared and cooked a day before, if you wish, and will warm with no loss of taste.

SERVES 4

4 pigeons, wood or squab	225 g (8 oz) Shortcrust Pastry (see p.251)

For the Peas

50 g (2 oz) green split peas	150–300 ml (5–10 fl oz) Vegetable Stock
75 g (3 oz) mixed carrot, onion, celery,	(see p.259) or Chicken Stock
chopped into 5 mm ($\frac{1}{4}$ in) dice	(see p.258)
A knob of unsalted butter	Salt and freshly ground black pepper

For the Sauce

The central carcasses of the pigeons	1 sprig of fresh thyme
A little oil	1 bay leaf
2 glasses of red wine, about 300 ml	300 ml (10 fl oz) Veal or Beef *Jus*
(10 fl oz)	(see p.261) or alternative (see p.262)

Pre-heat the oven to 200°C/400°F/gas 6.

To prepare the pigeons, remove the legs and then remove the central carcass, leaving the breasts still attached to the breast bone. Roasting the breasts on their part of the carcass will prevent them from shrinking and will also keep them moist. The legs can be roasted separately and served (only if using squab pigeon – wood pigeon legs are even smaller) with the rest of the pigeon. I personally just chop them up and use when making the sauce. Another alternative is to cook (confit) them in oil in a pan in the oven for 15–20 minutes. This will make them very tender, but still with little meat.

To cook the peas, cook the vegetables in a pan with a small knob of butter for 1–2 minutes before adding the peas. Cover with the stock and bring to a simmer. Cover with paper and a lid and cook in the pre-heated oven for 30–40 minutes. During the cooking time, check and stir to ensure even cooking. If at any time the mix appears to be a little too dry, then add more stock. At the same time be careful not to allow the mixture to be too thin, this will result in a soup consistency when puréed. When completely cooked and breaking when stirred, season with salt and pepper and blitz to a purée with an electric hand blender or push through a sieve. The peas are now ready.

To make the sauce, chop the carcasses (and legs) and fry in a little oil in a pan until brown and sealed. Add the red wine, thyme and bay leaf. Boil to reduce the wine by three-quarters, then add the *jus* or gravy. Bring to a simmer and cook on a low heat for 15–20 minutes. If the sauce is becoming too thick, then loosen with water. Check the sauce for seasoning with salt and pepper and then strain through a sieve. The sauce will now have a good pigeon/game flavour.

While the sauce is simmering, pre-heat the oven to 200°C/400°F/gas 6. Butter and lightly flour 4 × 7.5 cm (3 in) tartlet moulds.

Roll out the shortcrust pastry and use to line the moulds. Line the pastry with greaseproof paper and fill with baking beans or rice and bake in the pre-heated oven for 15–20 minutes until golden and crispy. Remove the paper and beans.

To roast the pigeons, season with salt and pepper. Colour in a frying or roasting pan and then roast in the pre-heated oven with the breasts sitting up for 12–15 minutes. Once cooked, remove from the oven and leave to rest and relax.

To serve the dish, fill the tartlets with pea purée. Remove the breasts from the bone and slice each into three and arrange on top of the peas, allowing two breasts (one pigeon) per portion. Sit the tarts on plates and simply finish by pouring the rich sauce around.

Note

The breasts can be left whole and just set on top of the tarts. If you are using pigeon legs, then simply serve them on top of the tart with the breasts. The pigeon can also be roasted for 8–10 minutes (particularly if you are using wood pigeons) for a more pink finish.

Turkey Saltimbocca

Saltimbocca is an Italian dish using a veal escalope that has been wrapped in Parma ham with sage leaves. Well, this is exactly what I'm doing using an escalope of turkey breast instead. An escalope is actually just a slice of meat or fish. When using meat, depending on which cut and variety, you may find that it will need to be slightly batted out between pieces of clingfilm. This will give you a thin slice that will cook quite quickly when pan-fried.

This dish came to me when I was looking for Christmas lunch alternatives. I wanted to stick with turkey – capture all the traditional Christmas tastes – but at the same time make a complete dish that doesn't need the endless garnishes that we all have. I wanted to keep things lighter and easier, instead of roast turkey and pork with bacon, sausages, stuffing, bread sauce, cranberry sauce, roast potatoes, sprouts, parsnips, carrots, gravy. I'm worn out writing it, let alone eating it! And remember that's just the main course!

But you certainly don't have to think about just keeping this recipe to serve at Christmas; the turkey can be eaten at any time of the year. Or you could perhaps replace the turkey with chicken breast batted out into an escalope and prepared with the Parma ham and sage, then served with some cheesy noodles and olive oil. If you find it difficult to get Parma or Bayonne ham, then just use some smoked or unsmoked rashers of back or streaky bacon – it still eats well.

To make sure the dish really is complete, I'm serving it with Braised Pearl Barley, Cranberry Sauce with Orange and Crispy Cabbage. Mustard Dressing is used to bind with the barley to give it a risotto-style consistency. If you really don't like mustard, then just use a splash of cream and a squeeze of lemon juice to help the taste and consistency.

I feel I've just written a book about this recipe! So, here it is: it's worth every word and minute!

SERVES 4

4 × 100–175 g (4–6 oz) turkey breast
   escalopes about 5 mm ($\frac{1}{4}$ in) thick
4–8 slices of Parma ham or bacon
$\frac{1}{2}$ bunch of fresh sage
A knob of unsalted butter
Salt and freshly ground black pepper
1 quantity Braised Pearl Barley
   (see p.123)

2–3 tablespoons Mustard Dressing
   (see p.271)
1 quantity Cranberry Sauce with
   Orange (see p.264)
1 quantity Crispy Cabbage (see p.141)

The turkey can be prepared well in advance and kept chilled. Wrap the turkey escalopes in 1 or 2 rashers of Parma ham or bacon with a large sage leaf on the outside, reserving the rest of the sage for later. This can be held on with a cocktail stick. Season and pan-fry the escalopes in a knob of butter in a hot pan for a few minutes on each side, giving a golden brown colour on each side and crisping the Parma ham. Remove the cocktail sticks.

Chop the remaining sage while the turkey is cooking. Warm the pearl barley and add the sage. Moisten to taste with the mustard dressing.

You can serve the dishes separately if you like, but the way I like to serve this dish is to spoon some cranberry sauce around the outside of the plate. In the centre of the plate, spoon some pearl barley, sit the turkey on top and finish with the crispy cabbage sitting on top of the turkey. For a little extra taste, I like to trickle some extra mustard dressing over the cranberry sauce. The dish is now finished – it really is easy to make and, as you can see, it looks exciting and, of course, tastes delicious!

Turkey Saltimbocca.

Roast Turkey Breast with Lemon and Herb Stuffing

Christmas Day cooking can be quite a nightmare, especially if you only finished wrapping the presents at midnight on Christmas Eve, went to bed at 1 a.m., then the children (if you have them!) woke you at 6.30 a.m. Christmas morning wanting to unwrap their presents. The next thing you know, it's 9 a.m., your guests are arriving in three hours and you haven't even started cooking!

You've eventually served lunch at 2.30 p.m., first a starter, then the main course – roast turkey, stuffing, bread sauce, cranberry sauce, gravy, bacon, chipolatas, sprouts, carrots, parsnips, roast potatoes and probably even more! Of course, pudding hardly gets a look in because we're already too full.

Well, this recipe keeps things a bit simpler; it won't give so many headaches but certainly will give you the traditional flavours! You'll have the lovely lemon-flavoured turkey with carrots all from the same pan. I would be tempted just to serve one other vegetable, perhaps French beans or Brussels sprouts with chestnuts, along with good roast potatoes. If you want to serve the other basic garnishes, such as chipolatas, bacon and cranberry sauce, you can include them as well. Cooking and carving this dish is like having another Christmas present. When you make the first cut the lemon and herb flavours just hit you. A great surprise – Happy Christmas!

SERVES 6–8

1 × 1.75 kg (4 lb) turkey breast
6–8 large carrots, halved lengthways
300 ml (10 fl oz) Chicken Stock (see p.258)

2–3 tablespoons Veal or Beef *Jus*
(see p.261) or alternative (see p.262)

For the Lemon, Onion and Herb Stuffing

1½ tablespoons cooking oil
4 large onions, finely chopped
1 garlic clove, crushed (optional)
Grated zest of 3 lemons
1 heaped teaspoon chopped fresh sage
½ teaspoon chopped fresh thyme
½ teaspoon chopped fresh tarragon

450 g (1 lb) fresh white breadcrumbs
Salt and freshly ground black pepper
Freshly grated nutmeg
Juice of 1–1½ lemons
1–2 eggs, beaten
A knob of unsalted butter

To make the stuffing, warm half the cooking oil in a pan and add the finely chopped onions with the crushed garlic, if using. Soften the onions over a medium heat. Add the lemon zest and chopped fresh herbs and continue to cook for 6–8 minutes until the onions are tender. Leave to cool. Once cooled, add the breadcrumbs and season with salt, pepper and nutmeg. Then mix in the juice of 1 lemon. Taste the stuffing, it should be rich in flavour with a bite from the lemon. If you feel it needs a little more bite, then add the juice of the remaining $\frac{1}{2}$ lemon. Now add enough egg to ensure that the stuffing holds together once cooked.

It's best to stuff the turkey a few hours before cooking, even the night before. Place the turkey breast on the work surface and make an incision with a long, sharp knife to make room for the stuffing at the thick end of the breast, not cutting quite through to the sides or other end. The turkey can now be filled with the stuffing. This will almost double the size of the breast. To hold the stuffing in the cut end during cooking, several methods can be used.

1. Simply hold together with 3 or 4 cocktail sticks.
2. Brush egg white on the turkey and press together. This will seal and set once hot. (It's a good idea to do this, then also use some cocktail sticks to be sure!)
3. The turkey can be sealed by sewing with cooks' string.
4. The turkey can also be wrapped in buttered foil. This will hold in the stuffing and also prevent the meat from becoming dry.

Any leftover stuffing can be placed in an ovenproof dish and cooked separately.

Pre-heat the oven to 200°C/400°F/gas 6.

To cook the turkey, first colour the turkey in a roasting pan with the remaining oil and knob of butter until golden. This will work even if the meat is wrapped in foil. If you want to be completely sure of good colouring, then colour the turkey before wrapping. Once coloured, I like to place the carrots in the pan and sit the turkey on top. This will prevent the meat from colouring too much on its base and becoming dry and leathery. Cover the turkey with some butter papers and place in the pre-heated oven. The turkey will take approximately $1\frac{1}{4}$–$1\frac{1}{2}$ hours. This will roast the bird and also cook and set the stuffing. During the cooking process, baste the breast every 10 minutes, not wasting any flavour.

Once cooked, remove from the oven and allow to relax for a further 15–20 minutes before carving. The carrots will also be roasted and full of turkey taste. These, of course, can be served as a vegetable. The juices left in the pan can be used as a gravy. Warm the pan on top of the stove and add the chicken stock. Bring to boiling point, releasing all the flavours in the pan. This can now simply be poured through a sieve and used as a cooking liquor or boiled to reduce by half and some *jus* or alternative added to give a sauce consistency. Then just slice the turkey and serve.

Pork and Black Pudding Patties

Every recipe has alternatives and this one certainly isn't going to miss out! It's a basic recipe for minced pork patties with the addition of black pudding. The black pudding gives a different texture to the dish and a lot more flavour.

As far as the alternatives are concerned, this recipe can be rolled into dumpling balls and braised with mushrooms, onions and red wine. Or go very British by braising them in beer and serving with spinach and mashed potatoes.

There's also a very quick and easy way of making this recipe. Simply buy a pound of good quality pork sausages, squeeze them out of their skins and mix them with 100–175 g (4–6 oz) of chopped black pudding and the mix is made!

SERVES 4

175 g (6 oz) black pudding
450 g (1 lb) pork belly including fat, coarsely minced
2 small or 1 large onion, finely chopped
1 garlic clove, crushed

$\frac{1}{2}$ teaspoon chopped fresh sage
A knob of unsalted butter
1 egg, beaten
1 thick slice of white bread, crumbled
Salt and freshly ground black pepper

The black pudding should first be peeled, and then either crumbled by hand or chopped before adding to the minced pork. Cook the onion, garlic and sage in a knob of butter for 2–3 minutes until softened. Leave to cool. Once cooled, mix with the pork and black pudding, add the egg and breadcrumbs and season with salt and pepper. The mix can now be shaped into 4 × 175–225 g (6–8 oz) patties approximately 2.5 cm (1 in) thick. The patties can now be cooked by either grilling (perhaps on a barbecue) or pan-frying for 6–7 minutes on each side until completely cooked through. Now to serve the patties there are endless alternatives.

I like to serve them topped with my Welsh Rarebit mix (see pp.130–1) and sitting on Irish Potato Cakes (see p.151) with Apple and Mustard Seed Relish (see p.257). A good mustard sauce also works very well with mashed potatoes, or why not just eat them in a good roll with salad and chips!

Pork and Black Pudding Patties, delicious in a bun or
served on their own with chips.

Variations

Here's a great alternative for this recipe – do you remember meat loaf, mashed potato and gravy from school dinner days? Well, that's exactly what this recipe can be turned into. Just follow the recipe and ingredients until the mix is made. Now instead of dividing it into patties, take a square of buttered foil and make the mix into a bloomer loaf. Wrap the foil around, then allow to set and firm in the fridge for 30 minutes. The next stage is to pan-fry in the foil for a few minutes before baking in a pre-heated oven at 200°C/400°F/gas 6 for 25–30 minutes. All you have to do now is remove the foil, slice into 4–6 portions and serve. The mix can also be spiced up with Worcestershire sauce or perhaps add some chopped chestnuts and thyme for a Christmas supper. Adding some Dijon mustard to the accompanying mashed potatoes works very well, as does the onion gravy from *Rhodes Around Britain*. Strain off the onions once cooked to give a smooth onion-flavoured sauce. This will be the best school dinner you'll have ever had!

Note

It is best to leave some of the black pudding in 1 cm ($\frac{1}{2}$ in) pieces mixed with the pork. This gives a better texture and an exciting bite to the patties.

Confit of Pork Belly with Rich Sherry Lentils

A 'confit' of any meat really means a preserve. This is a process of cooking the meat in fat, then storing the meat encased and covered in the fat. Kept chilled, the meat will keep for at least a month. There is, of course, more to the technique than just preserving. The method of slow cooking in the fat keeps the meat very moist and tender. The pork belly should be bought already portioned. Simply ask your butcher to prepare it for you, boned and skinned.

I like to serve the dish with Rich Sherry Lentils or noodles. Or for a starter, cook some smaller portions of pork and sit them on top of my Sweet Pepper and Chilli Relish (see p.280).

Serves 4

900 g (2 lb) lard
4 × 225 g (8 oz) pork belly portions, each a 10 cm (4 in) square (1 cm ($\frac{1}{2}$ in) squares for starters)

A knob of unsalted butter
2 tablespoons clear honey (optional)
1 quantity Rich Sherry Lentils (see p.136)

Pre-heat the oven to 190°C/375°F/gas 5.

Melt the lard in a flameproof, ovenproof dish and add the squares of pork. Bring to a simmer, then cover and place in the pre-heated oven to cook for 1–1½ hours. After the first hour, pierce the pork belly with a knife. If it feels tender right through, then just remove from the oven and allow to cool. If not, leave for a further 20 minutes, then test again.

If you want to keep them chilled, then leave until cold. Remove the pork from the fat and place in a bowl or tray, then strain the fat back on top to cover the meat completely. It will keep refrigerated for at least 1 month.

When you are ready to eat the pork, pre-heat the oven to 180°C/350°F/gas 4.

Remove the meat from the fat and score the fat side diagonally with a knife. Heat a little butter in an ovenproof frying-pan, sit the pork in, fat-side down, and fry for a few minutes until golden. Turn the pork over and cook in the pre-heated oven for about 15 minutes until golden and heated through. The confit of pork is now ready. To make it even richer, spoon a little honey on top and glaze under a hot grill.

To serve, spoon the hot lentils into a large soup plate and sit the golden pork belly on top.

Caramelized Pork Fillets

These pork fillets are quick and easy to prepare. The caramelizing is created by seasoning with granulated sugar as well as salt and pepper. On contact with the hot pan, the sugar begins to dissolve and caramelize, giving you an almost burnt look to the pork but with a rich bitter-sweet taste.

I prefer to eat pork fillets pink inside, and for best results you should leave them to relax while you make a quick sweet and sour sauce from the residue in the pan.

SERVES 4–6

2 × 450 g (1 lb) pork fillets
Salt and freshly ground black pepper

1 tablespoon groundnut oil
50 g (2 oz) granulated sugar

For the Sauce

2 tablespoons white wine vinegar
1 teaspoon tomato purée or ketchup
150 ml (5 fl oz) Chicken Stock
   (see p.258) or water

A knob of unsalted butter (optional)
A dash of Worcestershire sauce
   (optional)
A dash of Tabasco sauce (optional)

Pre-heat the oven to 200°C/400°F/gas 6.

Season the pork fillets with salt and pepper. Heat a frying-pan with the oil until hot. Coat the pork with the sugar, then add it to the pan. As the pork is caramelizing, turn in the pan to ensure equal colouring. Once a rich golden colour, which will only take a few minutes, finish in the pre-heated oven for 12–15 minutes (or 6–8 minutes longer if you like them well done) until cooked to your liking. Remove the pork from the oven and pan and leave to rest.

Now it's time to make a quick sweet and sour sauce. Add the white wine vinegar to the pan and boil to reduce. This will happen immediately due to the heat of the pan. Add the tomato purée or ketchup and the chicken stock or water. Bring to the boil and cook for a few minutes. The sauce can now be sieved and finished with a knob of butter and spiced with a little Worcestershire and Tabasco sauce, if liked. The pork fillets can now be sliced and served with the sauce.

BELOW *Caramelized Pork Fillets (see p.93)*.

RIGHT *Roast Loin of Lamb with Lemon, Garlic and Mint (see p.96)*.

Roast Loin of Lamb with Lemon, Garlic and Mint

The three flavours of lemon, garlic and mint all work so well with lamb. However, it's not often you find three that work well on their own that can also be mixed and work even better! You'll find that all three flavours can be recognized without overpowering the sweetness of the lamb.

For this recipe you'll notice that I am using loins of lamb. This is the cut of meat taken from the best end (lamb cutlets). This gives you individual portions. These flavours also work very well on a roast leg of lamb, making a gravy from the residue left in the pan. I'm sure you can imagine the flavours you'll achieve.

I like to serve the loins on spinach warmed through with the cream sauce. The spinach and cream certainly prevent the predominant flavours taking over the lamb. The gravy is really an optional extra. I like just to serve a tablespoon over the top of each portion of spinach. It does eat very well, making the dish even richer.

SERVES 4

2 boned loins of lamb, cut in half to make 4 portions
Finely grated zest of 2 lemons
1 large garlic clove, crushed
1 tablespoon chopped fresh mint

Pig's caul to wrap loins (optional), soaked overnight in cold water
A knob of unsalted butter
Salt and freshly ground black pepper
900 g (2 lb) spinach, picked and washed

For the Cream Sauce

1 shallot or ½ onion, chopped
2 garlic cloves, roughly chopped
1 glass white wine, about 150 ml (5 fl oz)
Juice of 1–2 lemons

300 ml (10 fl oz) Chicken Stock (see p.258)
150 ml (5 fl oz) double cream
Salt and freshly ground black pepper

For the Gravy

150 ml (5 fl oz) Veal or Beef *Jus* (see p.261) or alternative (see p.262)

5 teaspoons Home-made Mint Sauce/ Reduction (see p.277) or mint sauce

Pre-heat the oven to 220°C/425°F/gas 7. To make the sauce, place the chopped shallot or onion in a pan with the garlic. Add the white wine and bring to the boil, then boil to reduce by two-thirds. Add the juice of 1 lemon and the chicken stock. Bring to the boil, then boil again to reduce by half. It's now time to add the double cream. The sauce can now be brought to the simmer and cooked for a few minutes. Taste the sauce for consistency and seasoning. It's not a thick cream sauce that we are after, just one that barely coats the back of a spoon. The overall taste should give you the flavour of garlic and natural acidity of lemon. Once you feel the flavour is right, simply strain through a sieve to leave you with a smooth cream sauce. You should have about 300 ml (10 fl oz).

To make the gravy, all you have to do is bring the *jus* or gravy to the boil and add the mint sauce reduction or mint sauce from a jar. If you do this, strain the sauce through a sieve. You should have about 150 ml (5 fl oz). Any not used will set when cold and can be refrigerated or frozen.

To cook the spinach, plunge it into boiling salted water and cook only for 1–2 minutes before straining off and refreshing in ice cold water. This will keep the deep green and freshness of the spinach. It also means it can be cooked well in advance and re-heated when needed. Spinach microwaves very well once cooked. Another option for cooking it is to melt a knob of butter in a pan. Once bubbling, add the spinach and cook quickly on a fast heat. The spinach, after being washed, will have some water content. This will help create a steam and cook the spinach a lot quicker. With this method the spinach should be served immediately.

To prepare the lamb, mix the lemon zest with the garlic and chopped mint. Roll the lamb in the lemon mix to give a thin coating of all the flavours. This can be rolled several hours in advance or just before cooking.

I like to then cover the lamb in pig's caul. This is quite difficult to get hold of but holds all the mix on to the lamb. Pig's caul must be soaked in cold water, this makes it easier to use, then drained. It's almost like using clingfilm, just roll it around the meat and it will cling. If caul is unavailable, cook without a covering or wrap foil around the lamb before cooking.

To cook the lamb, heat a roasting pan and add a knob of butter or cooking oil. Season the lamb with salt and pepper, then colour and seal in the pan. The meat must now be finished in the pre-heated oven. Loins of lamb will only take 8–12 minutes to cook to a medium rare to medium stage. For completely well done, cook for 15–20 minutes. Whenever roasting meats, whether they be individual portions or complete joints, it's important to allow resting time. This relaxes the meat after cooking in a hot oven. These portions will need between 5–10 minutes, legs of lamb or beef joints should always have 20–30 minutes.

Warm the spinach and add the cream sauce. The creamed spinach eats so well, every bite of spinach gives you the creamy garlic lemon flavour.

Spoon the spinach on to plates or bowls. Pour a tablespoon of the gravy, if using, on top of each spinach portion. The portions of lamb can now be cut into three, giving you three medallions of pink lamb per portion. Sit them on top of the spinach and serve. It looks a very simple dish that releases so many textures and tastes.

Roast Chumps of Lamb with Spring Greens and Pickled Red Onions

Chumps of lamb are normally sold as chump chops. These aren't; they are the chump joint taken off the bone, the same place the chops come from (rear end of the saddle), but to be served as individual portion roasts. They need trimming of some fat and tidying up, then you have a wonderful portion of lamb with just 1–2 mm of fat covering and ready for roasting.

The pickled red onions are really good. I promise you, when you've made these once you'll be designing dishes to go with them – I have! They will keep very well chilled and can be used for many other dishes and salads. You will notice that we don't have a sauce or gravy here. The marinade from the onions works well enough. Also any excess oil, vinegar can be used again.

SERVES 4

4 lamb chumps, trimmed	675 g (1½ lb) spring greens, stalks
Salt and freshly ground black pepper	removed and cut in 1 cm (½ in) strips
	A knob of unsalted butter

For the Pickled Red Onions

450 g (1 lb) red onions	90–120 ml (3–4 fl oz) balsamic vinegar
95–120 ml (3–4 fl oz) olive oil	A squeeze of fresh lemon juice
95–120 ml (3–4 fl oz) groundnut oil	

The red onions can be made well in advance. Cut the onions into 6 or 8, making sure the core is kept intact as this holds the onions together. Bring a pan of water to the boil, add the onions and cook for 1–2 minutes. Meanwhile, warm together the oils, balsamic vinegar and lemon juice. When the onions are ready, drain off the liquid and add the onions to the vinegar mix, keeping them off the heat. Season with salt and pepper. The onions are now marinating and should be turned over every now and again to ensure even flavouring. It's best to make these at least 1–2 hours before eating. They should then only be served warm; if they become too hot the real flavour is lost.

Pre-heat the oven to 200°C/400°F/gas 6.

The lamb should now be seasoned and started in a roasting pan on top of the stove over a medium heat. Add the lamb fat-side down and start to colour and cook for a few minutes before turning in the pan until each side is sealed and browned, then cook in the pre-heated oven for 12–15 minutes for a pink finish, depending on the size of the cut. It's very important to give chumps of lamb a good 8–10 minutes resting time once cooked to relax the meat.

While the lamb is resting, the spring greens can be blanched in boiling salted water for 30 seconds to 1 minute, before draining off the water and adding a knob of butter and seasoning with salt and pepper.

To serve, spoon the greens at 6 o'clock on the plate with the red onions and some of the dressing at 12 o'clock. Now all we need to do is carve the chumps of lamb and sit them on top of the greens.

Note

The pickled red onions and spring greens will also complement roast lamb for a really satisfying Sunday lunch.

Another great idea is to add the pickled red onions to the roasting pan for the last 10 minutes so that they absorb the wonderful flavours of the roast itself.

Pot Roast Shoulder of Lamb

This is a variation of a Great British dish, using a classic cooking method of pot roasting, slowly braising to allow the meat to take on all the flavours of the ingredients and become more and more tender at the same time. This recipe takes on one or two spices to give it a whole new taste. Shoulder of lamb is one of the tastiest cuts of lamb. For this recipe it has been boned, rolled and tied, removing any excess fat from the centre. Marinating the lamb for two or three days with all the ingredients helps to increase the flavour.

SERVES 4–6

1 shoulder of lamb, boned and rolled, about 675 g (1½ lb)	2 star anise
1 orange, cut into 6–8	2 tablespoons demerara sugar
1 lemon, cut into 6–8	2 glasses of dry sherry, about 150 ml (5 fl oz)
1 cinnamon stick	100 ml (3½ fl oz) soy sauce
6 cloves	450 ml (15 fl oz) water
10 black peppercorns	

Pre-heat the oven to 160°C/325°F/gas 3.

Mix together all the ingredients except the lamb and the water. The lamb can now be marinated in this mix and kept chilled for 2–3 days. The lamb is now ready to pot roast.

Sit the lamb in a deep ovenproof dish with the marinade and add the water. This will cover the lamb half-way. Bring the pan to a simmer, then cover with a lid. Place the dish in the pre-heated oven and cook for 2½–3 hours, basting every 20 minutes until the lamb is totally moist and tender through the whole joint. For the last hour of cooking, remove the lid. This will allow the liquor to reduce, and the continual basting will help the lamb become golden brown and glazed.

Once cooked, drain off any excess liquor. This will have some fat content from the lamb. Strain the liquor through a sieve into a pan and bring to a simmer, skimming off any excess fat that rises to the top. This cooking liquor can be used as a natural *jus* for the dish, or mixed with a gravy to give a good flavoured sauce – you should have about 450 ml (15 fl oz) in all. If the sauce is too strong, simply add water.

A boned and rolled shoulder is ideal for carving. I like to carve straight through, giving good rounds of succulent, rich lamb. It also eats well just sitting on top of mashed potatoes with the rich savoury liquor poured on top.

Pot Roast Shoulder of Lamb.

Lambs' Kidneys 'Chasseur' and Others

Eating offal isn't everyone's favourite, but liver and kidneys seem to be on every household menu at some point. Kidneys can make a very quick and easy dish, just diced and sautéed in hot fat with mustard, or served with a paella-style rice dish with peas, peppers and mushrooms.

A classic chasseur is normally made with onions or shallots, mushrooms, tomatoes, tarragon and parsley in a white wine sauce. This one can be just that, but I thought about having the garnish 'dry': roasted button onions, sautéed button mushrooms and maybe garlic cloves roasted in their skins. Pea purée makes a good vegetable accompaniment.

As for the 'others', well, kidneys eat very well in a mushroom risotto; roasted and sliced on top of the Pea Tart (see p.84); or served with Spring Greens and Pickled Red Onions (see p.98). Kidneys can also be roasted encased in their own fat, which protects them and gives you nothing more than good, succulent meat inside, or sautéed in some of their own fat for a few minutes, keeping them rich and moist. Veal kidneys can be used and cooked in exactly the same way.

SERVES 4

10–12 lambs' kidneys	25 g (1 oz) unsalted butter
2 glasses dry white wine, about 300 ml	12–16 button onions
(10 fl oz)	8 garlic cloves with skin on (optional)
300 ml (10 fl oz) Veal or Beef *Jus*	16–20 button mushrooms
(see p.261) or alternative (see p.262)	Salt and freshly ground black pepper
2 tomatoes, blanched, skinned and diced	
1 teaspoon chopped fresh tarragon	

To make the sauce, boil the white wine until reduced by three-quarters. Add the *jus* or alternative, bring to simmer, then add the tomatoes and tarragon.

Remove the fat from the kidneys if you have not bought them already trimmed. Halve them lengthways and remove any sinew from the centre. These can now be left at this size, this will give you between 5–6 halves per portion, or halved again. If you have some kidney fat, then save it for sautéing them in. Heat a frying-pan and add one or two knobs of kidney fat or butter. Add the kidneys, making sure the pan stays very hot otherwise the kidneys will begin to stew. Fry, turning them in the pan for 2–3 minutes, then remove and keep warm. This pan can now be used to cook the button onions. Add a little more fat and pan-fry until the onions are golden brown. Add the garlic and continue to cook until they are also golden. Now add the mushrooms, making sure the pan stays hot. Season with salt and pepper. The cooking time for the mushrooms will be between 3–4 minutes, during which time the onions and garlic will finish cooking. Add the kidneys to re-warm. The sauce can now be served separately or all mixed together.

Variations

If you prefer to serve the kidneys in the sauce, just use ½ crushed garlic clove. Boil the white wine with the crushed garlic to reduce by three-quarters. Add the *jus* or alternative and bring to a simmer, then cook for 8–10 minutes before adding the cooked mushrooms, button onions, tarragon and diced tomato. The sauce is now ready just to have the kidneys added and served.

If you wish to try roasting kidneys, it's best to buy them totally encased in their own fat. This can be coloured on the outside in a roasting pan, then finished in a pre-heated oven at 200°C/400°F/gas 6. Lambs' kidneys will only take about 20 minutes, large veal kidneys will take between 50 minutes to 1 hour. Once cooked, simply remove the fat, carve and serve.

Note

If using whole garlic cloves, the raw flavour can be weakened by blanching them four or five times in boiling water and then sautéing them to give a milder finish.

Peppered Roast Beef with Beetroot Crisps

At first impression, you might think the pepper flavour would mask the flavour of the beef, which can happen with a peppered steak because the whole of the outside of the cut is covered. When you pepper a joint of beef, however, it is going to be served sliced. This means that the beef itself has the predominant taste, with a fire of pepper just round the edges to lift it. So for your next beef roast, have a go at this recipe. The best cuts of beef to use are sirloin, topside or rib. If using a rib of beef, ask just for the eye of the joint, which will give you a better cut with few trimmings.

Peppered roast beef is also very good served cold or just warm with a raw Pickled Red Cabbage (see p.42) or a good beetroot salad with horseradish dressing. The beetroot crisps provide a tasty garnish. The quantities are not really important for this recipe; make as much as you like!

SERVES 8

675–900 g (1½–2 lb) topside, sirloin or rib of beef	Salt
	Cooking fat or oil
2–3 tablespoons black peppercorns, finely crushed	

For the Beetroot Crisps

2 raw beetroots	Oil for deep-frying
Plain flour for dusting	Salt

Pre-heat the oven to 220°C/425°F/gas 7.

Roll the beef in the crushed peppercorns until completely covered. Season with salt. Seal the meat in a hot roasting pan, then place in the pre-heated oven. A joint of this size will take between 20–40 minutes to cook, but this very much depends on how you would like to eat it. Cooking for 20 minutes will keep it rare, 30 minutes medium and 40 minutes medium to well done. Once cooked, leave the meat to rest for 15–20 minutes before carving. This will relax the meat and it will become even more tender.

To make the beetroot crisps, first peel the raw beetroot and slice absolutely paper thin, using a mandoline, the slicer on a food processor or a very sharp knife. Dry on a cloth. Heat the oil in a deep-fat fryer or heavy-based pan to 180°C/350°F. Lightly dust the beetroot slices in flour and deep-fry in batches for 15–20 seconds. Drain and lightly salt before serving.

Peppered Roast Beef with Beetroot Crisps.

Grilled Calves' Liver Steak with Spiced Potatoes

If calves' liver is hard to find, then simply replace it with lambs' liver, which eats equally well in this dish. In fact, the spiced potatoes, or 'Aloo Bhaji', work with so many other meats, fish and vegetarian dishes.

SERVES 4

4 × 175 g (6 oz) calves' liver steaks or slices 2.5 cm (1 in) thick	Salt and freshly ground black pepper ½ quantity Soured Cream, Lime and
Oil for frying	Mint Yoghurt (see p.276)

For the Spiced Potatoes

4 tablespoons oil	Pinch of chilli powder
1 onion, sliced	¼ teaspoon ground ginger
2 garlic cloves, crushed	A pinch of salt
2 teaspoons black mustard seeds	450 g (1 lb) potatoes, peeled and cut into
1½ teaspoons ground coriander	1 cm (½ in) dice
½ teaspoon ground turmeric	150–300 ml (5–10 fl oz) water

To make the spiced potatoes, warm the oil and add the sliced onion, garlic and all the spices and cook for 2–3 minutes. Add the potatoes and continue to cook for a few minutes before adding the water, just enough almost to cover the potatoes. Bring to a simmer and cook until the potatoes are tender. This will take 15–20 minutes. As the potatoes are simmering, stir gently for an even cooking. The water will reduce, being absorbed by the potato. Do not add any more during cooking or you will be left with a bland potato soup. However, if the liquor does seem to be too thin, then once cooked, drain off the excess stock and boil the stock to reduce before returning it to the potatoes. This will give you a better consistency and taste.

The calves' liver can now be brushed lightly with oil and seasoned with salt and pepper. These eat very well cooked on a grill or pan-fried. I like to eat liver at medium stage. This will take 2–3 minutes cooking on each side, or 4–5 minutes for well done.

To finish the dish, mix 1–2 tablespoons of the soured cream with the hot spiced potatoes and divide on to plates. The liver steaks can now be sliced into three and layered on top. Serve with the remaining soured cream.

Note

I also like to serve Red Wine Dressing (p.274) over each portion of liver.

Steak with Spinach and Café de Paris Butter

A good grilled or fried steak — whether it is a sirloin, rump or rib steak — still seems to be one of the most popular main courses in the UK. Well, there's nothing wrong with that; a good tasty tender steak will suit me any day of the week! This recipe just takes a basic dish a bit further and certainly makes the steak worthy of any special occasion or dinner party.

I'm not really quite sure where the Café de Paris butter originated from but it's one that has been around for some time. This recipe makes about 350 g (12 oz).

SERVES 4

4 × 225–350 g (8–12 oz) steaks (your choice!)
A knob of unsalted butter
2 tablespoons water

A pinch of salt
900 g (2 lb) spinach, picked and washed
Salt and freshly ground black pepper

For the Café de Paris Butter

225 g (8 oz) unsalted butter
1 bay leaf, finely crushed
A pinch of chopped fresh thyme
$\frac{1}{2}$ teaspoon snipped fresh chives
$\frac{1}{2}$ teaspoon chopped fresh tarragon
$\frac{1}{2}$ teaspoon chopped fresh chervil.
A pinch of cayenne pepper

$\frac{3}{4}$ teaspoon Madras curry powder
1 large gherkin, finely chopped
1 heaped teaspoon chopped capers
1 garlic clove, crushed
1 teaspoon chopped fresh parsley
2 egg yolks
2 shallots or 1 small onion, finely chopped

Put all the Café de Paris butter ingredients except the egg yolks and shallots or onion into a food processor or liquidizer and blend together. The shallots and egg yolks can now be added. Shape the butter into a 15 × 5 cm (6 × 2 in) cylinder, wrap in clingfilm and chill.

To cook the steaks, just heat a grill plate or frying-pan and cook them to your liking. For rib and rump steaks I find it best to eat them between medium rare and medium. This helps break down the coarser texture. Cooking them rare can result in chewy steaks. It's always best to allow some resting time for the steaks after they have been cooked; a few minutes will do. This relaxes the meat, making it more tender.

While the steaks are cooking, melt a knob of butter in a pan and add the water. Bring to the boil and add the spinach. This will now take just a few minutes to cook, stirring from time to time. Do not cook with a lid on as this will result in the loss of colour from the spinach. Season the spinach with salt and pepper.

Pre-heat the grill. Finish the dish by putting 1 cm ($\frac{1}{2}$ in) slices of the Café de Paris butter on top of the steaks. Pop these under the grill for 1–2 minutes so the butter begins to melt. Divide the spinach between plates and sit the steaks on top. Pour any excess butter on top.

American Corned Beef Hash

Corned Beef is a dish I featured in More Rhodes Around Britain. *I believed that was really the only way to make it and there would be no other corned beef dish without using that. Well, how wrong I was. It's absolutely true you can never stop learning in this job; there's always another method to learn.*

While I was in New York I just had to try a good corned beef hash and guess what? I found it. The beef itself is still salted for 3 days but after that it's simply boiled and left to cool. All you do then is simply shred it finely and then fry it. Could it be easier and tastier? I don't think so!

For me this is the best way to eat a good corned beef hash and the dish certainly has many options when to serve it. It eats very well as breakfast, lunch or dinner especially with fried eggs 'sunny-side up' or 'easy over'!

SERVES 6–8

900 g (2 lb) beef skirt (corned beef)	3 onions, sliced
2 large jacket potatoes, about 900 g (2 lb)	A knob of unsalted butter
Salt and freshly ground black pepper	

You can buy the meat already salted, but if you want to do it yourself, it is quite simple. It's very important to order well in advance as the meat must be soaked for 3 days before cooking. Simply add enough salt to some water (enough to cover the beef) to keep a new potato afloat, cover and soak in the fridge for 3 days.

Once soaked, remove the beef and discard the water. Rinse the meat to release any excess salt. Cover the beef skirt with cold water in a pan and bring to a simmer. Cook for about $2\frac{1}{2}$ hours until completely tender. Once cooked, leave to cool in the cooking liquor.

Now it's time to take the beef from the stock. The beef can now be chilled and kept for several days or used immediately.

Peel the potatoes and cut into 5–10 mm ($\frac{1}{4}$–$\frac{1}{2}$ in) dice. These should now be cooked in boiling salted water for 3–4 minutes until tender. Pour off the water and leave the potatoes to one side. Shallow-fry the onions in the butter until golden brown.

Using a sharp knife, shred the beef, including all fat content, as thinly as possible. This will keep it very tender and moist. The beef can now be seasoned with salt and pepper and then fried off with the onion and the pre-cooked potatoes. Once all has warmed, increase the heat and continue to fry until a crispy golden base has formed. The hash can now be turned over and an equally crispy base repeated. It's not essential to form an omelette-style cake, but the change in textures from crispy to succulent is certainly very important.

You now have American Corned Beef Hash. And to keep with American traditions, why not serve it with the Home-made Ketchup on page 268.

American Corned Beef Hash.

Home-made Haggis

This traditional Scottish dish goes back to the 1600s, although it didn't really become a common dish until the mid 1700s in Edinburgh. It's not one that's going to be made on a daily basis, but if you do feel like having a go and you've never eaten it before you will be more than pleasantly surprised.

Haggis has a faggot-like consistency that certainly isn't short of flavour. I personally love to eat a good haggis with mashed turnips, the real Scottish way. The mashed 'turnips' in Scotland are, in fact, mashed 'swedes' to us in England! Mixing the swedes with mashed potatoes eats very well with this dish.

This recipe was first cooked for me by Stuart Busby, a chef I've worked with for many years. It was Burns Night, 25 January – well what else can you eat?

I like to make this recipe into individual portions. It can also be made into a steamed haggis pudding by simply making the recipe and placing it into 2 × 1.75 litre (3 pint) pudding basins. Cover it with buttered foil and then steam it for 3½ hours. This can then be served with gravy made from the cooking liquor.

SERVES 4–6

1 × sheep's pluck (lungs, heart and liver)
Chicken Stock (see p.258) or water
Carrot, onion, celery and leek, chopped
    (optional)
6 large onions, finely chopped
25 g (1 oz) unsalted butter
A drop of oil
175 g (6 oz) pinhead oats
100 g (4 oz) shredded suet
½ teaspoon chopped fresh thyme

½ teaspoon chopped fresh sage
2 teaspoons salt
A pinch of cayenne
A pinch of black pepper
Finely grated zest and juice of 1 lemon
    (optional)
225–450 g (8–16 oz) pig's caul to wrap
    the haggis (optional, needed if not
    using pudding basins), soaked
    overnight in cold water

To Serve

Mashed swede

Mashed Potatoes (see p.154)

If it is difficult to buy a complete sheep's pluck (containing the lungs, heart, liver and lights), then simply buy a sheep's heart, lung and liver separately. These can then be cooked in the same way. Wash the pluck, place in a pan and cover with chicken stock or water. Obviously chicken stock will give you a stronger flavour and more of a jellied finish. It's best to add some chopped carrot, onion, celery and leek to the stock or water to increase the flavour. The windpipe from the pluck should be left hanging out of the pan and left to drip into an empty pan. This can now be simmered for $1\frac{1}{2}$ hours. Once cooked, leave to cool in the pan, then set in stock overnight.

The windpipe can now be removed. The hearts, lung, lights and liver can now be minced through a medium mincer or chopped; you will need about 1.1 kg ($2\frac{1}{2}$ lb) in total. The liver obviously has a very powerful taste; I prefer only to use half to balance the flavours.

The cooking liquor should be tasted for flavour and seasoning. Should it taste a little weak, then simply return to the boil and boil to reduce and increase the depth of flavour. Up to 600 ml (1 pint) of stock may be added to the haggis mix to give a good moist texture.

The onions can be lightly softened without colour in the butter or drop of oil, then allowed to cool. The pinhead oats can be toasted to a golden brown colour. All the ingredients can now be mixed together, including the herbs, salt, pepper and cayenne. The stock can now be added to finish the mix. The mix should be well seasoned, giving a full flavour with a bite from the cayenne pepper. Lemon zest and juice can also be added to this mix to lift the other flavours.

If you are using pig's caul, drain the soaked caul, squeeze out excess water and lay it on a chopping board. Divide the mix into 8–10 portions and wrap each portion in the caul to make oval shapes. To keep the shape and prevent the caul from splitting, also wrap each portion in buttered foil. If pig's caul is unavailable, then simply wrap each portion in clingfilm twice, then also in foil. Alternatively, you can use 2×1.75 litre (3 pint) pudding basins or 300 ml ($\frac{1}{2}$ pint) ones for individual portions.

To cook, simply boil any remaining stock with the addition of water to give enough quantity to cover the haggis. The haggis portions can now be cooked in the simmering liquor for 45–60 minutes. Once cooked, they will keep hot in the stock. Some stock can be strained off and made into a gravy for the haggis. I always like to eat them straight from the stock, the mix being moist enough because of the added stock.

Of course, while it was cooking the mashed turnips/swedes will also be on the stove along with mashed potatoes to finish the dish.

Variation

While I was staying in Glasgow and feeling peckish – it was probably 9.30–10.00 p.m. – I decided to pop into a fish and chip shop for a bite to eat. To my surprise I ended up eating the speciality of the house. It was Battered Deep-fried Haggis with Curry Sauce! Certainly a dish I hadn't tried before and probably what worried me was that I really loved it!

So there's another option, if you have any haggis left over. Once it's cold just lightly flour, dip in batter (lager mixed with self-raising flour to a thick consistency makes a brilliant batter), and deep-fry until golden. Now just serve a good curry sauce to go with it.

Vegetarian Dishes

When you look through these recipes, you'll see some of the favourites I have featured in earlier books – I just couldn't leave them alone. One of these is the risottos, with their almost unlimited uses and variations. The Tomato, Spinach and Parmesan Risotto (see p.120) is particularly good and very different, having been made with my natural Tomato Stock (see p.263); you feel you're eating fresh tomatoes from the flavour. This is a great main course dish that can be served with just a green salad and one or two spoons of the Red Wine Dressing (see p.274). So there's one more for the list.

Vegetarian dishes are becoming more and more popular, and so they should be. The best feature about vegetarian foods as well as just vegetables is their freshness. I don't think any fish or meat can match being picked one minute and cooked the next.

Oh, and by the way, you simply must have a go at the Mushroom Pancake Gâteau (see p.132). You'll love it.

Broccoli – cooked so it still holds its shape, colour and of course its taste. (see p.146).

Rice

I thought I would give you some information about rice because I was absolutely amazed myself to find just how much is produced worldwide. It's a food commodity that in Britain we tend to use as a side dish, normally just to mop up the sauce.

About 500 million tonnes of rice are produced each year and at least half of the world's population eat rice as their staple food. This basically works out that for every single person living on earth, 65 kilos are produced a year.

Rice originated in India, which is still one of the world's foremost growers. Today, over 100 million tonnes are produced there annually. This includes over 8000 different varieties. Rice was taken to China from India around 2000 BC. China has since become the world's largest rice producer, producing over 180 million tonnes a year. That's about a third of world production. The people of China eat about 80–100 kg (176–220 lb) per person a year. Rice was also introduced to Japan from China in the third century BC. Japan now produce about 15 million tonnes annually. Here are a few more countries who produce rice: Thailand, 20 million tonnes per annum; USA, 7–8 million tonnes per annum; Spain, 500,000 tonnes per annum. Other European countries produce rice, for example Greece and France produce approximately 100,000 tonnes each.

There are so many varieties to choose from which give us so many different dishes. We are familiar with these basic varieties.

Patna: probably the most common to us. This is a long-grain which is used for boiled or braised (pilaf) dishes.

Carolina: this is our short-grain pudding rice for classic baked rice puddings.

Ground: this basically cooks to a creamy rice pudding texture for desserts.

Arborio: an Italian rice most famous for risottos.

Wild rice: this is an American relative of the rice family, with a nutty taste.

Basmati: this must be the king of all rice. It is grown in India at the foot of the Himalayas. Basmati is more expensive than patna and has a fine, longer grain with an almost perfumed flavour. If ever you are simply cooking some boiled or braised rice, try some basmati; it really is as good as its reputation tells us.

Rice, as I have said, has become and, in fact, always has been one of the most eaten foods. Rice cooked very simply, braised, boiled, etc. and without butter is a very healthy food to eat with very few calories.

Well that's enough information, now I'm going to give you some recipes to try.

Braised Rice

Using this recipe, you can make a simple braised rice or a spicy version. Choose your stock to go with whatever dish you are serving.

SERVES 4–6

225 g (8 oz) basmati or patna rice, washed
1 tablespoon cooking oil
2 onions, finely chopped
Salt and freshly ground black pepper
450 ml (15 fl oz) Vegetable Stock
(see p.259), Chicken Stock (see p.258), Fish Stock (see p.260) or water
A knob of unsalted butter (optional)

For Spicy Braised Rice

2–3 cloves
½ cinnamon stick
1 garlic clove, crushed
5–6 cardamom pods
A few saffron strands (optional)
1 bay leaf

Pre-heat the oven to 200°C/400°F/gas 6.

Warm the cooking oil in a braising pan and add the chopped onion. If you are making the spicy version, then add all the other ingredients except the stock, otherwise just add the rice. Cook for a few minutes until the onions have softened. Pour on the stock or water. Bring to a simmer, cover with greaseproof paper and a lid and place in the pre-heated oven. This should now be cooked for approximately 20–25 minutes, stirring occasionally to keep an even cooking. While the rice is cooking, check the stock. If the rice seems to be very dry, then simply add more stock or water to moisten. It is, however, important that the rice does absorb the stock and still have a very slight bite in texture. The rice when forked up will remain light and fluffy. If too much stock is used and the rice cooks too long it will become very heavy and stodgy. The maximum the rice will take is 30 minutes. Once cooked, season with salt and pepper and serve. A knob of butter can also be forked into the rice to enrich the texture and taste.

The spicy rice should have the cinnamon, bay leaf and cloves removed before serving. To make this easier these can be tied in muslin before being added. The flavours will not spread quite so much but will still lend good taste.

Variations

The rice eats very well if bound with the Soured Cream, Lime and Mint Yoghurt (see p.276). Great as a vegetarian dish with grilled vegetables or spinach and toasted flaked almonds added to it.

Braised Nutty Rice

This dish has the same basic ingredients as the Braised Rice but also has plenty of extras that can be added. The addition of butter is what is going to give it the nutty taste. The butter will first be cooked to a nut-brown, bubbling stage before colouring the rice. I have only listed vegetable stock in this recipe because I prefer to keep this recipe vegetarian. If you prefer to use chicken or fish stock, you can use either.

SERVES 4–6

225 g (8 oz) basmati or patna rice, washed
75 g (3 oz) unsalted butter
1 onion, very finely chopped

450 ml (15 fl oz) Vegetable Stock (see p.259)
Salt and freshly ground black pepper

Pre-heat the oven to 200°C/400°F/gas 6.

Melt the butter in a braising pan and cook to a nut-brown stage. The butter at this stage will be bubbling and have a nutty colour and aroma. Add the rice immediately, before the butter becomes burnt. Now the rice should be cooked until it becomes a nut-brown colour. At this point, add the finely chopped onion and continue to cook for a few minutes. Now add the stock and bring to a simmer. Cover with greaseproof paper and a lid and cook in the oven for 20–25 minutes until tender. During the cooking time, check the rice has sufficient stock. The rice should be cooked, absorbing the stock and still having a slight bite. The maximum time the rice will need to cook is 30 minutes. Once ready, season with salt and pepper and serve.

Variations

Extra flavours that can be added for a different taste and texture are: toasted chopped pine nuts; diced tomato flesh; chopped fresh coriander; a dash of Tabasco sauce. All these can be added together. I also like to beat 1–2 eggs, then add them at the last moment to create a scrambled egg effect running through the rice.

Rice and Peas

This isn't quite as it sounds because the peas are, in fact, kidney beans. However, this is the traditional name for this Caribbean speciality that I have grown to love. It's a dish that can be eaten hot or cold and once you've had one taste you just can't stop eating.

It can go with so many dishes, whether they be dry spicy curries, fried chicken, fish kebabs or salads – all work very well. The flavour of the kidney beans works through the rice, making them very predominant. The whole dish is also enriched with the addition of coconut cream.

SERVES 6–8

350 g (12 oz) long-grain rice, washed
175 g (6 oz) kidney beans, soaked in water for a minimum 8 hours
About 1.2 litres (2 pints) water
75 g (3 oz) coconut cream (block), cut into pieces
2 onions, finely chopped
4 garlic cloves, crushed
½ teaspoon chopped fresh thyme
25 g (1 oz) unsalted butter
Salt and freshly ground black pepper
Water

Place the kidney beans in a pan and cover with the water. Bring to the boil, then turn down to a simmer. The beans will now settle in the pan. Now any impurities should be skimmed off. Now add all the other ingredients except the rice and coconut. The beans can now be left to simmer until they become tender, stirring occasionally. This will take 45–60 minutes. During this time the onions and other ingredients will have cooked to a purée and totally flavoured the beans.

Now it's time to add the block of coconut cream and cook for a few minutes until dissolved. Once dissolved, add the rice. There should still be sufficient water to cook the rice. Continue to simmer for 15–20 minutes, stirring occasionally. During this time, the rice will become tender and absorb the excess liquor. The rice will take on the flavour and a slightly pink colour from the kidney beans. Season with salt and pepper and serve.

Risottos

Risottos became quite a big feature in More Rhodes Around Britain. *I didn't want to take you over repeat recipes, but I do want to share as many of my thoughts and dishes with you as possible. My original basic risotto recipes included between 100–175 g (4–6 oz) of butter, which gives you a wonderful creamy rich texture, but can be quite expensive and too rich for some taste buds. So for these recipes I'm only suggesting 50 g (2 oz). This does make quite a difference to the fat content. If that amount still worries you then simply only add a small knob of butter at the very end, just to finish off the dish and give it a good shine. The other basic quantities remain the same: 225 g (8 oz) of Arborio rice (speciality risotto rice from northern Italy) and 1.2 litres (2 pints) of Vegetable, Chicken or Fish Stock (see pp.259, 258 or 260). These will give you four main-course servings of risotto with a good creamy consistency.*

Although the basic method of making risottos will always be the same, the actual flavours can be totally different. Those featured here are all vegetarian with their own textures and tastes.

Why not try a Tomato and Spinach Risotto Tart finished with Stilton Rarebit (see p.130). Line some 10 cm (4 in) tartlet moulds with thin Shortcrust Pastry (see p.251), adding 25–50 g (1–2 oz) of freshly grated Parmesan to the pastry recipe. Bake these blind. Once the risotto is made, spoon it into the tartlets and top with Stilton rarebit, making sure the pastry edges of the tart are completely covered. Finish under the grill until golden.

The risotto list could just go on and on. I do have a couple more ideas here for you to try, both using the basic risotto recipe.

The first one is a Sweet Pepper Risotto. All you need is to take 3–4 red peppers and cut them into a 1 cm (½ in) dice or 5 mm (¼ in) strips and cook them with a chopped onion before adding the rice and hot stock and cooking in the normal way. This releases all the pepper juices, giving a rich flavour and colour to the dish. One or two finely diced red chillies can also be added to fire up the finished taste. The vegetable stock can also be helped by adding one or two peppers to the basic vegetables. To finish the dish, stir in some freshly grated Parmesan, a knob of butter and an extra trickle of olive oil.

Another way of cooking this dish is to turn it into a Ratatouille Risotto. Just use a red and green pepper with the chopped onion and also add some sliced mushrooms. Once the risotto is cooked, finish it with cooked diced courgettes, chopped tomato flesh and freshly grated Parmesan cheese. To lift the tomato base, use half Tomato Stock (see p.263) and half Vegetable Stock (see p.259). This will give you a good tomato / ratatouille flavour.

For the ultimate finish, I use crispy deep-fried aubergine slices. These are just very thin half slices dusted in flour flavoured with cayenne pepper (2–3 tablespoons of flour to 1 teaspoon of cayenne). They are then deep-fried in hot fat until golden and crispy. Lightly salt and sit them on top of the ratatouille risotto.

One more risotto can be made by just taking half the recipe, i.e. 100 g (4 oz) of Arborio rice and 600 ml (1 pint) of vegetable stock. This is then mixed with an equal quantity of braised lentils cooked in vegetable stock with sherry vinegar (see p.136). Once both have been mixed and loosened with more stock, I like to finish the dish with soured cream or Crème Fraîche (see p.275). This replaces the usual butter and Parmesan. This creamy Lentil Risotto eats very well as a winter dish or can accompany several fish and meat dishes. Home-made herb and pork sausages would work very well or perhaps a good portion of roasted cod.

So there are a few more to try. I think that's the last of the risotto recipes, well, at least the rice-based ones!

Tomato, Spinach and Parmesan Risotto

Sun-dried tomatoes give a rich finish to this dish. The tomatoes are literally left out to dry in the sun. This dries out all the juices in the tomato flesh, concentrating the flavour. I only use a tablespoon to help flavour this dish along with the tomato stock and fresh diced tomato flesh.

You can buy sun-dried tomatoes completely dry or in oil. It's best to buy them in oil, which makes them ready to use and very tender. Also the oil can be used to help flavour the risotto. The tomatoes in oil are also sometimes flavoured with garlic and chilli. This helps add spice to the finished dish. Completely dry tomatoes will need to be placed in boiling water and left to stand for up to 1 hour to soften.

SERVES 4–6

225 g (8 oz) Arborio rice
600 ml (1 pint) Tomato Stock (see p.263)
600 ml (1 pint) Vegetable Stock
   (see p.259)
2 tablespoons olive oil
2 onions, finely chopped
225 g (8 oz) spinach, picked and washed

2–3 tomatoes, skinned and diced
1 tablespoon sun-dried tomatoes, finely
   diced (optional)
2–3 tablespoons freshly grated Parmesan
50 g (2 oz) unsalted butter
Salt and freshly ground black pepper
Freshly shaved Parmesan flakes

Preferably use a braising pan to make the risotto, as this gives space for the stock to cook the rice evenly. Warm the olive oil in the pan, add the onions and cook for a few minutes without colour until tender. The two stocks should be mixed together in a separate pan and brought to simmering point. This is important as risotto can only be made with a hot stock. This breaks down the outside of the rice, creating a creamy texture. Also the stock is only added 1–2 ladlefuls at a time, and kept on the move with stirring, creating a constant braising.

Add the rice to the onions and continue to cook for a few minutes. Add a ladle of the stock (about 150 ml/5 fl oz) and cook and stir over a medium heat. Once the stock has been absorbed by the rice, add another ladle and continue to cook, repeating the same process until the rice becomes tender with the slightest bite left in. This will take about 20 minutes. Meanwhile, blanch the spinach in boiling water for a few seconds until just wilted, then drain and roughly chop.

Now it's time to finish the dish. Add the diced tomato flesh, sun-dried tomatoes, grated Parmesan and butter to the risotto. Once completely warmed through, add the spinach and check the consistency. You will probably find the mix to be too thick, due to the Parmesan absorbing the stock. Add more stock until a loose consistency is achieved. Season with salt and pepper. The risotto can now be served and finished with Parmesan flakes.

Variation

Another good finish for this risotto is a nut-brown vinaigrette. This is simply 25–50 g (1–2 oz) of butter cooked in a hot frying-pan until it begins to bubble and take on a nut-brown colour and flavour. At this point, and no further otherwise it will burn, pour into a bowl with 4–6 tablespoons of Basic Vinaigrette (see p.276). Season with salt and pepper and spoon over the risotto. The nutty flavour works very well with the sweet acidic tastes of the tomatoes.

Tomato, Spinach and Parmesan Risotto.

Roast Winter Vegetable Risotto

This risotto has a great texture with plenty of the roasted winter vegetables giving flavours and, of course, colours to the dish. It's as basic as our other risotto dishes but leaves a totally different taste.

To finish this dish, I've made what I call a Roast Gravy Dressing. It certainly doesn't sound vegetarian, but it is. The gravy taste comes from the reduction of Madeira. When reduced, Madeira can give a sweet but almost 'meaty' rich flavour. Also, once the vegetables have been roasted and removed from the pan, the dressing can be used to remove any taste residues left in the pan. So this is a good example of how I don't like to waste any flavours!

The 'roasted' flavour can be increased if when you make the vegetable stock, you first roast the vegetables. They need to be well coloured in the pan before adding any water. This will give a good nutty roast taste.

SERVES 6–8

225 g (8 oz) Arborio rice
1.2 litres (2 pints) Vegetable Stock
(see p.259)
2 tablespoons olive or vegetable oil
2 onions, finely chopped
2 carrots, cut into 1 cm ($\frac{1}{2}$ in) dice

2 small white turnips, peeled and cut
into 1 cm ($\frac{1}{2}$ in) dice
$\frac{1}{2}$ swede, cut into 1 cm ($\frac{1}{2}$ in) dice
2 parsnips, cut into 1 cm ($\frac{1}{2}$ in) dice
75 g (3 oz) unsalted butter
2 tablespoons freshly grated Parmesan
Salt and freshly ground black pepper

For the Roast Gravy Dressing

120 ml (4 fl oz) Madeira
1 heaped teaspoon finely chopped
shallots (optional)

6 tablespoons Basic Vinaigrette
(see p.276)

Pre-heat the oven to 200°C/400°F/gas 6.

Bring the vegetable stock to a simmer. Heat the oil in a pan or braising pan and add the chopped onions. Cook for a few minutes without colour until the onions begin to soften. Add the rice and continue to cook for a few minutes. It's now time to start adding the hot vegetable stock, just 1–2 ladles at a time to break down the layers of the rice and create a classic risotto texture. For even cooking it's important to stir the rice as the stock is added.

While the risotto is being made, heat a frying-pan and add a knob of butter. The carrots can be the first to be fried as these will take the longest to cook. Fry the carrots until a good golden colour, almost burnt at the edges, is achieved. Once coloured, transfer to a roasting pan and continue to cook in the pre-heated oven. Repeat the frying process with the turnips and swede, then add them to the carrots. Now finish by frying the parsnips. All the vegetables mixed together will now take a maximum 15 minutes to cook in the oven. The carrots take the longest which is why we start with them first. Basically, the vegetables should have a roasted, tender taste.

All we need now is to finish with the dressing. Boil the Madeira, and shallots, if using, until reduced by half, then add to the vinaigrette. You should have about 150 ml (5 fl oz). Another method is once the vegetables have been cooked in the roasting pan, remove them, then pour the Madeira into the hot pan. This will almost immediately reduce in quantity and at the same time lift the flavours from the pan. Strain through a sieve into the dressing.

When the risotto is ready, you can add either all or just half the vegetables. You may also need to add a little more stock with the Parmesan to maintain the creamy texture. Add the remaining butter and adjust the seasoning with salt and pepper. The risotto can now be divided between bowls. If only half the vegetables were added, then the rest can now be sprinkled on top to give a coarser and more colourful finish. Spoon the roast gravy dressing over the risotto and serve.

Braised Pearl Barley

Perfect for the Turkey Saltimbocca (p.86), this is also a great side dish for grilled meats.

SERVES 4

100 g (4 oz) pearl barley	600 ml (1 pint) Chicken Stock (see p.258)
1 large onion, finely chopped	or Vegetable Stock (see p.259)
15 g (½ oz) unsalted butter	Salt and freshly ground black pepper

Pre-heat the oven to 200°C/400°F/gas 6.

In a warm ovenproof pan, soften the chopped onion in the butter. Add the pearl barley and cook for a further minute. Add the stock and bring to a simmer. Cover with a lid and transfer to the oven for about 30–40 minutes, stirring from time to time, until the barley becomes tender. Once cooked, remove from the oven. The barley can now be seasoned with salt and pepper and used immediately or left to cool and re-heated later in a pan or in the oven with a little more stock or water.

Mustard Pearl Barley Risotto with Parsley Coulis

This dish will probably create a few raised eyebrows. After all, I've always stated that risotto can only be made with Arborio rice, and I still believe that.

It's unusual for me to use a cookery term that doesn't really apply. That's normally something that irritates me. So many chefs will put a navarin of lamb (a classic braised lamb dish) on the menu and when you receive the dish you find it's lamb fillet medallions with turned baby vegetables. A nice well presented dish but certainly not a navarin!

So do I have a better excuse? No, is the answer. I'm basically calling it a risotto because this dish is being finished in a similar way; extra stock and butter being added to give a creamy texture. Once you've tried it you'll know exactly what I mean: the tender soft barley bound with the creamy stock is so good to eat. It also has, as for risotto, almost unlimited variations. Any of my risotto recipes will work so well with this recipe.

I like to serve this with main course fish or meat dishes: this creamy risotto with either grilled fillet or chunks of salmon running through it are a delight to eat. Chicken is also a perfect meat to go with this, whether it be a plain roast accompanied by a large bowl of savoury thyme barley risotto, or chicken escalopes cooked on a barbecue, or simple chicken breasts. All work very well.

The basic recipe is made with vegetable stock, but fish and chicken stocks can be used; it really depends on what you are serving with the dish. The mustard I'm using is Dijon enhanced with the Mustard Dressing (see p.271). Another good mustard to use is a grain mustard such as Meaux mustard.

This pearl barley dish also eats very well cold loosened with basic dressing. Many other flavours can be added: peas, tomatoes, spring onions, olives – endless combinations. If you want to serve the dish as a starter or side dish, you can halve the quantities.

The parsley coulis couldn't be more basic with so few ingredients, but has so much flavour, with the strength of continental parsley coming through. It keeps very well chilled for a few days. It can also be served with many dishes: rice or barley risottos, pasta dishes and salad dressings.

SERVES 4–6

225 g (8 oz) pearl barley
1.2–1.5 litres (2–2½ pints) Vegetable
    Stock (see p.259)
2 tablespoons olive oil
2 large onions, finely chopped

2 tablespoons Dijon mustard
50 g (2 oz) unsalted butter
4–6 tablespoons Mustard Dressing
    (see p.271)
Salt and freshly ground black pepper

For the Parsley Coulis

1 large bunch of fresh flatleaf parsley,
    about 40 g (1½ oz)

2 tablespoons ice cold water
4 tablespoons olive oil

To make the coulis, very quickly blanch the parsley in boiling water and immediately refresh in cold water. Squeeze out the excess water and blitz in a liquidizer with the 2 tablespoons of ice cold water. Slowly add the olive oil until totally blended in. Season the coulis with salt and pepper, then strain through a very fine sieve. This will leave you with a rich green parsley coulis with a coating consistency. This can now be kept in a bottle or bowl and chilled until needed. You will have about 150 ml (5 fl oz) of coulis.

Pre-heat the oven to 200°C/400°F/gas 6.

Warm the olive oil in an ovenproof braising pan and add the chopped onions. Cook over a medium heat without colouring, until softened. Add the pearl barley and mustard and continue to cook for a few minutes. Add 900 ml (1½ pints) of the vegetable stock and bring to a simmer. Cover with greaseproof paper and a lid and cook in the pre-heated oven for 40–45 minutes for a very soft, almost souffléd finish. After 20–25 minutes, check the barley. It may need another 300 ml (10 fl oz) of stock to finish the cooking.

Once tender, add the butter and mustard dressing. You may find a little more mustard dressing or Dijon mustard is needed to give a stronger taste. Loosen the barley with more stock to give a creamy consistency. Adjust the seasoning with salt and pepper and serve in bowls with the parsley coulis drizzled over the top.

Chestnut, Onion and Brussels Sprout Risotto Cake with Brandy Herb Butter

The real feature of this dish is it is completely vegetarian but has a good Christmas feel and taste. It's also great for a complete Boxing Day meal using up all the Christmas leftovers.

You can make the risotto cakes well in advance and breadcrumb them ready for frying. Or you can just serve all your friends with a large bowl of Christmas risotto and a mixed salad. In the risotto, you can shred up some left-over cooked turkey, bacon rashers and chipolatas and add them to the finished dish, if you prefer. I like to finish it in the normal fashion with some grated Parmesan. I also chop up any left-over stuffing, fry it until crispy and sprinkle it over the top. Whichever version you choose, there's a festive sauce to accompany it, which eats brilliantly.

SERVES 4–6

For the Risotto Mix

225 g (8 oz) Arborio rice
225 g (8 oz) Brussels sprouts, finely
    shredded
100 g (4 oz) unsalted butter
4 onions, finely chopped

1.2 litres (2 pints) Vegetable Stock
    (see p.259), hot
2 tablespoons freshly grated Parmesan
Salt and freshly ground black pepper
50–75 g (2–3 oz) shelled chestnuts,
    chopped

For the Cakes

3 tablespoons plain flour
2–3 eggs, beaten

225 g (8 oz) fresh white breadcrumbs
Oil for deep-frying

For the Brandy Herb Butter

1 tablespoon chopped shallots
2 tablespoons brandy
300 ml (10 fl oz) Vegetable Stock
    (see p.259)

25–50 g (1–2 oz) unsalted butter
$\frac{1}{2}$ teaspoon chopped fresh flatleaf parsley
Salt and freshly ground black pepper

To Garnish

About 20 fresh sage leaves
Flour for dusting

A pinch of cayenne pepper

If the shredded sprouts are raw, cook them quickly in boiling water for approximately 1 minute, then drain.

To make the risotto, melt the butter in a large pan and add the chopped onions. Cook for a few minutes until softened, without colouring. Add the rice and continue to cook for a few minutes. As with all risottos, the stock must be hot before using. Add 1–2 ladlefuls at a time, stirring and allowing the stock to be absorbed before adding more. The cooking process will take between 20–25 minutes, until the rice is tender with just a slight bite. It's now time to add the Parmesan cheese and season with salt and pepper. Mix in the sprouts and chestnuts. A drop more stock may be needed to loosen the mixture slightly. The risotto is now ready to serve as it is.

If you are going to make the cakes, then pour the risotto into a 25×15 cm (10×6 in) tray lined with clingfilm and spread, making sure the risotto is 2.5 cm (1 in) deep. Leave to cool, then chill to set firm. Once chilled and set, the risotto can be turned out; the clingfilm will make this very easy. Cut out the risotto with 7.5–10 cm (3–4 in) round cutters or simply cut into 7.5–10 cm (3–4 in) squares.

Lightly flour the risotto cakes, then pass through the beaten eggs and breadcrumbs. Repeat the process through the eggs and crumbs, tidying up the shapes with a palette knife. A criss-cross effect can be made on top with a knife. Heat the oil to 160°C/300°F. Deep-fry the cakes for about 6 minutes to heat and cook through. If you find them colouring too quickly, then simply pop them into a pre-heated oven to finish. The cakes can also be just shallow-fried in oil and butter.

To make the brandy herb butter, place the chopped shallot in a shallow pan and warm. Flambé with the brandy, then boil to reduce until almost dry. Add the vegetable stock and boil to reduce by two-thirds. Whisk in 25 g (1 oz) of the butter. If you'd prefer the sauce a little thicker and richer, then simply add more butter. Finish with the chopped herbs and season with salt and pepper.

As a garnish for the top of the cakes, I like to dust some sage leaves, about 4–5 per portion, with flour seasoned with cayenne pepper and deep-fry them until very crispy.

To serve the dish, sit the cakes on to plates and spoon the sauce around. Sit the crispy sage leaves on top. The dish is now ready to eat.

Variations

If you are making round cakes, the remaining risotto left after being cut can be rolled into balls and also breadcrumbed for deep-frying. These are very good if rolled small and used as hot crispy canapés.

ABOVE *Chestnut, Onion and Brussels Sprout Risotto Cake with Brandy Herb Butter (see p.126).*

LEFT *Chard Potato Cake with Stilton Rarebit (see p.130).*

BELOW *Mushroom Pancake Gâteau (see p.132).*

Chard Potato Cake with Stilton Rarebit

Chard is an interesting vegetable, one that is picked like spinach but without throwing the stalks away! It can also be braised or pan-fried as a vegetable, having the consistency of a soft celery. The leaves are like a spinach with a slightly coarser texture and are best cooked in boiling salted water for a minute until tender. They can then be finished in butter and seasoned with salt and pepper. Chard can be finished in the same way as most spinach dishes; however, it doesn't hold its colour quite as well. If it is hard to find, substitute spinach for this dish.

The Stilton rarebit is a variation of my classic Welsh rarebit, and you can make that by simply using all Cheddar. The strength of flavour of the Stilton is up to you; use 100 g (4 oz) of Stilton and 225 g (8 oz) of Cheddar if you prefer a milder taste. This mix will make quite a large quantity of finished rarebit; you won't need it all for the recipe. It can be used for many dishes or simply grilled on toast for a snack. The mix also freezes very well for use later.

MAKES about 450 g (1 lb) rarebit to serve 4

For the Stilton Rarebit

225 g (8 oz) Stilton, chopped
100 g (4 oz) Cheddar, grated
75 ml (3 fl oz) milk
25 g (1 oz) plain flour
25 g (1 oz) fresh white breadcrumbs

½ tablespoon English mustard powder
1–2 shakes of Worcestershire sauce
1 egg
1 egg yolk

For the Potato Cake

2 large cooked jacket potatoes, about
    450 g (1 lb)
50 g (2 oz) unsalted butter
Salt and freshly ground black pepper
Freshly ground nutmeg

675 g (1½ lb) chard, picked, blanched
    and refreshed
50 g (2 oz) walnuts, chopped (optional)
175 g (6 oz) Stilton Rarebit

Butter 4 × 7.5 cm (3 in) flan rings for individual portions or 1 × flameproof vegetable dish. To make the rarebit, put the Stilton and Cheddar into a pan and add the milk. Slowly melt over a low heat, making sure it does not boil as this will separate the cheese. Once the mix begins to bubble mildly, add the flour, breadcrumbs and mustard and cook for a few minutes, stirring over a low heat until the mixture comes away from the sides of the pan and begins to form a ball shape. Add the Worcestershire sauce and leave to cool.

When cold, place the mixture in a food processor, turn on the motor and slowly add the egg and egg yolk. If you don't have a food processor or mixer, then just beat vigorously with a spoon. When the eggs are mixed in, chill for a few hours before using.

Pre-heat the grill.

Halve the jacket potatoes and fork the potato into a bowl. Add half the butter and season with salt, pepper and a pinch of nutmeg. Spoon the mix into the buttered rings or vegetable dish.

Blanch the chard in boiling salted water for 1 minute and refresh in iced water, squeezing out any excess. (Chard can be prepared in advance and refrigerated.) Heat the chard in the remaining butter and season with salt and pepper. Add the chopped walnuts, if using. Sit the chard on top of the potatoes. Mould the Stilton rarebit to cover the chard. Finish under a hot grill until the rarebit is golden.

Variations

The potato and chard can be moulded and allowed to cool and chilled. When needed, simply microwave until warm, then cover with the rarebit before finishing under the grill.

As a starter, these can be served in the potato skins. Simply spoon the creamy potatoes back into the skins, top with chard and finish with glazed rarebit.

Chard also works well blanched in boiling water, then sautéd with sliced mushrooms and walnuts. Finish the dish with chopped Stilton cheese added at the last moment, and if you want it to be very rich, simply add 2–3 tablespoons of double cream!

Mushroom Pancake Gâteau

This is a great vegetarian dish that can be served with equal success as a starter or main course. The recipe came to me from a chef in New York. His name is Jean-Georges Vongerichten, probably the most famous chef in the United States. I've eaten his food many times (he has restaurants in New York and London) and each time I get a new inspiration.

This is basically savoury pancakes that are layered with a mushroom stuffing, a duxelle. Wild mushrooms can also be used in the filling but, if they're available, I prefer just to use them in the finished sauce. This can be a simple mushroom sauce with the shallots and herb, or become a chunky sauce with the addition of wild mushrooms. The selection of wild mushrooms is really up to you: you can use oyster mushrooms or a mix of chanterelles, ceps, trompettes de la mort and girolles. If wild mushrooms are unavailable, then just use some button mushrooms.

This gâteau keeps very well and can be cut and warmed in the microwave.

SERVES 4–6

For the Pancakes

100 g (4 oz) plain flour
Salt and freshly ground black pepper
1 egg
300 ml (10 fl oz) milk

25 g (1 oz) unsalted butter, melted
2 teaspoons chopped fresh parsley
Oil for frying

For the Mushroom Filling

900 g (2 lb) cup mushrooms
A knob of unsalted butter
2 large onions, finely chopped
1 large garlic clove, crushed

A pinch of chopped fresh thyme
225 g (8 oz) button mushrooms, sliced
(optional)
Salt and freshly ground black pepper

For the Mushroom Sauce

1 large shallot, finely chopped
8–12 tablespoons reserved mushroom
stock
100–175 g (4–6 oz) mixed wild
mushrooms or button mushrooms,
chopped
50 g (2 oz) unsalted butter

1 teaspoon chopped fresh flatleaf
parsley
Salt and freshly ground black pepper
2 tablespoons chopped chestnuts
(optional)
A squeeze of fresh lemon juice

To make the pancakes, sift the flour and season with salt and pepper. Add the egg with three-quarters of the milk and whisk in. Add the melted butter. Once mixed, check the consistency of the mix; it should barely coat the back of a spoon. If it appears to be a little too thick, then add the remaining milk and finish by adding the chopped parsley.

Heat a 20 cm (8 in) pancake pan or frying-pan and brush with oil. Add a ladle of pancake mix, tilting the pan so that it is totally covered in a thin layer of batter. Cook over a medium heat for about 30 seconds until golden. Turn the pancake over and cook for a further 20–30 seconds. Remove the pancake from the pan and place it on a square of greaseproof paper. Repeat the same process until all the mix has been used. For the gâteau recipe you will need 8–9 pancakes. This recipe may well give you between 8–10, depending on the size of the pan used.

To make the filling, mince or blitz the cup mushrooms in a food processor or liquidizer, then place them in a pan and bring to a simmer. The mushrooms will create a lot of water. Leave them over a medium heat for about 20 minutes so that the liquid is reduced, to intensify the flavour while the mushrooms are cooking. Half-way through the cooking time, strain off 8–12 tablespoons of the mushroom water. This is a natural mushroom stock that will be used to make the finished sauce for the dish. Allow 1–2 tablespoons of stock per portion of sauce. Continue to cook the mushrooms.

While the mushrooms are cooking, melt the butter in a pan and add the chopped onions with the garlic and thyme. These need to be cooked for a few minutes until the onions are soft and translucent. The sliced button mushrooms are an optional extra. I like to use them to give another bite to the dish. To cook just add to the onions and cook for a further 4–5 minutes. Mix the reduced mushroom mixture with the onions and season with salt and pepper.

To assemble the gâteau, spread the mushroom filling 2–3 mm ($\frac{1}{8}$ in) thick on to a pancake and then sit another pancake on top and repeat the process until at least 6 layers of mushroom have been spread. I prefer to have 8 layers of mushroom between 9 pancakes. This gives you a better height and look to the dish.

To make the sauce, place the shallot in a pan with the reserved mushroom stock, bring to a simmer and cook for 1 minute. Add the wild or button mushrooms and continue to cook for a few minutes. Now add the butter and stir in to give a slightly creamy finish. Add the parsley and season with salt and pepper. Stir in the chopped chestnuts, if using. Add a few drops of lemon juice and taste. You will find this has lifted all the other flavours.

The gâteau can now be cut into wedges like a cake. Sit a wedge of hot gâteau on a plate and spoon the wild mushroom sauce on top.

Mushroom Tart

This must be the only tart recipe without pastry! The mushrooms themselves are, in fact, the pastry.

This is a great vegetarian main course. The mushrooms I am using are large flat ones that have a good 'meaty' (excuse the expression!) texture. These are then topped with tomatoes, braised onions and Swiss cheese, all helped with garlic butter. You can sit these on top of pastry discs for extra texture, or just serve them on their own.

As for a dressing, well I've listed plenty to choose from in the book and they'll all work well.

SERVES 4

4 large flat mushrooms, cleaned and
    stalks removed
4 large onions, sliced
2–3 tablespoons water
A pinch of demerara sugar (optional)
Salt and freshly ground black pepper

4 teaspoons Garlic Butter (see below)
4 plum or salad tomatoes, sliced and
    ends discarded
8 slices of Gruyère or 100 g (4 oz)
    Cheddar, grated

For the Garlic Butter

50 g (2 oz) unsalted butter
1 large garlic clove, crushed
Freshly ground black pepper
1 teaspoon chopped fresh parsley
    (optional)

1 teaspoon very finely chopped shallot
    (optional)
Squeeze of lemon juice

To Serve

Tomato Dressing (see p.268),
    Spicy Tomato Dressing (see p.269),
    Watercress and Herb

Dressing (see p.270),
    Mustard Dressing (see p.271) or
    Hazelnut Dressing (see p.272)

The first job is to cook the onions. These can be placed in a heavy-based pan with the water and cooked on a very low heat, with a lid on, until softened. Then remove the lid and cook very gently, reducing the natural sugars in the onions, stirring occasionally. This will take to a caramelizing stage. At this point they only need to be a light golden colour, any more will be too strong for this dish. This will take between 2–3 hours. The finishing can be brought on by 30 minutes by adding the demerara sugar; this will sweeten the onions and they will caramelize quicker.

If the thought of waiting that long is too much (although I can promise you the finished taste is brilliant!) then simply pan-fry the onions for 6–7 minutes until golden. Now add the sugar and continue to cook for 2–3 minutes before seasoning with salt and pepper.

To make the garlic butter, soften the butter and mix in the garlic, pepper, parsley, lemon juice and shallot, if using. The butter is now ready and can be kept chilled.

Pre-heat the grill.

The mushrooms can now be cooked. Season with salt and pepper and top each mushroom centre with a knob of garlic butter. Cook the mushrooms under the grill for 7–8 minutes until just tender. Sit the sliced tomatoes on top and continue to cook for another minute. Spoon the onions on to the tomatoes and cover with the cheese. These can now be browned under the grill until melted and lightly coloured. The tarts are now ready to eat with the dressing of your choice or simply on their own.

Variations

There are, of course, many other flavours that can be added. Some sliced leeks, spinach or both mixed with the cooked onions work very well. Another garnish to use is the Crispy Spinach (p.141), which gives a real contrast of textures.

Try using Parsley and Tarragon Butter (see p.279) instead of the garlic butter.

Rich Sherry Lentils

Whether or not you are serving this with the Confit of Pork Belly (see p.92), this dish is best served in a large soup plate or bowl. It tastes great with other rich meat dishes, too. Puy lentils are tiny green lentils which are available in most large supermarkets; there is no need to soak them before you start cooking.

SERVES 4

100–175 g (4–6 oz) Puy lentils
40 g (1½ oz) unsalted butter
1 carrot, finely chopped
1 onion, finely chopped
2 celery sticks, finely chopped
1 small fennel bulb, finely chopped (optional)
2 tablespoons brandy

450–600 ml (15–20 fl oz) Chicken Stock (see p.258) or Vegetable Stock (see p.259)
2 tablespoons double cream (optional)
Salt and freshly ground black pepper
1 tablespoon sherry vinegar or more for a sharper taste
1 tablespoon chopped fresh flatleaf parsley

Pre-heat the oven to 200°C/400°F/gas 6 if you are cooking the dish in the oven.

Melt 15 g (½ oz) of the butter and cook the chopped vegetables without colouring for 2 minutes. Add the lentils and brandy and boil to reduce until almost dry. Add 450 ml (15 fl oz) of the stock and bring to a simmer. Cover with a lid. The lentils can now be cooked on top of the stove or in the pre-heated oven for about 30 minutes until the lentils are tender. During the cooking time you may need to add the remaining 150 ml (5 fl oz) of stock so that the finished lentils have a thick soup consistency.

To finish, add the remaining butter and the double cream, if using. Season with salt and pepper and add the sherry vinegar. The vinegar is added totally neat, without any reduction. It really lifts the flavour of the lentils. Finish with the chopped parsley and serve.

Note

Crème fraîche (see p.275) can be used in place of the double cream, to give a slightly sharper taste.

Pea Pancakes

Here's a great alternative for peas – home-made pea pancakes. This recipe works with fresh or frozen peas and goes beautifully with so many dishes: meat, fish or vegetarian. The pancakes are simple to make and can be served as a vegetable or part of a main course dish. For a vegetarian dish they eat very well topped with florets of cauliflower and grated cheese, browned under the grill and served with a tomato dressing. I also like to serve them with roast lamb. If you add 2 teaspoons of chopped fresh mint to the recipe you're adding a herb that suits both flavours, the lamb and the peas.

SERVES 4

225 g (8 oz) cooked fresh peas, or frozen
 peas, thawed
1 egg
1 egg yolk
3 tablespoons plain flour

3 tablespoons double cream
50 g (2 oz) unsalted butter
Salt and freshly ground black pepper
Oil or butter for frying

Place the peas, egg, egg yolk, flour and cream in a food processor or liquidizer and blitz to a smooth consistency. Heat a frying-pan and add the butter, allowing it to colour to nut-brown stage. Add the butter to the mix and season with salt and pepper. The mix is now ready to cook. Heat a frying-pan and add a trickle of oil or small knob of butter. The pancake mix can now be dropped in a tablespoon at a time. This will spread slightly, giving you small pea pancakes; you'll probably have room to cook 3–4 together, depending on the size of your pan. Cook until golden, then turn over and brown the other side. You should have enough for 10 to 12 pancakes in all. You can make the pancakes larger, if you prefer, by using a small ladle instead of a spoon to measure the batter.

Variation

To make the vegetarian dish with the cauliflower, simply sit cooked cauliflower florets on top and cover with grated Cheddar. Brown under the grill and serve with Spicy Tomato Dressing (see p.269).

Vegetables

Vegetables can be so exciting to eat. I often think about having a summer barbecue and grilling nothing but vegetables. Having leeks, asparagus, tomatoes, onions, broccoli, all with their own taste being lifted from the flavour of the grill bars would be so tasty. The vegetables featured in this section are packed with texture and flavour. The roasted tomatoes with a touch of sea salt, garlic, basil and olive oil just speak for themselves.

Vegetables just seem to grow and grow! By which I obviously mean in variety and selection. Springs, summers, autumns and winters appear at different times of the year all over the world. Consequently, virtually all vegetables and fruits are available 12 months of the year and most become available in Britain. Of course, this means we can buy and eat them when we want, but one thing is certain: you can't beat vegetables or fruits in the height of their season. Vegetables which are transported long distances are picked unripe and then ripen in transit, so you never quite get that just-picked flavour. So I say where possible buy and cook what's in season.

If you check the roads around Britain you'll find so many farms with pick-your-own strawberries, raspberries, runner beans and more. So basically you go and pick and choose your own and then go home and enjoy them. And if the season is short, eat as many as you can and then move on to another variety. As a guide, here are the best seasons to buy some of our favourites:

Asparagus	May–June	Cherries	June–August
Broad beans	May–September	Pears	August–February
Broccoli	May–June	Plums	July–October
French beans	June–September	Raspberries	July–September
Leeks	August–May	Rhubarb	December–June
Peas	May–October	Strawberries	May–June
Runner beans	July–October		
Tomatoes	March–November	Potatoes, cabbages, carrots,	
Apples	July–March	cauliflowers and spinach are 'in	
Blackberries	July–September	season' all year round.	

Cabbage

Cabbage has a history almost as long as the potato. Probably the most common variety in Britain is the Savoy. It arrived in Britain in the mid 1500s from the Netherlands, just as the potato was arriving in Europe. Before then we were eating a wild variety that apparently is still grown in Europe and northern Britain around the sea coasts. This was very different to the cabbages we now know. It was very bitter and consequently had a bad reputation. It took the Romans to develop the plant, taking away some of that bitter flavour but still only supplying the open-leafed kale variety and not the round ones of today. In the days of the bitter plant, it was eaten for medicinal purposes, apparently to be eaten with your drinks and prevent you from becoming drunk! It was the Dutch who mastered the cabbage as we know it; the titles Savoy and coleslaw both coming from Dutch names.

Over the years the cabbage has formed a very large family: green, Savoy, white, red, then we go on to spring greens, sea kale, curly kale, watercress, cauliflower, broccoli, and the list goes on adding many more relatives of one plant.

One of the beauties of cabbage is that it is an all-year-round vegetable that can stand up very well against cold and even icy conditions. It does, however, carry one or two problems. The first being that unsavoury smell of overcooked cabbage that lingers in the room. My school dinner days (25 and more years ago!) remind me of that. The cabbage had a dull, almost yellow colour with a bad odour to go with it! That's the second problem, understanding the cooking of cabbage so that we can eat it at its best.

I think the problem may have started hundreds of years ago when almost all foods were cooked by the slow braising method. This meant that the cabbage would be added to a stew or broth at the beginning of cooking and just continued to cook and cook. As with all cooking methods and recipes, the ideas were just passed on, and consequently we have continued the habit of overcooking it.

Cabbage, in fact, cooks to its best in just minutes, keeping all its natural tastes and colours and giving a really inviting nose rather than odour. You will find that I use cabbage in many recipes. When potatoes and cabbage arrived in Europe, Ireland was one of the biggest growers and eaters of both products. It just shows how good, simple dishes will never die and continue to be enjoyed for years.

I thought I would just give you one or two ideas of some cabbage dishes to be enjoyed.

The Dutch white cabbage eats at its best as sauerkraut or raw in coleslaw. The coleslaw idea can take on completely different tastes.

White cabbage must be shredded or grated very finely if being served raw. This prevents it from being too tough and bitter to eat. Instead of mixing it with carrots and mayonnaise, why not simply mix it with Thai Dressing (see p.159) or Hazelnut Dressing (see p.272).

Sweet and sour cabbage can also be made by boiling 1 tablespoon of caster sugar with 4 tablespoons of white wine vinegar. Bring to the boil and pour over the finely shredded cabbage, season with salt and leave to cool.

Green and Savoy cabbages can also be finely shredded or grated and used in salads. It's important to serve them straight away, otherwise the acidity of vinegar or citrus fruit (lime works very well with ginger and cabbage) will discolour the leaves.

The golden rule whenever cooking any variety of green cabbage or, for that matter, any green vegetable, is to always cook in plenty of boiling salted water without a lid. Bring the water to the boil, remove the lid and add the shredded cabbage. This will now only take between 1–2 minutes to cook or until the water just begins to simmer again. Now the cabbage can be drained off, re-seasoned with salt and pepper, and a knob of butter added to finish. It's also important to serve the vegetables immediately.

Another alternative is to cook the cabbage in the same way, but then refresh in ice cold water. Once cold, drain off, then season and top with butter. This is now ready either to microwave or drop back into a hot pan to re-heat.

Cabbage can be cooked, again as soon as needed, by heating a few tablespoons of water with a knob of butter, then adding the cabbage, stirring for a few minutes on fast heat until tender. This method can be helped along with other flavours. Sliced onions and strips of bacon can be tossed in butter before adding the raw or pre-cooked shredded cabbage. This gives you a good vegetable dish or can be used as an accompaniment for a fish or meat dish.

If cabbage has been very quickly blanched in boiling water, just taking out the rawness, it can be sautéd to an almost golden brown tinge in butter or perhaps a flavoured oil. Sesame oil works very well, with sesame seeds. Also, prawns and a squeeze of lemon work beautifully with that sesame flavour. Pieces of pork scratchings mixed with sautéd cabbage also go very well.

Stir-fry dishes using all types of flavours give you really tasty vegetarian starters, main courses or vegetable dishes. The cabbage must be shredded very finely, then added at the last moment when cooking with other ingredients. How about mushrooms, onions, sweet peppers, leeks, bean sprouts, chillies, herbs, ginger, garlic, lemon, limes, tomatoes, the list could just go on and on. All are readily available, easy to cook and serve and go very well.

Here's one more idea: Winter Vegetable Cabbage Lasagne! It's great as a starter or main course. The 'pasta' is actually the cabbage. Cut the stalk from the leaves individually, then blanch the leaves in boiling water and refresh in iced water. Take a loose-bottomed

20 cm (8 in) cake tin and place 1–2 leaves on the base to cover. Now you need the winter vegetables, using 4–5 varieties. I suggest carrots, swedes, turnips, parsnips and maybe beetroot. These can now be roasted or puréed or a bit of both. If roasted, make sure they are slightly overcooked and tender. Now simply place either a roasted or puréed vegetable on top of the cabbage, then place some more leaves on top. This process should now be repeated until all the vegetables have been used, finishing with more cabbage.

This dish can now be kept chilled. Once you want to serve it, simply push from the ring and cut into wedges. This can now be microwaved as portions. You don't have to serve them individually. If you wish to present it as a whole dish, then simply build it on a plate and microwave the whole thing. It does, however, cut a lot easier if it has been chilled first. The individual wedges look very neat and colourful. If you have decided to use purées, make sure they are not too wet or this will prevent the lasagne from holding up so well.

This dish can be served with a dressing or make a vegetable and herb butter sauce to go with it. Just reduce the vegetable stock with some finely chopped shallots or onions. Add chopped fresh sage and thyme with a squeeze of lemon juice. Now just whisk in a little butter to emulsify. Season with salt and pepper and serve.

So there are a few cabbage ideas to be working with. Eating at The Savoy is one thing, but cooking and eating it is something else!

Crispy Cabbage

This recipe cuts through the myth that cabbage is tasteless and soggy!

SERVES 4–6

½ Savoy cabbage

Oil for deep-frying
Salt

Cut the cabbage half into 3 wedges, removing the core. It's important to use the outside leaves as well as this will give you a good contrast in colours from deep green to light. The cabbage now needs to be cut into 2.5 cm (1 in) strips.

Heat the deep-frying oil to 180°C/350°F. It is very important to use a lid on the fryer or pan when frying cabbage. This is due to cabbage having a high water content. For the first few seconds of frying the cabbage will spit hot fat.

Add the cabbage to the pan and put on the lid. Once the crackling has stopped, the cabbage should be ready with just a little colouring around the edges. Drain off all excess fat on kitchen paper, then lightly salt.

Roast Tomatoes with Sea Salt and Basil

The best tomatoes to use for this recipe are plum tomatoes. These have a much better taste and hold up better when cooked. If you are using salad tomatoes, only cook for 5–6 minutes. This dish eats well as a vegetable or vegetarian main course finished with chopped black olives, capers and Mozzarella or Parmesan (almost pizza-like) browned under the grill. They also eat very well with grilled fish or meat, in particular, lamb.

SERVES 4

6–7 plum tomatoes, eyed and halved	12 fresh basil leaves
4 tablespoons olive oil	1 teaspoon coarse sea salt
1 garlic clove, halved	Freshly ground black pepper

Pre-heat the oven to 200°C/400°F/gas 6.

Heat 1 tablespoon of the olive oil in a roasting pan with the garlic pieces. Fry the tomatoes seed-side down until coloured. Add 6 leaves of the basil and the remaining olive oil. Turn the tomatoes and sprinkle with the salt and pepper. Cook in the pre-heated oven for 6–7 minutes.

Once cooked, remove 12 tomato halves and keep warm in a serving dish. Heat the remaining 2 tomato halves in the oil on top of the pan and mash with a fork. This dressing can now be pushed through a sieve, leaving you with a tomato and olive dressing. Tear the remaining 6 basil leaves in half and sprinkle on top of the 12 tomato halves. Finish by spooning the dressing over the tomatoes and serve.

Quick Sweet and Sour Onions

These eat really well as a vegetable or to serve with another dish. Grilled chicken breasts or wings is delicious with these sweet and sour onions, as is grilled or sautéd liver. But one of my favourites is roast turbot or halibut with the onions trickling over, giving that sweet and sour flavour to work with the bitter-sweetness of the fish.

SERVES 4–6

450 g (1 lb) button onions
25 g (1 oz) unsalted butter
25 g (1 oz) caster sugar

50 ml (2 fl oz) white wine vinegar
Salt and freshly ground black pepper

Blanch the onions in boiling water for 5 minutes. Drain off the water. Melt the butter in a frying-pan. Once bubbling, add the onions and cook over a medium heat until golden. Add the sugar and continue to cook for a further 1 minute. Now add the white wine vinegar and boil to reduce until almost dry. Alternatively, the sugar and vinegar can both be added at the same time to create a syrup and almost sauce consistency. Season with salt and pepper and serve.

ABOVE *Quick Sweet and Sour Onions*
(see p.143).

RIGHT *Roast Tomatoes with Sea Salt*
and Basil (see p.142), just before they go in
the oven.

Broccoli

Good, firm broccoli is a very attractive and tasty vegetable. Broccoli comes in various sizes and varieties. My favourite is calabrese. This is the broccoli that grows in individual florets with a thick stalk. These really keep their colour and are very tender to eat, needing very little cooking. There is also the purple sprouting broccoli, which I believe was the first to grow. These also cook very tender but never quite keep that rich purple colour.

SERVES 6–8

900 g (2 lb) broccoli
Salt and freshly ground black pepper

A knob of butter

Boil some salted water in a deep pan. Trim the stalks of the broccoli florets; these can be kept and also boiled to be used as another vegetable dish. Once the water is boiling, drop in the florets, making sure the lid is left off. These will only take between 2–5 minutes to become tender but still with a little bite, depending on the size of the florets. Once cooked, remove from the water and, if not using immediately, plunge into iced water to stop the cooking and retain their green colour. These can simply be re-heated by dropping once again into boiling water for 1 minute or microwaving.

The broccoli can now be seasoned with salt and pepper, buttered and served.

Variations

Here are some more ideas of how to serve broccoli once cooked: top with Stilton Rarebit (see p.130) and finish under the grill; sprinkle with Parmesan and brown under the grill; fry in Garlic Butter (see pp.134); fry with flaked almonds; finish with hollandaise sauce; finish *à la Française* with bacon, onions and lettuce.

Braised Onions

These are a wonderful vegetable to go with your roast Sunday lunch. They will give you your gravy already made! With the caramel onion taste along with slices of roast beef and good crispy Yorkshire puddings, second helpings become a standard procedure!

SERVES 4–6

450 g (1 lb) small onions
A knob of unsalted butter
A pinch of sugar
150 ml (5 fl oz) Chicken Stock
(see p.258)

5 tablespoons Veal or Beef *Jus* (see
p.261) or alternative (see p.262)
Salt and freshly ground black pepper

Pre-heat the oven to 200°C/400°F/gas 6.

Blanch the onions in boiling water for 2–3 minutes. This will take out the absolute rawness of the onion. Heat a braising pan and add the butter. Add the onions and colour on top of the stove for about 8 minutes until completely coloured with almost burnt tinges. Add the pinch of sugar and chicken stock and bring to a simmer. The onions can now be cooked in the pre-heated oven for 10 minutes without a lid until they become tender.

Once cooked, boil the stock with the onions and reduce until thick and syrupy. This will create a sweet glaze around the onions. Add the *jus* or gravy and bring to a simmer. The braised onions are now ready to check for seasoning before serving.

Fried Onion Rings

Here's a quick recipe for fried onion rings. Slice the onions into thin rings and separate. Dip through milk, then seasoned flour. Fry in hot fat at 180–185°C/350–360°F until golden and crispy. Season with salt and serve.

Potatoes

Potatoes have always played an important role in my menu planning. I don't mean so much as a vegetable but as part of each individual dish. I almost become afraid that I would over-use them and have to come up with a new idea without potato.

But should I be afraid? After all they are one of our staple foods. They are eaten with just about every main course whether it be fish, meat or vegetarian – and let's not forget frozen chips (they were once potatoes!) and crisps. Crisps, in fact, are made from one of the best and tastiest varieties that can be used for baking. They are grown mostly in Northern Ireland and Scotland and yes, you've guessed it, they are called Golden Wonder. It's also almost impossible to obtain the seed potato, so forget it, you have no chance of telling your friends that you are growing your own Golden Wonders!

The British repertoire of everyday potato dishes is fairly limited; they are normally boiled, mashed, fried or roasted. Restaurants around Britain have become a lot braver, taking influences mostly from France and Italy with garlic, saffron, olive oil, cream and herbs all being used. The French must have one of the widest repertoires of potato dishes: over a hundred are featured in Le Répertoire de La Cuisine alone!

I'm going to give you one of the most famous, Pommes Parmentier, which was popular in the mid 1700s. By that time, the potato had already been a staple food in Ireland for a hundred years, and its first introduction to Europe was the mid 1500s, when it was brought from the New World. Its origins stretch back to South America around 3000 BC. I found much of this from reading Lindsey Bareham's In Praise of the Potato. She tells the full story of the potato, then gives a massive selection of recipes to go with it. What I'm going to do is just give you an idea of which potato to use for what and, hopefully, you'll find the 'spud you like'.

I have already mentioned the Golden Wonder. This potato has the reputation of having a good, full flavour, it's perfect for all-round use: mashing, roasting, baking and chips. Alternative varieties include Maris Piper, Estima, Wilja and King Edward. All these make a good mashed potato, the potato texture breaking down to give quite a light, creamy finish. The Maris Piper and King Edward also work well for roasting along with Désirée, Romano and Cara.

New potatoes obviously have a totally different taste and texture, usually called waxy. Virtually all new potatoes are good for boiling, salads and shallow-frying. The texture is quite dense and firm and will hold together for these cooking methods.

Probably the best known is the Jersey Royal. It's one we all love to eat because it has so much flavour, although we may not always be so keen to wash and scrub it. Plenty more varieties are now becoming available: the Pink Fir Apple is a very tasty pink potato with an uneven, knobbly finish; the Charlotte is grown both in Britain and France; others include La Ratte, Belle de Fontenay, Salad Blue and Aura.

Sauté potatoes can also be prepared in many different ways. Old or new potatoes both work well. The new potato will give you more of the perfect finished shape, whereas the old will break down around the outsides, giving a broken, flaky texture. The old potato will also colour better, giving a more natural look. I prefer using an old potato; they might not look as good but I feel they eat better. For all sauté potatoes, the potatoes must first be boiled or steamed in their jackets until cooked. They can then be peeled and cut into 5 mm (¼ in) slices. All you have to do now is pan-fry them in butter until golden, season with salt and serve.

Many of the dressings and sauces in the final chapter (see p.255) go very well with potato dishes. The Red Wine Dressing (see p.274) dribbled over sauté potatoes to go with a beef dish is delicious to eat.

Sliced fried onions mixed with sliced potatoes and fried gives you another classic combination. Again, bacon can also be added, or maybe strips of sweet red and green peppers.

Red peppers, finely diced and cooked in butter along with diced cooked ham, work very well in mashed potatoes. This can be served in vegetable dishes or spooned into individual moulds before being topped with grated cheese and put under a hot grill until golden brown. Mustard Dressing (see p.271) also works very well in mashed potatoes, simply poured in to taste at the last minute. Perhaps add either a leek purée or cooked sliced leeks to the mash as well – leeks and mustard work so well together.

New potatoes eat at their best cooked with the skins on, rolled in butter and seasoned. However, when I use them in salads and starters, once cooked, I usually peel them, then marinate in some form of dressing before using. The Charlotte new potato also roasts very well. Boil until three-quarters cooked, then peel the potatoes and colour golden brown in hot oil. These can now be finished in a pre-heated oven at 180°C/350°F/gas 4 for 20 minutes. The finished colour is fantastic. They have a golden touch but come through with a deep yellow glaze that's the natural colour of a rich, new potato. And, of course, they also taste very good.

These really are just a few ideas from an almost unlimited number. We probably only know up to twenty types of potato, but Europe has had about 400 varieties in 400 years. So dig deep in your thoughts for new recipe ideas for me!

Pommes Parmentier

One of the first potato dishes taught at catering college is Pommes Parmentier. This is a 1 cm ($\frac{1}{2}$ in) diced potato that is shallow-fried in butter, then finished with chopped parsley – an attractive potato dish as well as good to eat. While at college you never think to ask how the dish got its name. As with many recipes, which are frequently named after people and places, this dish takes the name of the man who made the French public aware of the potato in the mid to late 1700s.

SERVES 4

675 g (1½ lb) potatoes, peeled and cut into 1 cm (½ in) dice
2–3 tablespoons cooking oil

25–50 g (1–2 oz) unsalted butter
Salt
Chopped fresh parsley (optional)

Once the potatoes have been cut, wash them, then dry them in a cloth. It's best to fry them in stages; trying to cook them all at once will reduce the heat and also totally overcrowd the pan, giving you uneven colouring.

Simply heat a frying-pan and add a drop of the oil and a knob of butter. Add just enough potatoes to cover the pan and begin to shallow-fry (sauté) over a medium heat for 10–12 minutes, turning the potatoes for an even, all-round golden colour.

Once the potatoes are coloured, remove from the pan and transfer to a roasting tin. Repeat the same process until all are cooked. The potatoes should now all be tender and ready to serve. They can be placed in a hot oven to finish cooking or simply heat through. Season with salt and sprinkle with chopped parsley, if liked, before serving.

Variations

The Parmentier has many variations. Crushed garlic, crispy bacon or mixed herbs can be fried with the potatoes. I like to fry off pieces of smoked bacon and onions, then mix them with the raw potato dice. This can now be placed in an ovenproof serving dish, having the potatoes just roughly sitting above the dish. Now pour in some Chicken Stock (see p.258), filling three-quarters of the dish. Brush the potatoes with butter and bring to a simmer. These can now be baked in a pre-heated oven at 220°C/425°F/gas 7 for 30–40 minutes. During this time the potatoes will become golden brown and crispy on top with moist fluffy potatoes underneath, having absorbed all the stock. These are great to serve straight on the table at a dinner party or Sunday lunch. Here's an extra thought. Why not sprinkle grated cheese on top and melt under the grill?

Irish Potato Cakes

Here's a recipe for Irish potato cakes if you fancy giving them a try. They are perfect with Pork and Black Pudding Patties (see p.90) and Apple and Mustard Seed Relish (see p.257).

MAKES 8

450 g (1 lb) mashed potatoes, made not too wet

100 g (4 oz) plain flour plus extra for dusting

15 g ($\frac{1}{2}$ oz) unsalted butter plus extra for frying

Salt and freshly ground black pepper

Pre-heat the oven to 200°C/400°F/gas 6.

Mix the potatoes with the flour and butter and season with salt and pepper. Divide into 8 balls, and then pat into rounds 1 cm ($\frac{1}{2}$ in) thick. Lightly flour and pan-fry in butter until golden brown on both sides. It's also best to finish them in the pre-heated oven for 2–3 minutes. This will cook out the flour added to the mix.

Variations

Of course, these potato cakes can be used with many other dishes and can also have many other flavours added. Chopped bacon, onions, spring onions, herbs, chestnuts, pesto, mustard and I'm sure many more. It's really just a question of using the flavours that suit the dish they are to accompany.

Note

It is important that the mashed potatoes listed in the ingredients are simply mashed, with no cream or butter added.

Soured New and Baked Potatoes

These potato dishes really excite me. They have such scope and variety, from a potato salad with a difference to an Indian curry side dish. The combination of flavours is unlimited, and I promise you if you don't usually like soured cream you certainly will in this recipe! This is not a strict ingredients recipe, the measurements are for guidelines. I'll give you the basic recipe for new potatoes, and you simply follow the same method for the baked potatoes.

SERVES 4

450 g (1 lb) new potatoes	Salt and freshly ground black pepper
2–3 tablespoons olive oil	3–4 tablespoons soured cream
Juice of 1 $\frac{1}{2}$–2 lemons	

To make the soured new potatoes, the new potatoes should be cooked in boiling salted water for 15–20 minutes until tender, then drained off. While still hot, mash with a fork, not making them too fine. With the new potatoes I prefer to leave the skin on. New potato skins hold a lot of flavour. If you prefer them skinned, then just peel once cooked.

Once the potatoes have been forked, add 2 tablespoons of the olive oil and the juice of 1 lemon. Season with salt and pepper. The oil and lemon will have loosened the potatoes slightly. If you feel they need more, then just continue to add until the mix has been softened and has quite a sharp flavour from the lemon. The potatoes up to this stage can be made in advance.

The soured cream should be added at the last minute before serving. Warm through the potatoes, then lightly mix in 3 tablespoons of the soured cream, adding the rest if necessary. Do not overmix the potatoes; if you do, the creaminess will be lost and the mix become almost chewy. Re-season with salt and pepper and serve.

Soured Baked Potatoes

This recipe is the same as the above using 4 baking potatoes in place of the new potatoes. Baked potatoes will take approximately 1 hour to cook in a pre-heated oven at 200°C/400°F/gas 6. Once cooked, split them lengthways and fork out the insides, saving the skins to serve the potatoes in. Mix the potato with the olive oil and lemon juice before adding the soured cream and seasoning with salt and pepper. Once creamed and seasoned, the potato can be spooned back into the skins before serving. I usually just spoon the filling into 4 skin halves, making them very full.

The remaining potato skins can now be quartered giving you 4 strips per half potato. I bet you can guess what I'm going to do with these! Yes! Deep-fried Crispy Potato Skins (see p.154).

Variations

If you're thinking of serving the soured baked potato in its skin, then top it with Swiss Gruyère or Cheddar and melt under a hot grill before serving.

Both recipes for soured new and baked potatoes have room for different flavours – chives, tarragon, basil, parsley, pesto, limes, tomatoes can all be used.

Soured New and Baked Potatoes, and Deep-fried Crispy Potato Skins (see p.154).

Deep-fried Crispy Potato Skins

These really are good and something we only normally eat in steak house restaurants. Well, why not make your own – they are so good. All you need are the skins (with 2–3 mm (⅛ in) of potato left on) of some baked potatoes, cut into strips. The skin strips will keep in the fridge to fry whenever you like. Just heat some oil in a deep pan to 180°C/350°F and add the skins. After a few minutes deep-frying they will become golden and crispy. Drain and lightly salt before serving.

These eat very well with the Peppered Roast Beef (see p.104) and a good mixed salad. You can also make a dip to go with the potato skins: take some soured cream and season to taste with fresh lemon juice, snipped fresh chives, salt and freshly ground black pepper.

Mashed Potatoes

I find Maris Piper are one of the best varieties for making mashed potatoes, one of my favourite vegetable dishes – then all you need to add is a little care.

SERVES 4–6

900 g (2 lb) jacket, floury potatoes, peeled and quartered	100 g (4 oz) unsalted butter
Salt and freshly ground white pepper	120 ml (4 fl oz) double cream or milk
	Freshly grated nutmeg

Boil the potatoes in salted water until tender, about 20–25 minutes depending on size. Drain off all the water and replace the lid. Shake the pan vigorously which will start to break the potatoes. Add the butter and cream or milk a little at a time, while mashing the potatoes. Season with salt, pepper and nutmeg. The potatoes will be light, fluffy and creamy.

Chips and French Fries

Chips and French fries are readily available in all shapes and sizes. There are many good quality frozen fries around, but I don't believe you can find any frozen chip that can beat good home-made fries. I use large jacket potatoes which will cool after pre-cooking and become tender without losing their potato texture. For each portion 1–1½ potatoes will be plenty. You really need a deep-fat fryer to make these and guarantee the right temperature. If you don't have one, they will have to be treated with even more care and attention to give you fluffy, tender, crisp potatoes.

SERVES 4–6

4–6 peeled jacket potatoes, about 1.5 kg (3 lb)	Salt Oil for deep-frying

Heat the oil in the deep-fat fryer or deep heavy-based pan to 95°C/200°F for blanching. For good large chips, trim the potatoes into rectangles. Now cut into 1 cm ($\frac{1}{2}$ in) thick slices, then cut again to give chips 1 cm ($\frac{1}{2}$ in) thick and 6–7.5 cm (2 $\frac{1}{2}$–3 in) long. If you want French fries, then simply halve the thickness, making them 0.5 × 6–7.5 cm ($\frac{1}{4}$ × 2 $\frac{1}{2}$–3 in). The chips now need to be blanched in the pre-heated fat fryer. This is very important to guarantee the chips will be totally cooked before serving.

Frying them at 95°C/200°F will cook them without colour. The large chips will take up to 10–15 minutes before becoming tender. The smaller fries will only need 6–8 minutes. Once cooked, check by piercing with a knife. When ready, remove from the oil and drain. The chips or fries can be left to cool on greaseproof paper and even chilled before finishing in the hot fryer.

To finish, pre-heat the oil in the fryer to 150°C/300°F. Once hot, place the chips into the fat. These will now take 2–3 minutes before becoming golden brown and crispy. Shake off any excess fat, and sprinkle with salt before serving.

Note

Using a domestic fat-fryer may require a temperature of 180°C/350°F to finish.

Sautéed Jerusalem Artichokes

These vegetables are most famous for a creamed soup known as Palestine. The soup, when cooked and creamed, has a very distinctive artichoke flavour with a rich, smooth, velvety consistency. They are also served roasted or puréed. The vegetable itself has a knobbly shape with a brown/green colouring and the flesh inside is white. Once peeled and trimmed, they must be kept in water with a dash of lemon juice or cooked immediately to keep that colour.

SERVES 4

900 g (2 lb) Jerusalem artichokes	Salt and freshly ground black pepper
50 g (2 oz) unsalted butter	

To Serve

2 tablespoons toasted flaked almonds	A squeeze of lemon juice
2 tablespoons chopped fresh parsley	

Pre-heat the oven to 200°C/400°F/gas 6.

Peel the artichokes with a sharp knife. Once completely trimmed, split in half. The chokes can now be cut into 2–3 mm ($\frac{1}{8}$ in) slices.

Heat a frying-pan and add a knob of butter. Once the butter is bubbling, add a handful of the artichokes. It's best not to fry too many at once as this tends to reduce the heat of the pan and stew the artichokes. Fry and toss the chokes until golden brown, then season with salt and pepper and transfer to a roasting pan while you fry the remaining artichokes. Finish in the pre-heated oven for 2–3 minutes. Sprinkle with the almonds, parsley and lemon juice and serve.

Sautéed Jerusalem Artichokes.

French Bean and Sesame Salad

The flavours of Seared Tuna with Garlic and Almond Cream (see p.38) eaten with this salad are just knock-out!

SERVES 4

225–275 g (8–10 oz) French beans

For the Sesame Dressing

25 g (1 oz) sesame seeds
2 tablespoons sesame oil
2 tablespoons groundnut oil

$\frac{1}{2}$ teaspoon soy sauce
$\frac{1}{4}$ teaspoon fresh lemon juice
Salt and freshly ground black pepper

Cook the beans in boiling salted water until just tender but still with a little bite. Drain, then refresh under cold running water.

To make the dressing, the sesame seeds need to be lightly toasted under a hot grill or in a dry pan until golden. Mix together the oils and blitz in a food processor or liquidizer with the toasted sesame seeds. The consistency we are looking for is like a pesto sauce, loose but reasonably thick. Add a few drops of soy sauce and a good squeeze of lemon juice. If the mix still seems to be too thick, then simply add more equal quantities of both oils. Season with salt and pepper and the dressing is made.

To serve the salad, warm the cooked beans in the dressing, then divide on to plates.

Warm Thai Salad

The ingredients in the salad itself are really very simple. The Thai flavours are given to us from the dressing which uses chillies, peanut oil, oyster sauce and the kaffir lime leaves. The dressing can be served either warm or cold. However, I find that all the flavours really liven up when served warm. The dish eats very well as a side salad or as a starter.

Kaffir lime leaves are dark green in colour and have a shiny finish. These can be bought fresh or dried from Indian shops. If you happen to find fresh leaves, then make them first choice. Any you don't use can be treated like bay leaves: just hang them up to dry. These leaves are, in fact, used in the same way as bay leaves, to add their sharp citrus flavour to the dish.

Oyster sauce can be bought in bottles and is made from oysters cooked with soy sauce and a brine. The sauce is a good seasoning in dressings, soups and many other savoury dishes. It's a sauce that also doesn't have to be matched with fish; many Chinese pork dishes are flavoured with it.

SERVES 4

For the Salad

1 small iceberg lettuce, shredded	12 fresh basil leaves
4–6 spring onions, thinly sliced	12 fresh coriander leaves

For the Dressing

2 garlic cloves, sliced	1 red chilli, very thinly sliced
2 tablespoons peanut oil	2–4 tablespoons oyster sauce
2 kaffir lime leaves, finely shredded	3 tablespoons water

Mix together the iceberg lettuce with the spring onions and herb leaves. Fry the garlic slices in the peanut oil, add the lime leaves and chilli and warm for a few minutes. Mix together half the oyster sauce and the water and whisk into the oil. Taste and add more oyster sauce, if liked. You will have about 120 ml (4 fl oz) of dressing. This can now be strained through a sieve and poured warm over the salad. Mix and serve the salad immediately.

Yorkshire Puddings

Served with roast beef, these must be the most famous of all our Great British dishes. A good basic Yorkshire pudding eats so well with a rich gravy, and these are perfect for that traditional lunch, served as individual puddings or larger puddings.

But why stop there? Yorkshire puddings can also have so many variations. The pudding mix itself can be flavoured with mustard, horseradish, fresh herbs and many other flavours. It really depends on what you want to serve them with. My favourite is a rich Onion Gravy (see p.162). Another great classic is to make Toad in the Hole. This is, of course, sausages that have first been fried to give a golden brown colour and then baked in the Yorkshire batter. These can be made in one large tray or cooked in individual flan cases.

I also like to make the 'complete roast' as a starter in individual puddings. With this I use sautéed or pan-fried potatoes, black pudding, pieces of sausage and peas. Sit all these in the moulds and just pour the batter over. Bake in a pre-heated oven at 200°C/400°F/gas 6 and in 20–25 minutes time you have an almost complete meal! I like to serve these as a starter with a drop of the onion gravy.

Yorkshire puddings also eat very well with fish. For this I add the grated zest of 1 or 2 lemons to the batter along with some roughly chopped parsley. Cook them in the normal way and then serve them with roast cod, turbot or salmon with Fish Gravy (see p.62) and you have a real Alternative Great British Dish.

Another favourite of mine is to serve Yorkshire puddings with curry – does that sound odd? Well, they eat almost like a home-made naan bread, but with a lighter texture. All you need to do is add the grated zest of 2 limes and about 2 tablespoons of chopped fresh coriander; a pinch of curry powder can also be added to fire them up, perhaps make your own by mixing a pinch of turmeric with ground ginger, coriander and chilli. Once baked, serve them with Soured Cream, Lime and Mint Yoghurt (see p.276). I can promise you they eat very well and create a lot of fun when you've cooked a home-made curry and rice for friends and then you bring a tray of Yorkshire puddings and sit them on the table! They certainly provide a good talking point. But just imagine when you break a piece of Yorkshire pudding, dip it into your curry and then spoon the soured cream on top – I told you it works.

But I still haven't finished with ideas for this recipe. Yorkshire puddings also eat very well as sweets. Golden syrup can be added to the mix to give a rich batter. Once cooked, trickle more syrup over and serve with fresh cream or Vanilla Ice-cream (see p.216). Or sweeten the batter by adding 25 g (1 oz) of caster or icing sugar, bake as individual cooked puds and serve with fresh cream. Serve with poached pears and Rich Chocolate Sauce (see p.248), or apples with honey or golden syrup. They also eat very well if baked to an almost burnt edge on top. Once cooked and garnished with the fruit of your choice, dust heavily with icing sugar to give a bitter-sweet taste.

Here's one more idea: how about Yorkshire Pudding 'Suzette', finishing the dish as you would for Crêpes Suzette – with reduced orange juice with caramelized caster sugar, Grand Marnier and maybe even a touch of brandy. Warm fresh orange segments in the sauce, spoon it over the puddings and serve the dish with clotted cream. So the next time you're having a dinner party tell your friends it's Yorkshire pudding for pudding!

MAKES 8 × 10 cm (4 in) puddings

225 g (8 oz) plain flour	1 egg white (optional)
A pinch of salt	300–450 ml (10–15 fl oz) milk
3 eggs	Oil, lard or dripping for cooking

Pre-heat the oven to 220°C/425°F/gas 7. Oil 8 × 10 cm (4 in) moulds or larger moulds and pre-heat in the oven until almost smoking.

Sift the flour with the salt. Add the eggs and egg white, if using. The egg white gives extra lift to the batter. Whisk in 300 ml (10 fl oz) of milk. This will give you a thick batter which works very well. To check the consistency, simply lift a spoon in and out. The batter should hold and coat the back of the spoon. If it seems to have congealed, then simply add the remaining milk. The batter is now ready to cook. It can be made up to 24 hours in advance and will still rise.

Once the fat in the moulds is almost smoking, it's time to add the batter. Bake individual puddings in the pre-heated oven for 20–25 minutes and large ones for 40–45 minutes.

Onion Gravy

This wonderful gravy is perfect with your Yorkshire Puddings (see p.160).

MAKES ABOUT 450–600 ml (15–20 fl oz)

4 large onions, finely chopped
2 tablespoons water

300–450 ml (10–15 fl oz) Veal or Beef
Jus (see p.261) or alternative
(see p.262)

To make the onion gravy, place the chopped onions in a pan with the water. This must now be cooked on a very low heat. This will slowly draw the natural sugar content from the onions, and together with its juices the two will caramelize. This is a slow process, possibly taking up to 2 hours. It is very important that this does not burn as this will create a bitter taste. Once a golden caramel flavour has been achieved, add the gravy. By adding just 300 ml (10 fl oz) you will have a thick onion marmalade. This eats very well just spooned into the cooked Yorkshire puddings. For a thinner sauce consistency, use 450 ml (15 fl oz) of gravy.

For a quicker caramelizing method, cook the onions to a golden brown colour in a knob of butter. Add a teaspoon of demerara sugar and cook for 1–2 minutes. Taste the onions for sweetness. If you feel they need more then repeat the same quantity until the flavour you are after is achieved. Now just add the gravy and cook for 6–8 minutes before serving.

Fish Gravy

This gravy eats very well with fish. The gravy itself should be of a thin sauce consistency. It can be made by simply adding gravy to the roasting pan once the fish is cooked and lifted from the pan, leaving all the juices to be mixed with the gravy.

Another alternative is to buy fish bones and roast them in a pan with onion, celery, leek, bay leaf and a sprig of tarragon. Once coloured, add 1–2 glasses of white wine and boil to reduce by three-quarters. Add the 300–600 ml (10–20 fl oz) of gravy (not too thick) and cook for 20 minutes. The sauce can now be strained through a sieve and used as a sauce for roast fish.

This sauce can also be made into a fish chasseur by simply adding some cooked chopped onion or shallot, sliced mushrooms, diced tomato flesh and chopped tarragon.

Crispy Spinach

This is wonderful with the Tuna Carpaccio (see p.37).

This is wonderful with the Tuna Carpaccio (see p.37).

SERVES 6–8

225 g (8 oz) spinach leaves, washed and picked (large stalks removed)

Oil for deep-frying
Salt
Cayenne pepper

Heat the oil to 150°C/300°F.

The spinach leaves should be carefully spun and well dried, removing all excess water from the leaves. Cut the spinach into thin strips. This can be either very fine (as for Chinese seaweed) or 5 mm ($\frac{1}{4}$ in) thick. Deep-fry in small batches in the hot oil until crispy. This will only take between 30 seconds and 1 minute. Shake off excess fat, then season with a pinch of salt and cayenne pepper. The crispy spinach is now ready to serve.

Puddings

This is usually everybody's favourite chapter. Delicious puddings with lots of cream, custard or chocolate. I must admit I get really excited making puddings and there are many here that have become firm favourites. The Jaffa Cake Pudding (see p.168) is so good it's almost reached the classic status of my bread and butter pudding. I've always been a fan of Jaffa Cake biscuits and so decided to have a go at making a pudding with the same theme. To say it works is an understatement.

ABOVE *Jaffa Cake Pudding (see p.168)*
LEFT *Clockwise from top: Dark Chocolate Mousse, White and Dark Chocolate Mousse, White Chocolate Mousse, individual portion of White Chocolate Mousse (see p.208) Chocolate and Prune Soufflé Cake (see p.171), Chocolate Truffle Cake (see p.196).*

Cutting through the chocolate, orange jelly and then into the sponge is a knockout. Three different textures and tastes that all go together so well.

This is a new pudding theme that I am on now, looking at all the biscuits we buy and how I can turn them into puddings or simply make the biscuits themselves. So there are also recipes here for Lemon Puffs Pudding (see p.174) and Fruit Shortcake Biscuits (see p.234). At the moment I'm working on chocolate bourbon biscuit pudding, coconut snowballs, Wagon Wheels, fig rolls and After Eight puds – all coming soon! And it's not just biscuit-puddings in this chapter. There's Turkish Delight (see p.220), Tutti-frutti and Ovaltine Ice-creams (see pp.219, 224) or an Iced Neapolitan Parfait (see p.228). I've also included a recipe I picked up in New York, American Cheesecake (see p.202), delicious on its own or with a spoonful of Home-made Cherry Jam (see p.249) just trickling over the top. Scrumptious!

Wild children hunting for truffles – the cake mix variety of course!

Black Treacle Pudding

This recipe comes from Northern Ireland and is actually made with black treacle, unlike what we usually call a treacle pudding which is, in fact, a golden syrup sponge. That is lovely, too, but now you have the recipe for the real thing. For an even stronger taste, use the soft brown sugar instead of caster sugar.

I like to eat this with pouring cream and Anglaise (Fresh Custard) Sauce (see p.246), but if you feel like being really rich, then try the Rum Sabayon (see p.232) to go with it (perhaps with the cream and custard as well!), or even with the Liquorice Ripple Ice-cream (page 216).

SERVES 4–6

225 g (8 oz) self-raising flour
A pinch of salt
2 teaspoons mixed spice
100 g (4 oz) unsalted butter
6 tablespoons black treacle
50 g (2 oz) caster sugar or soft
   brown sugar

$\frac{1}{2}$ teaspoon bicarbonate of soda
6 tablespoons milk
2 eggs
2 tablespoons golden syrup, warmed
   (optional)

Butter and flour a 1.2 litre (2 pint) pudding basin. Sift together the flour, salt and mixed spice. Work in the butter to a breadcrumb texture. Warm the treacle with the sugar. Mix the bicarbonate of soda with the milk and eggs. Add both to the dry ingredients, then fill the prepared basin with the mixture. Cover with foil, loosely, on the top to allow the pudding to rise, and place the basin in a pan filled with water to come half-way up the basin. Bring the water to the boil, cover and steam for $1\frac{1}{2}$–2 hours, topping up with more water as necessary. The sponge is now ready to turn out. To make it really shine, spoon some more treacle or golden syrup on top. Now that is a rich pudding!

Jaffa Cake Pudding

There are three stages to this recipe: the sponge base, the orange jelly and the chocolate topping. It's important to make the jelly first. This can be made a few hours ahead of time, or up to 24 hours in advance. The jelly itself will keep for up to a week, chilled, and also freezes well. Yorkshire pudding moulds make good individual jelly discs to sit in the sponge. If you use bought fresh orange juice, add the grated zest from 3 large oranges for extra flavour. The sponge recipe is a basic vanilla sponge with the addition of orange zest. To make it even easier, you can make it as one large pudding using one of those sponge base flan cases that are sold in most supermarkets. Add some orange syrup, place one large disc of jelly in the middle and finish with the chocolate ganache spread.

I can promise you these eat so well. You might not be able to dunk them in your tea but when you've finished one you'll be looking for another!

Serves 6–8

For the Jelly

1 × 11 g sachet of powdered gelatine
300 ml (10 fl oz) fresh orange juice
 (approximately 4–5 oranges)

Finely grated zest from all oranges used
75 g (3 oz) caster sugar

For the Sponge Base

3 eggs
75 g (3 oz) caster sugar
75 g (3 oz) plain flour

Finely grated zest of 1 orange
40 g (1½ oz) unsalted butter, melted

For the Orange Syrup

Grated zest and juice of 1 orange   50 g (2 oz) caster sugar
2 tablespoons water

For the Ganache

300 ml (10 fl oz) double cream   Finely grated zest of 1 orange
2 tablespoons Cointreau or   2 egg yolks
   Grand Marnier (optional)   25 g (1 oz) caster sugar
250 g (9 oz) good quality plain chocolate

For the Shiny Topping

100 g (4 oz) good quality plain chocolate   25 g (1 oz) unsalted butter, softened
120 ml (4 fl oz) double cream

For this recipe I am making individual portions using small, round 9 cm ($3\frac{1}{2}$ in) moulds 2.5 cm (1 in) deep, buttered and floured. One large 'Jaffa' can be made instead, in which case you will need a 20 cm (8 in) cake tin or flan mould. For the jelly, line a cake tin, baking tray or Yorkshire pudding moulds with clingfilm. The base should also be lined with greaseproof or silicone paper.

To make the jelly, dissolve the gelatine in a little hot water. Boil the orange juice with the zest and caster sugar. Simmer for 2 minutes, then remove from the heat and add the gelatine. The syrup jelly can now be strained through a sieve. This will remove the zest, preventing the syrup from becoming over bitter and strong. Now it's best to test a tablespoon of the mix on a saucer and chill. If the jelly has set well once cold, then the mix is ready. If it seems to be a little too soft, then add a little more dissolved gelatine. Pour the jelly into the lined cake tin or tray so that it is 1 cm ($\frac{1}{2}$ in) thick. Set the jelly in the fridge. When set, cut out 6–8 × 6 cm ($2\frac{1}{2}$ in) discs of jelly. Freeze any left over to use another time.

Pre-heat the oven to 190°C/375°F/gas 5. To make the sponge, whisk the eggs and sugar together in a bowl over a pan of hot water until light, creamy and at least doubled in volume. Remove from the heat and continue to whisk until cold. Gently fold in the flour, orange zest and melted butter. The mix can now be poured into the moulds so that they are three-quarters full and baked in the pre-heated oven for 15–20 minutes. If you are using one large mould, then cook for 25–30 minutes. Once cooked, leave to cool.

Now a central disc can be cut out to make space for the jelly. To do this take a 6 cm ($2\frac{1}{2}$ in) diameter cutter and press into the sponge 1 cm ($\frac{1}{2}$ in) deep, leaving a 5 mm ($\frac{1}{4}$ in) border and a 5 mm ($\frac{1}{2}$ in) thick base, or if you are making a large one, cut out a disc of sponge 2 cm ($\frac{3}{4}$ in) deep, leaving a 1 cm ($\frac{1}{2}$ in) border and base. You will now find that the sponge simply lifts out, leaving you that space. In both cases, do not cut through the base.

As an added extra and something that will really lift the texture and flavour of the sponge, I like to make a rich orange syrup to soak the sponge bases. Mix the orange zest and juice, water and sugar in a pan. Bring to a simmer and cook for 1–2 minutes to a rich orange syrup. Now pour 1 tablespoon of syrup into each sponge base. The discs of orange jelly can now be placed in the sponge base.

Now it's time to make the chocolate ganache filling. Melt together half the cream, the Cointreau or Grand Marnier, chocolate and orange zest. Whisk the egg yolks and sugar together until the mixture trails off the whisk in ribbons. Lightly whip the remaining cream. Mix the egg and sugar mix with the melted chocolate mix, then gently fold in the whipped cream. The mix can now be left to cool, stirring occasionally until it has reached piping consistency. The chocolate ganache can now be piped or spooned on top of the jelly sponge, making sure you have a 1 cm ($\frac{1}{2}$ in) topping. This can now be rippled with a palette knife for that 'Jaffa' finish.

To give the ultimate 'Jaffa' effect, here is a recipe for a shiny topping.

Melt the chocolate with the cream, add the softened butter and then spoon a thin layer on top of the puddings. The puddings are now finished and can be chilled. They eat at their best at room temperature. This prevents the chocolate from becoming over-set.

To serve, remove the puddings from the moulds and for a real shiny finish place them under the grill for a few seconds or fire with a gas gun.

Note

The orange jelly can also be made by quartering 3 oranges and poaching them in 150–300 ml (5–10 fl oz) of stock syrup for 1 hour. Liquidize the orange with the syrup and push the mixture through a sieve, giving you a totally fresh orange taste. Then just add the gelatine and set before using.

Variations

When making the ganache, you can leave out the egg yolk and sugar mixture and simply fold the whipped cream into the melted mix.

I also like to serve on Orange Anglaise Sauce with this dish. Simply follow the basic Anglaise (Fresh Custard) Sauce recipe (see p.246) omitting the vanilla and adding the zest from 2 oranges to every 600 ml (1 pint) of milk or cream used. Once made, Cointreau, Grand Marnier or brandy can be added.

For a quick 'Anglaise', simply add one of the liqueurs to some tinned custard. If none of these takes your fancy, then why not just have pouring cream? It eats just as well.

Any ganache left over can be rolled into small balls and then rolled in cocoa powder for home-made *petit four* chocolates.

Chocolate and Prune Soufflé Cake

This recipe gives you a rich chocolate pudding with the rich prunes to help moisten and provide extra flavour. I usually cook these in individual moulds, but a 15–20 cm (6–8 in) cake tin or flan mould can be used. If so, cook the pudding for 35–40 minutes instead of 20 minutes. The pudding rises and has an almost soufflé consistency when warm, but once cold becomes a sunken soufflé, giving it an even more puddingy texture. The cakes are light to eat and can be served as puddings or cakes. As a pudding, I like to serve them with thick whipped or clotted cream or perhaps an Anglaise (Fresh Custard) Sauce.

SERVES 8

8–10 prunes, stoned and cut into strips	100 g (4 oz) unsalted butter
1 tablespoon brandy	4 eggs, separated
225 g (8 oz) dark plain chocolate	100 g (4 oz) caster sugar

To Serve

Whipped or clotted cream or Anglaise
(Fresh Custard) Sauce (see p.246)

Pre-heat the oven to 180°C/350°F/gas 4.

You will need individual, loose-bottomed 9 cm ($3\frac{1}{2}$ in) cake tins 2.5 cm (1 in) deep, lightly dusted with flour and base-lined with greaseproof paper.

Before using the prunes, soak them in the brandy until plump and soft.

Melt the chocolate and butter together in a bowl over a pan of warm water, not allowing the water to boil or come into contact with the bowl. Once melted, remove the bowl from the pan and allow to cool to room temperature.

Whisk together the egg yolks and sugar until the mixture is pale and has thickened so that it trails off the whisk in thick ribbons. Fold the egg yolk mix into the chocolate, making sure both are at room temperature. Whisk the egg whites until they form soft peaks, then carefully fold them into the chocolate mix. Divide the mix between the moulds and add the prunes. Bake in the pre-heated oven for approximately 20 minutes until the cakes have risen like soufflés. Once removed from the oven, they will take on a sunken soufflé look. Leave in the tins for 5 minutes, then carefully remove and serve as a cake or pudding. Accompany with Anglaise sauce, cream or both! You can also garnish the plates with a dusting of icing sugar or cocoa.

Spotted Dick

Spotted Dick was always one of those puddings I would look forward to at school. The moist dough with currants or raisins topped with loads of custard (usually lumpy!) was a treat. Like most of my recipes, this has so many variations. I always like the grated zest of 1 lemon added to the mix; this really helps lift all the other flavours. So how about exchanging or adding to that the grated zest of a lime or orange? If it's orange you're going to use, then add chopped hazelnuts – the orange and nut flavours work so well together – or add some chocolate chips to the orange mix, another classic combination. The dish can be served with thick cream or custard and also eats very well drizzled with honey or golden syrup.

SERVES 6–8

300 g (11 oz) plain flour	100 g (4 oz) currants
10 g (¼ oz) baking powder	Finely grated zest of 1 lemon
150 g (5 oz) shredded suet	About 150 ml (5 fl oz) milk
75 g (3 oz) caster sugaer	

Mix together all the dry ingredients with the currants and lemon zest. Add enough milk to give you a binding/dropping consistency. Roll the mix with a rolling pin or by hand into a 15 cm (6 in) cylinder about 5 cm (2 in) in diameter. Either lightly dust a tea towel with flour or butter some greaseproof paper and wrap around the cylinder, leaving enough space for the sponge to rise. Tie the towel or paper at both ends. This can now be placed in a hot steamer and cooked for about 1 hour. Once cooked, remove the towel or paper and the pudding is ready to serve. Cut it into slices at least 2.5 cm (1 in) thick to keep a good texture.

Variations

The quantity of grated lemon zest can be doubled to give a strong lemon taste. This pudding can then be served with the Lemon Anglaise (Fresh Custard) Sauce (see p.246).

Steamed golden syrup sponge log is also very good. Simply omit the sugar and milk and replace with 5–6 tablespoons of golden syrup. The richness of this pudding eats so well, especially with clotted cream.

In the introduction I mentioned adding orange zest and chocolate chips. This works very well, but if you want to make it even richer then replace 50 g (2 oz) of the flour with cocoa. This will give you a Chocolate and Orange Spotted Dick!

Another favourite is adding chopped Medjool dates and dried figs, about 50–75 g (2–3 oz) of each works very well, with 2–3 tablespoons of honey. This gives you a steamed suet fig roll. If you don't want to put the honey in the mix then simply trickle some over every slice or add some to taste to the Anglaise (Fresh Custard) Sauce.

So there are some ideas of how to turn a Spotted Dick pudding into something completely different – and still as good to eat.

Spotted Dick.

Lemon Puffs Pudding

This pudding is really a combination of two of my favourite recipes: a glazed lemon tart with a puff pastry palmier biscuit. I'm sure you can imagine just how well these work together. The crisp but light puff pastry mixed with the soft delicate lemon 'mousse' that has a sharp bite behind it. Use a home-made puff pastry or simply buy a block of frozen. The palmier biscuits can also be made from any puff pastry trimmings you may have frozen.

MAKES 8 biscuits

For the Biscuit

Icing sugar, sifted	225 g (8 oz) Puff Pastry (see p.250)

For the Lemon Puff Filling

8 eggs	Juice of 4 lemons
350 g (12 oz) caster sugar	Finely grated zest of 2 lemons
300 ml (10 fl oz) double cream	

To Serve

Icing sugar	Pouring cream

Pre-heat the oven to 220°C/425°F/gas 7. Lightly grease and dampen a baking sheet.

To make the biscuit, dust the work surface with icing sugar and roll out the pastry into a rectangle. Fold in each end to reach the middle, then simply close like a book. This should now be rested for 15 minutes. Dust the surface with more icing sugar and roll out the pastry to 3 mm ($\frac{1}{8}$ in) thick. Trim the edges to make a square, then liberally sprinkle icing sugar over the pastry before rolling up into a cylinder about 5 cm (2 in) in diameter. This can now be chilled for a further 15 minutes.

Remove the pastry cylinder from the fridge and cut into discs 5 mm ($\frac{1}{4}$ in) thick. You will need 2 biscuits per portion. These should now also be lightly flattened into 7.5–9 cm (3–3$\frac{1}{2}$ in) discs on icing sugar with a rolling pin, then lightly dusted with icing sugar before being placed on the baking sheet. Bake in the pre-heated oven for 5 minutes, then turn over and cook for a further 5 minutes until golden and crisp. Leave to cool on a wire rack. For a darker caramel crisp finish, dust with more icing sugar and place under the grill or use a gas gun. These biscuits are now ready to use or will keep for 24 hours in an airtight container.

Reduce the oven temperature to 150°C/300°F/gas 2. Grease and base-line a 20 cm (8 in) loose-bottomed flan ring or 8 × 6 cm (2½ in) tins.

To make the lemon filling, mix the eggs and caster sugar together until smooth, then add the cream, lemon juice and zest. This mix can now be poured into the tin or tins and should be 2.5–4 cm (1–1½ in) deep. Bake in the pre-heated oven for 45–50 minutes until the filling has just set. The small tins will only take 20–25 minutes. Remove from the oven and leave to cool. To make the mix slightly firmer and easier to use, chill for 30 minutes before cutting.

To finish the puddings, use a warm knife to release the filling mix from the edge of the case(s). For the small cases, dip very quickly in hot water to release the greaseproofed base. It's best to sit one of the palmier biscuits on top of the mould and turn the case upside down. This will immediately sit the filling on the biscuit. Remove the greaseproof and then sit another palmier on top to complete the dish.

If using a large tin, then simply turn out on to a large tray, or if loose-bottomed simply push out. Now the filling can be cut out with a 6–7.5 cm (2½–3 in) ring and carefully lifted on to a biscuit using a spatula or fish slice. The filling is very delicate and will need careful handling. You can then assemble the biscuits. Obviously, when using a tray, you will be left with some trimmings. I always find it best just to eat and enjoy them! To serve, I simply sit the lemon puffs on the plate, dust around with icing sugar and serve with pouring cream.

Note

The lemon 'mousse' trimmings can be whisked with some pouring cream and then set in glasses for an extra pudding.

Variation

If you want an extra garnish, then cook some thin strips of lemon zest in a stock syrup. This can be made by boiling 150 ml (5 fl oz) of water with 100 g (4 oz) of caster sugar until a syrup is formed. Serve with the lemon puffs.

Steamed Lemon Sponge with Prunes, Damson or Tutti-frutti

Lemon must be one of the most versatile flavours we have. It lends itself to such a variety of dishes, whether they be sweet or savoury. It also makes us think about menu compilation; starting off with a plate of smoked salmon, which is normally served with lemon, then following with chicken with lemon and parsley and finishing with one of these sponges, wouldn't really be a good idea. But I have found that using any of these three flavours with a lemon sponge, rather than just a basic vanilla recipe, really lifts all their tastes. First I'll give you the lemon sponge, followed by the alternatives.

MAKES 1 × 900 ml (2 pint) sponge or 4 × 150 ml (5 fl oz) sponges

For the Sponge

100 g (4 oz) unsalted butter
150 g (5 oz) caster sugar
Finely grated zest and juice of 1 lemon
2 eggs

1 egg yolk
200 g (7 oz) self-raising flour
1–2 drops of milk (optional)

For the Prune Pudding

About 12 stoned, ready-to-eat prunes

A little Stock Syrup (see p.210) (optional)

For the Damson Pudding

About 8 ripe damsons, stoned
    and halved

For the Damson Coulis

175 g (6 oz) stoned damsons,
    each cut into 4

40 g (1½ oz) caster sugar
50 ml (2 fl oz) water

For the Tutti-frutti Pudding

225 g (8 oz) mixed crystallized fruits
    and raisins such as glacé cherries,

strawberries, melon, orange, lemon,
angelica and raisins, chopped

For the Honey Stock Syrup

40 g (1½ oz) caster sugar
5 tablespoons water

1 tablespoon honey or golden syrup

Butter and flour 1 × 900 ml (2 pint) mould or 4 × 150 ml (5 fl oz) moulds. Beat together the butter and sugar with the lemon zest until almost white and the sugar has dissolved. This is easily achieved in an electric mixer. It does take a little while for the sugar to dissolve. Beat in 1 egg at a time, making sure that after each egg is added the mix is beaten until mixed and fluffy again. Once both eggs have been added, repeat the same process with the egg yolk. Fold the flour into the mix well, then add the lemon juice and milk, if needed, to give a dropping consistency. So that's the basic mix made. Here are the alternatives to go with it.

For the prune pudding, use stoned, ready-to-eat prunes as these are already tender. They can be made even softer by soaking in warm stock syrup. If you are going to soak them for the base of the moulds, do not allow them to become too wet as this will loosen the sponge mix and prevent the base from cooking. Just place 2 or 3 stoned prunes in each of the individual moulds before spooning the mix on top. As the pudding begins to cook the mix will soften the prunes. The prunes can also be cut into small dice and simply added to the pudding mix.

For the damson pudding, I simply take 1½–2 ripe damsons per portion, stoned and halved, and sit them in the bottom of the moulds before adding the sponge mix. To finish and enrich the dish, I like to serve stewed damsons (by cooking for 2–3 minutes) or coulis over the top, or both. Put all the coulis ingredients into a pan and bring to a simmer. Then cook for 5 minutes and push through a sieve. This eats very well with custard and fresh cream.

The tutti-frutti pudding simply needs 100–175 g (4–6 oz) of the glacé and crystallized fruits bound into the lemon sponge mix before being steamed. The remaining fruits can be warmed in a honey stock syrup made by heating and dissolving the caster sugar with the water and honey or golden syrup. Trickle the fruits and syrup on top of the sponge and serve with Vanilla Ice-cream (see p.216).

For any of the puddings, steam individual puddings for 40 minutes or a large pudding for 1½ hours, topping up with boiling water as necessary. Turn out the puddings and serve with the sauces or creams of your choice.

Variations

To lift the flavour of the prune sponge, I serve it with Lemon Curd and Prune Ripple Ice-cream (see p.225), along with a Lemon Anglaise (Fresh Custard) Sauce (see p.246). If you wish just to serve the custard, it's best to dice 2 or 3 more prunes per pudding and add them to the sponge mix. This will obviously give you a much stronger prune flavour.

The same quantity of fruits and raisins used in the tutti-frutti pudding can be added to Frangipane (see p.252) and cooked in tartlets as for the Cherry and Almond Tart (see p.184).

Christmas Rice Pudding with Honey and Rum Glacé Fruits

The glacé fruits can be of your choice. Most of the superstores sell a mixed 350–450 g (12–16 oz) tub which hold some very interesting fruits – melon, pear, fig, mandarin, plum and pineapple, as well as the classic cherries and lemon.

The quantities here assume you will have guests – but you can easily halve the recipe.

Serves 10–12

225 g (8 oz) short-grain pudding rice	6 egg yolks
1.2 litres (2 pints) milk	300 ml (10 fl oz) double cream
100 g (4 oz) caster sugar	Icing sugar, sifted
50 g (2 oz) unsalted butter	

For the Fruits and Syrup

150 ml (5 fl oz) water	25 g (1 oz) sultanas
25 g (1 oz) caster sugar	25 g (1 oz) raisins
2 tablespoons rum, or more to taste	225 g (8 oz) glacé fruits
3 tablespoons honey	

Butter a 1.75 litre (3 pint) pudding basin or 10 individual 150 ml (5 fl oz) moulds. Place the rice in a pan and cover with cold water. Bring to the boil then refresh under cold water and drain. Boil 1 litre (1¾ pints) of the milk, half the sugar and the butter in a pan, then add the rice. Bring to a simmer and cook for 15–20 minutes until tender and soft. Beat the egg yolks and remaining sugar together in a bowl. Boil the cream and remaining milk. Pour the milk on to the eggs and sugar, mixing all the time. Stir this custard into the hot rice and cook gently for another few minutes. The rice mix will now thicken. Pour into the prepared mould or moulds and leave to cool before setting in the fridge for 1–2 hours.

To prepare the sultanas, raisins and glacé fruits, boil the water and sugar together. Remove from the heat and add the rum and honey to taste. Cut the glacé fruits into halves or wedges and mix all the fruits, including the sultanas and raisins, with the warm syrup.

Turn out the pudding on to a large plate. This is easily achieved by sitting the bowl in warm water for a few seconds to release. Now simply spoon the fruits over and around the pudding and finish with a sprig of holly or mint and dust with icing sugar.

Christmas Pudding

I always plan my Christmas puddings well ahead of time. They are usually made by August, giving them time to mature and improve the flavour. I like to make several, as it's always a very nice gift to give: a good home-made Christmas pudding.

This pudding mix can also be kept chilled for a week before cooking. This gives the raw ingredients time to work their tastes together. It should at the least have 24 hours before cooking.

MAKES 3 × 1.2 litre (2 pint) puddings

225 g (8 oz) plain flour
1 teaspoon baking powder
225 g (8 oz) fresh white breadcrumbs
225 g (8 oz) shredded suet
100 g (4 oz) ground almonds
550 g (1¼ lb) dark muscovado sugar
1 teaspoon mixed spice
½ teaspoon freshly grated nutmeg
½ teaspoon cinnamon
175 g (6 oz) stoned prunes
175 g (6 oz) carrots

750 g (1½ lb) mixed currants, sultanas
   and raisins
50 g (2 oz) chopped mixed peel
2 apples, peeled, cored and chopped
Juice and grated zest of 1 orange
Juice and grated zest of 1 lemon,
5 eggs
4 measures rum
4 tablespoons black treacle
4 tablespoons golden syrup
300 ml (10 fl oz) stout

Sift the flour with the baking powder. Add the breadcrumbs, suet, ground almonds, muscovado sugar and spices. The prunes and carrots should be minced together through a medium mincer and then added to the mix together with the currants, sultanas, raisins, mixed peel, apples and lemon and orange zest. Beat the eggs and add to the mix with the orange and lemon juice, rum, treacle, golden syrup and stout. The pudding ingredients can now be totally mixed together; you should have about 3 kg (7 lb) in weight. This mix should have a loose consistency; if it feels too dry then simply add a little more stout. Cover and keep in a cool place for 24 hours to a week; if it's still bland, add more spices and rum.

Butter and lightly flour 3 × 900 g (2 lb) pudding basins. Fill three-quarters full with the mix and top with a circle of lightly greased greaseproof paper. The pudding basins can now be covered with parchment paper, leaving a fold in the paper. These should now be steamed for 4 hours. topping up with boiling water as necessary.

Once cooked, leave to cool before chilling, or store in a cool, dark place. The puddings will simply mature, becoming more tasty as the time goes on. If they take up too much space in your fridge, keep them well sealed in a cool place.

To serve the puddings on The Day, they will need to be steamed for a minimum 1 hour to bring them back to a tender pudding texture.

Apple Pies

This recipe can be used as individual pies or, of course, as one large one. I really don't mind either but it is nice to have your own personal apple pie! I like to place a disc of sponge in the base of the pies. This collects any apple juices and prevents the pastry from becoming soggy on the base. It also gives you a tasty sponge once cooked. You can use home-made or simply buy a Victoria sponge from any supermarket. This method and recipe could also have many other combinations: raisins and currants can be added, or you can make apple and cherry, blackberry or blackcurrant pies. The choice is yours!

SERVES 4

350 g (12 oz) Shortcrust Pastry (see p.251)

$\frac{1}{2}$ Victoria Sponge (see p.192) (optional)

For the Filling

350–450 g (12–16 oz) Bramley cooking apples, peeled, cored and cut into 1 cm ($\frac{1}{2}$ in) dice

Juice and grated zest of $\frac{1}{2}$ lemon

$\frac{1}{2}$ teaspoon grated orange zest

$\frac{1}{2}$ teaspoon ground cinnamon

2 tablespoons demerara sugar

For the Glaze

2 tablespoons apricot jam, sieved

4 tablespoons water

Pre-heat the oven to 200°C/400°F/gas 6. Grease and flour 4 × 9 cm (3$\frac{1}{2}$ in) loose-bottomed flan rings or tartlet tins or 1 × 15 cm (6 in) mould.

Roll out half the pastry, cut into 4 strips and use to line the inside of the rings, making sure it's slightly higher than the ring to fold some over. Cut the remaining pastry into 8 discs, 4 for the base and 4 for the lids. The bases can now be placed in the moulds. Cut the sponge into 5 mm ($\frac{1}{4}$ in) thick discs and place on top of the bases.

Mix together all the filling ingredients, then pack the filling into the moulds, making sure the moulds are absolutely full and brimming. This is basically because during the cooking time the apples will break down in texture and reduce in quantity. Brush the pastry edge with water and sit the lids on top. Trim off all excess pastry. The pies are now ready to cook. Cook in the pre-heated oven for 20–30 minutes for individual moulds and 40–45 minutes for one large pie. Once cooked and golden brown, allow to rest for 10–15 minutes before removing the mould.

To give an overall shiny glaze, bring the jam and water to a simmer, adding a little more water if the glaze is too thick, then brush over the complete pie. These are now ready to eat and go well with custard, clotted cream or ice-cream.

Apple Pie.

Cooking Fruits: Cherries, Plums, Greengages, Gooseberries and Damsons

All these fruits eat very well with different dishes. This recipe is really for cherries and plums, both of which are featured in the book, but also for the less frequently used fruits, gooseberries, greengages and damsons. Cherries, and in fact all of these fruits, once stoned, can be cooked in a knob of butter with sugar. The fruits will create their own liquor/syrup and are then ready to use. For every 450 g (1 lb) of fruit you will need only 25 g (1 oz) of butter to 50–100 g (2–4 oz) of caster sugar, depending on the ripeness of the fruit. So there's one basic recipe already. Here are a couple more alternatives.

MAKES about 600 g (1¼ lb)

450 g (1 lb) cherries, gooseberries or damsons, washed and stoned	4 tablespoons water 100 g (4 oz) caster sugar

All the ingredients can be placed in a pan and brought to the boil. Remove from the stove and allow the fruits to cool in the liquor. These can now be kept in their own liquor and chilled, or the liquor can be used to soak sponges or boiled until reduced by half and used as a glaze to finish flans and tarts.

Variation

A liqueur can be substituted for half the water; for example, try 2 tablespoons of kirsch and 2 tablespoons of water when cooking cherries.

Cooking Plums, Damsons and Greengages

This method is best for fruits being used in fruit tarts and sponges; they keep their shape but also become very tender. All you need to do is halve and stone the fruits and place on a baking sheet skin-side down. Sprinkle liberally with icing sugar and cook in a pre-heated oven 200°C/400°F/gas 6 for 4–6 minutes. The sugar will dissolve and sweeten the fruits as they soften. As the fruits cook on the baking tray, a little natural syrup will be created. It's best to save this and use it for a glaze.

These fruits will also work in the first recipe. However, plums and fruits from the same family, such as greengages, will not hold up so well when mixed with water. In fact they will purée very quickly which, of course, is fine if you're making a coulis or purée.

Fruit Purées and Coulis

A classic fruit coulis is really just fruit sieved to give you a purée. So for every 225 g (8 oz) of fruit just add 50 g (2 oz) of caster sugar and the juice of $\frac{1}{2}$ lemon. Blitz all together, then pass through a sieve. There you have a coulis. This recipe is very similar but gives you more of a sauce consistency rather than just a purée.

MAKES 750 ml ($1\frac{1}{4}$ pints)

450 g (1 lb) fruit such as plums, raspberries, etc.
100 g (4 oz) caster sugar

150 ml (5 fl oz) water
Juice of 1 lemon

All the ingredients can be mixed together and brought to the simmer for a few minutes until the fruits become tender. If the fruit is very sharp, the sugar quantity can be doubled to 225 g (8 oz). Once tender, after about 6–8 minutes, the mix can now be blitzed and pushed through a sieve. Once cold, this coulis will have a good sauce consistency to use with many puddings.

Cherry and Almond Tart with Pear Sorbet

In some ways, I suppose, this is similar to my Plum and Almond Slice (see p.190). These, however, are individual tarts. They can, of course, be made in a 15–20 cm (6–8 in) flan ring to give you a single cherry and almond tart, but when you make them individually and then shape some pear sorbet and sit it on top, the dish not only looks good but eats even better.

Serves 4

225 g (8 oz) Shortcrust Pastry (see p.251)
1½ tablespoons Cherry Jam (see p.249) or bought
225 g (8 oz) cherries, cooked as on p.182, the cooking liquid boiled to reduce by half for glaze

275 g (10 oz) Frangipane (see p.252)
300 ml (10 fl oz) Anglaise (Fresh Custard) Sauce (see p.246)
1–2 measures Poire William liqueur to taste (optional)
Pear Sorbet (see p.214)

Pre-heat the oven to 180°C/350°F/gas 4. Lightly grease 4 × 10 cm (4 in) fluted, round, loose-bottomed moulds about 2.5 cm (1 in) deep.

Roll out the pastry and line the tart cases. Spread 2 teaspoons of cherry jam into each mould, and then divide half the cherries between the moulds, reserving a few. Fill the moulds with the frangipane, and then finish by sitting the reserved whole cherries on top. Cook in the pre-heated oven for 30–35 minutes, covering with foil or greaseproof paper at the end of cooking if they are browning too quickly. Once cooked, allow to cool to a warm temperature. These can now be glazed with the reduced cherry syrup.

Flavour the Anglaise sauce with Poire William, if available. If Poire William is difficult to find, then simply use Anglaise sauce.

The pudding can now be finished. Spoon some Anglaise sauce on to a plate. Remove the tart from its mould and sit it in the centre. Shape the sorbet between 2 serving spoons and sit it on top.

Note

Tinned or griottine cherries (the latter steeped in alcohol) can also be used.

Cherry and Almond Tart with Pear Sorbet.

Hazelnut and Orange Cake with Orange Anglaise and Mascarpone Caramel Cream

This is a very light cake. You'll notice there's no flour in the ingredients; the sponge is set by the egg yolks and whisked egg white. It's also best eaten at room temperature. This is because of the chocolate: if the cake is chilled, the chocolate sets and changes the texture, so keep this cake in an airtight container rather than refrigerating it.

The cake eats very well as a dessert with caramel mascarpone cream and an orange Anglaise sauce, so both of those recipes are included here. If all of that sounds a bit too rich for you then simply eat the cake as it is – light and tasty!

This cake can be baked in a cake tin, but I prefer to cook it in a loaf tin. This gives you the same shape as the classic Jamaican Ginger Cake.

MAKES 2 × 900 g (2 lb) loaf cakes

150 g (5 oz) skinned hazelnuts, toasted
150 g (5 oz) good quality plain
   chocolate, chopped
1 teaspoon finely grated lemon zest

2 teaspoons finely grated orange zest
6 eggs, separated
100 g (4 oz) caster sugar

For the Orange Anglaise

Anglaise (Fresh Custard) Sauce
   (see p.246)
Zest of 2 oranges

1–2 measures Grand Marnier or
   Cointreau (optional)

For the Mascarpone Caramel Cream

250 g (9 oz) caster sugar
150 ml (5 fl oz) water

250 ml (8 fl oz) double cream
250 g (9 oz) mascarpone

Pre-heat the oven to 180°C/350°F/gas 4. Grease and line 2 × 900 g (2 lb) loaf tins or 2 × 15–20 cm (6–8 in) cake tins.

To make the cake, place the hazelnuts, chocolate, lemon and orange zest in a food processor or liquidizer and blitz to a fine consistency. Whisk the egg yolks and half the sugar together until pale and the mix trails off the whisk in ribbons, then fold in the hazelnut and chocolate mix. Whisk the egg whites to a firm stage. Add the remaining sugar and continue to whisk to a thick meringue stage. This can now be folded in to the main mixture. This mix can now be poured into the loaf or cake tins and baked in the pre-heated oven for 25–30 minutes until just firm in the centre. Once cooked, leave to cool and rest before turning out of the mould.

To make an orange Anglaise to go with the loaf, simply follow the Anglaise recipe on p.246, swapping the vanilla for the orange zest and then cooking as for custard, removing the zest at the last moment. To lift the flavour even more, add the Grand Marnier or Cointreau.

To make the mascarpone caramel cream, bring the caster sugar and water to the boil and simmer gently until you have a dark amber caramel. Bring the cream to the boil and add to the caramel, whisking as you're adding. Return the mix to the heat and allow to simmer for a few minutes, then strain through a sieve if the mix is not completely smooth. Allow to cool and set. You will have about 450 ml (15 fl oz). Whisk the mascarpone to soften it, then add half the caramel cream (more can be added if you prefer a richer flavour!). The mix can now be whisked and mixed until almost peaked. This is now ready to use or can be kept chilled until needed.

To serve the pudding, sit a slice of cake on to a plate and spoon some orange Anglaise around. The caramel mascarpone can now be shaped between 2 large serving spoons and placed on top of the sponge. The remaining basic caramel cream can now be warmed for the ultimate richness and dribbled with a teaspoon across the complete pudding.

Pear and Hazelnut 'Pasties'

The last time I called a dish a pasty (it was a lamb dish), I was inundated with letters telling me I didn't have a clue what a real pasty is! Well, after being shown several times since, I certainly do now. So please don't send me any more letters over this recipe. This is what I call using artistic licence!

All I'm really doing is taking the pasty shape and turning it into a pudding. The pastry I'm using is puff rather than a short/puff/crumbly pastry that's normally used. The frangipane made with ground hazelnuts rather than almonds immediately gives you a new flavour. Of course, almond frangipane can also be used. One of the advantages of this dish is that it can be made well in advance before being baked.

One of my joys of cooking is the number of variations each recipe can have. This recipe can be made with almost any fruit: apples, plums and cherries are just a few examples. I still have this run of 'Black Forest' ideas, so how about using Chocolate Frangipane (see p.252), mixing in some chocolate chips and topping the frangipane with poached cherries and cherry jam on the base. So there's a fun idea: Hot Black Forest Pasties served with Chocolate Sabayon (see p.244) and clotted cream – another classic!

SERVES 4

For the Pears

4 small pears, peeled, halved and cored
½ lemon
1 vanilla pod (optional)

1 cinnamon stick (optional)
600 ml (1 pint) water
225 g (8 oz) caster sugar

For the Pasties

350–450 g (12–16 oz) Puff Pastry
  (see p.250) or frozen
175 g (6 oz) Hazelnut Frangipane
  (see p.252, about ½ quantity) using
  ground hazelnuts

2 tablespoons chocolate chips (optional)
1 egg, beaten

Optional Extras to Serve

Rich Chocolate Sauce (see p.248),
  Chocolate Sabayon (see p.244),
  Anglaise (Fresh Custard) Sauce

(see p.246) or Chocolate Custard
(see p.247)

Pre-heat the oven to 200°C/400°F/gas 6.

Rub the pear halves with the lemon, then place in a pan with the remaining lemon juice, the vanilla pod and cinnamon stick if using, the water and sugar. Cover with greaseproof paper and bring to the boil. Allow to simmer for a few minutes, then remove from the heat. Leave the pears to cool in the syrup to allow them to finish cooking.

The next stage is to roll out the puff pastry into 4 × 20 cm (8 in) diameter circles. If using chocolate chips, add them to the hazelnut frangipane. Also, if it's plum, cherry or any red fruit you are going to use in this pasty, I always spoon some jam of the fruit flavour on the pastry before sitting the frangipane on top. Cherry jam can also be used with this pear recipe.

Divide the hazelnut frangipane between the pastry circles, spreading it on one half only and also leaving a 1–2 cm (½–¾ in) border to seal the pasty. The pears can now be placed on top, allowing 2 halves per portion. These should be placed core-side down, leaving a good domed top to fold the pastry over.

Beat the egg and brush around the border. The pastry can now be folded over and sealed. To shape the edge, this can be twisted as for a classic pasty or marked with a fork or perhaps cut to give a fluted finish. Brush the pasties with the remaining beaten egg to give them a shiny finish. These can now be chilled to rest for 10 minutes before cooking. If you are making them in advance – and you can even make them the day before – do not glaze them until you are ready to cook.

Bake the pasties in the pre-heated oven for 20–25 minutes. If they seem to be colouring too quickly, then simply cover lightly with foil or greaseproof paper and continue to cook. They're now ready to eat. Serve with pouring or clotted cream.

Variation

The pasties will also work very well with tinned pear halves. Of course they don't have quite the same strength or taste as fresh pears, but they still eat well.

Plum and Almond Slice with Cognac Zabaglione

In each book I like to include a frangipane or bakewell tart, so this one is not missing out. Instead of being a round flan I'm using a rectangular 'ring' 20 × 10 × 4 cm (8 × 4 × 1½ in), but if you can't find one use a 20 cm (8 in) flan ring. When a slice is cut you see the plums running through. It looks and eats really well, with the moist frangipane holding it all together. As for the cognac zabaglione, this is an optional extra that is so delicious with the flan. It just gives the whole dish a special edge. Just cream, clotted cream or custard can be served with this dish or, if you're feeling very greedy, why not have the lot!

SERVES 6–8

225 g (8 oz) Sweet Shortcrust Pastry (see p.251)	Icing sugar, sifted
4 tablespoons plum jam	½ quantity Frangipane (see p.252)
10 plums, halved and stoned	2–3 tablespoons water (optional)
	Icing sugar, sifted (optional)

For the Zabaglione

4 egg yolks	25 ml (1 fl oz) dry white wine
40 g (1½ oz) caster sugar	25 ml (1 fl oz) brandy or cognac

Grease and flour a 20 × 10 × 4 cm (8 × 4 × 1½ in) cake tin or 20 cm (8 in) flan ring. Sit the mould on to a greaseproof-papered baking tray.

Roll out the pastry and use to line the prepared tin. When lining, it's best to leave the excess pastry around the edges just folded over. This will prevent the pastry from shrinking in the mould and, once cooked, can simply be trimmed with a knife. Spread half the plum jam into the pastry case. The remaining jam will be used to help glaze the finished dish. This can now be left chilled while the plums are being prepared.

Pre-heat the oven to 180°C/350°F/gas 4.

Sit the plums skin-side down on a roasting tray and dust generously with icing sugar. Bake in the pre-heated oven for 4–6 minutes until softened. The cooking time will really depend on the ripeness of the plums. Once softened, drain off any excess liquor, adding it to the remaining jam, and leave to cool. Once cold, sit 10 plum halves in the mould skin-side up. These can now be covered with the frangipane, 2–3 mm ($\frac{1}{8}$ in) from the top of the mould. The remaining plums will not be used until 10–15 minutes before cooking time. If they are put on now they will sink without trace during cooking!

The flan can now be cooked in the pre-heated oven. It will take approximately $1\frac{1}{4}$ hours to cook. After 45–50 minutes, sit the remaining plums on top and finish cooking.

The jam and liquor can now be warmed to glaze. A little water may also be needed to loosen the jam. To give the tart an even richer colour before glazing, sprinkle liberally with icing sugar and finish under the grill or with a gas gun. This will give you one or two burnt edges, creating a bitter–sweet top. Trim the excess pastry from the edges, then brush with the jam glaze. Once cooled slightly, the flan ring or mould can be removed. This pudding can be served warm or cold.

To make the zabaglione to accompany the pudding, beat together the eggs and sugar until light in colour. Add the white wine and cognac and sit the bowl over a pan of simmering water and whisk vigorously (an electric hand mixer reduces the hard work) until light, thick and frothy. This will take at least 8–10 minutes. The zabaglione should be thick enough to form soft peaks when drawn back on itself.

To serve the dish, take a slice of the plum and almond cake, present on a plate and spoon some zabaglione on the side. I also like to serve clotted cream as well and have the zabaglione just falling off the slice.

Greengage and Lime Sponge Pie

Greengage is a fruit we just don't see enough of. The greengage is a member of the plum family and probably more sweet and perfumed than basic plums. With this recipe they can be used completely raw, if very ripe. If the only ones you can find are under-ripe and firm, then it's best to soften them through in the oven with icing sugar before using – I'll explain this in the recipe.

These fruits in France are known as the reine-claude, *named after France's first queen. So the next time you're in France and have ordered a* Tarte Reine-Claude *you now know you'll be eating a greengage tart or pie. This recipe gives you a combination of all these elements: it's in pastry, so there's the tart connection; and it's also set in a sponge, so there's the pie or gâteau connection.*

MAKES 1 × 20 cm (8 in) pie

175–225 g (6–8 oz) Sweet Shortcrust Pastry (see p.251)
400 g (14 oz) fresh greengages, halved and stoned

Icing sugar (optional)
2–3 tablespoons greengage jam or lime marmalade

For the Victoria Sponge

50 g (2 oz) unsalted butter
50 g (2 oz) caster sugar
1 egg

50 g (2 oz) plain flour (or use self-raising for a lighter finish)
Grated zest and juice of 1 lime

To Glaze and Finish

1 tablespoon greengage jam or lime marmalade (optional)

2 tablespoons water (optional)
Icing sugar for dusting (optional)

Pre-heat the oven to 200°C/400°F/gas 6. Grease a 20 cm (8 in) flan ring.

Line the flan ring with the pastry, leaving any excess pastry over the edge of the ring. Line with greaseproof paper and baking beans or rice. Cook in the pre-heated oven for 20 minutes. The greaseproof paper and beans or rice can now be removed and excess pastry trimmed off.

If the greengages are very ripe, then these are ready to use. If they feel firm and under-ripe, then sit them on a baking tray, skin-side down and dust generously with icing sugar. These can now be cooked and softened in the pre-heated oven for 4–6 minutes.

To make the sponge, cream together the butter and sugar. Beat the egg and then add it slowly to the butter mix. Fold in the flour with the zest of lime. The lime juice can now be added to finish the mix.

Reduce the oven temperature to 180°C/350°F/gas 4. To make the pie, spoon the greengage jam or lime marmalade into the pastry and spread over the base. The sponge mix can now be spread into the case. Sit the greengages skin-side up on top of the sponge mix. This can now be baked in the pre-heated oven for 35–40 minutes. As the pie is cooking, the sponge will rise around the fruit. Once cooked, remove from the oven and leave for 10 minutes before serving. This dish eats very well warm or cold.

For an extra glaze finish, heat the jam or marmalade with the water and brush over. For a simple rustic finish, dust round the edges with icing sugar and serve.

Variation

This recipe has so much scope. It can be made with plums, cherries, raspberries, damsons, apricots, more or less any fruit. All you need to do is use the right jam or marmalade to go with it.

Victoria Sponge

This is a basic sponge mix that can be used in so many puddings. I'm using a Victoria Sponge recipe with the addition of lime in the Greengage and Lime Sponge Pie (see p.192).

I thought it would be a good idea to include this recipe because it's easy and quick to make. So if you're really stuck for time, make this recipe and join the sponges with whipped double cream and jam. There you have a real English cake: fresh cream Victoria Sponge.

MAKES 1 × 18 cm (7 in) sponge sandwich

175 g (6 oz) unsalted butter
175 g (6 oz) caster sugar
1 scraped fresh vanilla pod (optional)

3 eggs, beaten
175 g (6 oz) self-raising flour

Pre-heat the oven to 190°C/375°F/gas 5 and grease and flour 2 × 18 cm (7 in) sandwich tins.

Beat together the butter, caster sugar and fresh vanilla, if using, to a creamy consistency. Slowly mix in the eggs until all is accepted. Fold in the flour. Pour into the prepared tins and bake in the oven for 20–25 minutes until well risen and golden and spring back when pressed with a finger. Turn out and leave to cool on wire racks.

Variations

Other flavours can be added to give a different taste: the finely grated zest of 1–2 lemons and/or 1 orange can be added for a citrus flavour; 25 g (1 oz) of the flour can be replaced with 25 g (1 oz) of cocoa for chocolate sponges.

Vanilla Sponge (Genoise)

This sponge can be used for many things: cakes, gâteaux, trifles or puddings. If you keep a couple of vanilla pods in an airtight jar with your caster sugar, you will have vanilla sugar ready whenever you need it.

MAKES 1 × 20 cm (8 in) SPONGE

6 eggs
175 g (6 oz) caster sugar flavoured with
   a vanilla pod

175 g (6 oz) plain flour
50 g (2 oz) unsalted butter, melted

Pre-heat the oven to 200°C/400°F/gas 6. Grease a 20 cm (8 in) round cake tin and dust with flour.

Whisk the eggs and sugar together in a bowl over a pan of hot water. Continue to whisk until the mixture has doubled in volume and is light and creamy. Remove from the heat and continue to whisk until cold and thick. This is called the ribbon stage as the mixture will trail off the whisk in ribbons when you lift it out of the mixture. Lightly fold in the flour and melted butter. Gently pour the mix into the prepared tin and bake in the pre-heated oven for about 30 minutes. The easiest way to test is with a skewer, which will come out clean when the sponge is ready.

Allow to cool for 10 minutes in the tin, then turn out on to a wire rack.

Chocolate Vanilla Sponge (Genoise)

To make a chocolate sponge, replace 25 g (1 oz) of the flour with 2 tablespoons of cocoa.

Chocolate Truffle Cake

The quantities of chocolate and cream in this recipe are quite frightening: it's really 450 g (1 lb) to 600 ml (1 pint), a lot of chocolate and cream. But remember, there are always times when we want to spoil ourselves and indulge in rich foods. So if it's Christmas, Easter or perhaps a birthday, then this is the cake for you. This recipe will fill a 25 cm (10 in) cake tin at least 7.5 cm (3 in) deep. The recipe can be halved for a 15 cm (6 in) cake tin.

I'm also using a Chocolate Vanilla Sponge (Genoise) (see p.195) for the base. Once cooked and cooled, I'm cutting the sponge in half horizontally to give a round slice for the base of the cake. Any remaining sponge can be frozen and kept ready for the next time. I like to soak the base sponge with a rum syrup – it's optional, but tasty! The chocolate topping recipe will give you enough to cover the top of the cake. If you want to cover the entire cake, you'll need to double the quantities.

MAKES 1 × 25 cm (10 in) cake

1 × 25 cm (10 in) Chocolate Vanilla Sponge (Genoise) (see p.195), cut in half horizontally to give a 1 cm ($\frac{1}{2}$ in) thick slice (freeze any left)

For the Rum Syrup

85 ml (3 fl oz) water
50 g (2 oz) caster sugar

Rum to taste

For the Cake

450 g (1 lb) good quality plain chocolate
600 ml (1 pint) double cream

4 egg yolks
50 g (2 oz) caster sugar

For the Chocolate Topping

100 g (4 oz) good quality plain chocolate
50 ml (2 fl oz) double cream

25 g (1 oz) unsalted butter, softened

Place the chocolate sponge in the base of a 25 cm (10 in) loose-bottomed flan ring.

To make the rum syrup, boil the water with the sugar and add rum to taste. This can now be used to soak the sponge in the base. You will have about 120 ml (4 fl oz).

To make the cake, melt the chocolate with half the cream in a bowl over a pan of hot water. Whisk the egg yolks and sugar together until pale and fluffy. Whip the remaining cream to soft peaks. Once the chocolate has melted, remove from the heat and beat in the egg mixture. Fold in the whipped cream and pour the truffle mix into the cake tin on top of the sponge base. Leave to set, refrigerated, for 2–4 hours (overnight is best).

Once set, remove the cake from the tin and finish with the chocolate topping. Melt the chocolate with the double cream. Add the butter and remove from the heat. Leave to cool and thicken, then spread over the top of the sponge. To ensure a glossy finish, place each slice under the grill or glaze with a gas gun for a few seconds before serving.

Chocolate Fudge Cake

This is a recipe for the children to make for you with very little help. This is a recipe that has all the ingredients sitting in our cupboards. It's also great to make for children's birthday parties or one of the cakes to present to their teacher.

MAKES 1 × 20 cm (8 in) CAKE

225 g (8 oz) plain or milk chocolate	Juice and finely grated zest of 1 orange
100 g (4 oz) unsalted butter	4 tablespoons brandy
25 g (1 oz) caster sugar	(for adult version only!)
1 egg	225 g (8 oz) digestive biscuits, crushed

Line a 20 cm (8 in) loose-bottomed cake tin with greaseproof paper.

Gently melt the chocolate with the butter in a heavy-based pan. Beat the sugar with the egg and orange zest over a pan of warm water until the mixture trails off the whisk in thick ribbons. Pour the chocolate mix into the egg and stir well. Stir in the orange juice, brandy, if using, and the crushed digestive biscuits. Now just pour into the cake tin and leave to cool and chill overnight. Once set and cold just turn out, cut and serve.

Note

The sugar, egg and orange zest can be whisked by machine without using the pan of hot water. This is obviously a safer method for children.

Whole Orange and Almond Cake

I like to visit local schools, fêtes and jumble sales. The reason for going is to find the cakes that are always on offer. This recipe reminds me of those sorts of cakes: often quite simple but absolutely packed with flavour. This one is certainly both. It's made with whole oranges which give it a good, sharp taste and make it very moist to eat, either as a cake or as a pudding served with Marmalade Cheesecake Cream (see page 205). The quantities are quite large, but using three oranges gives a stronger finished taste. You could ask: why not just cut the recipe down to a third using just one orange? Well, I promise you the flavour is not as full and good. Also, this cake freezes so well for up to a month, so it will save you having to make one the next time you fancy a slice!

MAKES 3 × 900 g (2 lb) CAKES

3 whole oranges
350 g (12 oz) ground almonds
350 g (12 oz) caster sugar

$\frac{1}{2}$ teaspoon baking powder
9 size 3 eggs

Pre-heat the oven to 180°C/350°F/gas 4. Grease 3 × 900 g (2 lb) loaf tins. To cook the oranges, cover with cold water and bring to a simmer. Simmer the oranges for 1 hour until completely cooked. Remove from the water and cut into quarters. Drain well. Remove pips, then blitz all the orange (including pith and zest) to a purée in a food processor. Leave to cool.

To make the sponge, mix together the almonds, sugar and baking powder. Whisk the eggs until the mixture trails off the whisk in thick ribbons. Fold in the almond and sugar mixture, then add the orange purée. Pour the cake mix into the prepared tins, only filling about two-thirds full and using about 1.2 litres (2 pints) in each tin. Bake for about 40–45 minutes. The cake should be firm to the touch and, if pierced with a knife, should leave the knife clean. The cake is now cooked and can be left to cool before turning out. If the cake has sunk in the centre once cooled, this will have no effect on the finished result – the cake will still be lovely to eat. The cake will keep for several days in an airtight tin.

Variations

The recipe will also work well using 4 lemons instead of the 3 oranges, or perhaps using a combination of lemons and limes.

Whole Orange and Almond Cake.

Rich Stout Cake

This is a chocolate cake with a difference. It's a basic chocolate cake recipe with the addition of rich stout which makes a very deep, rich cake, not only with the flavour of stout but also the colour to go with it. Guinness works very well in this recipe. The combination of the soft brown sugar and stout gives you fuller texture and taste. Also 100–225 g (4–8 oz) of plain chocolate can be grated into the mix to give an even stronger taste. It's very good to eat as a cake, or for real chocoholics, you could warm a slice in the microwave and serve it with a Rich Chocolate Sauce (see p.248).

MAKES 1 × 20–25 cm (8–10 in) cake

225 g (8 oz) unsalted butter	$\frac{1}{2}$ teaspoon baking powder
350 g (12 oz) soft brown sugar	2 teaspoons bicarbonate of soda
4 eggs, beaten	400 ml (14 fl oz) stout (Guinness)
225 g (8 oz) plain flour	100 g (4 oz) cocoa

Pre-heat the oven to 180°C/350°F/gas 4. Butter a 20-25 cm (8–10 in) deep cake tin.

Cream together the butter with the soft brown sugar. Gradually add the beaten eggs. Sift together the flour, baking powder and bicarbonate of soda. Mix the stout with the cocoa powder. Now add the flour and stout mixes alternately to the butter and eggs until completely and evenly bound. You will find the consistency to be quite soft.

Spoon into the prepared tin and bake in the oven for 1–1$\frac{1}{4}$ hours until set. You may need to cover with a piece of brown paper after an hour to prevent it browning too much. Allow to cool before removing from the tin. The stout cake is now ready – cheers!

Variations

Pouring a glass of stout always leaves you with a lovely finish on the top. You can do exactly the same with this cake. Melt 100–175 g (4–6 oz) of grated white chocolate with 100–175 g (4–6 oz) of butter and 1–2 measures of Irish whiskey until just softened, then leave to cool. You now have a rich white chocolate icing to spread on top of the cake.

To make a glass of Stout Cake Pudding, simply blitz some of the cake to a crumb stage and spoon into 300 ml ($\frac{1}{2}$-pint) glasses, leaving 1–2 cm ($\frac{1}{2}$–$\frac{3}{4}$ in) clear at the top. Soak the sponge crumbs in a flavoured syrup or perhaps add freshly grated chocolate or even fruits or raisins. Finish the dish with Irish Whiskey Sabayon (p.245) and pour on top. This, as you can imagine, looks just like a real half pint of thick creamy stout and tastes just as good!

Baked Orange Tart

This really is a simple pudding to make that certainly isn't short of taste! The flavour of the oranges, the bitter-rich taste of the zest, together with the sweetness of the juice working together give a lovely aroma as well as flavour. Of course the total flavour of this dish can be changed by simply replacing the oranges with lemons or perhaps lemon and lime. For the cake crumbs, simply use a basic Vanilla Sponge (Genoise) (see p.195) or Victoria Sponge (see p.194), or use a bought cake.

MAKES 1 × 20 cm (8 in) TART

2 oranges
50 g (2 oz) caster sugar
50 g (2 oz) cake crumbs
25 g (1 oz) unsalted butter, diced
150 ml (5 fl oz) milk

2 eggs
1 × 20 cm (8 in) flan ring lined with
    175 g (6 oz) Shortcrust Pastry or
    Sweet Shortcrust Pastry (see p.251)

Pre-heat the oven to 180°C/350°F/gas 4.

Finely grate the orange zest and mix the zest with the sugar until a yellow/orange colour is achieved. Add the cake crumbs and the butter. Warm the milk and pour over the crumb mix. Stir until the butter has melted.

Squeeze the juice from the oranges; you'll need 150 ml (5 fl oz). Separate the eggs, adding the yolks and orange juice to the mix. Whisk the egg whites to a soft peak, then gently fold into the mix. This can now be carefully spooned into the pastry case and baked in the oven for 30–35 minutes until set and light golden brown. Allow to relax for 20 minutes before serving warm, or leave until cold. To capture the rich orange flavour I like to eat it just warm, almost at room temperature, and of course with a spoonful of fresh cream.

American Cheesecake

While making Rhodes Around Christmas *in 1995 in New York, we visited a restaurant, baker, coffee shop – it really was all of these and more rolled into one – in Brooklyn. It's called Junior's. Junior's has been there for many years and has a great reputation for most of its food; everything is made fresh on the premises. But one dish is voted every year the best in New York. Yes you've guessed it, it's American cheesecake.*

I helped in the kitchen for a day and just couldn't believe how many they make daily and send all over the USA – literally thousands! It took me some time to squeeze this recipe from them, so please give it a try! At Junior's they serve it either natural or topped with strawberries, nuts and jam, the choice is yours. I have included a recipe for Home-made Cherry Jam (see p.249) which is not over-sweet and is lovely served with the cheesecake.

The sponge base used is a basic Vanilla Sponge (Genoise); if you don't use all the sponge, any remaining slices can be frozen and kept for next time. Failing that, simply buy a vanilla sponge base and cut it to fit the base.

SERVES 6–8

25 cm (10 in) Vanilla Sponge (Genoise) (see p.195) or ready-made vanilla sponge base
225 g (8 oz) caster sugar
3 tablespoons cornflour

675 g (1½ lb) full-fat soft cream cheese
2 eggs
1 teaspoon vanilla essence
300 ml (10 fl oz) whipping cream

Pre-heat the oven to 180°C/350°F/gas 4. Butter a 25 cm (10 in) loose-bottomed cake tin.

Cut the sponge horizontally into 1 cm (½ in) thick slices. Line the prepared cake tin with one slice of the sponge (the remaining slices can be frozen).

Mix together the sugar and cornflour, then beat in the cream cheese, making sure it's mixed to a creamy texture. Beat in the eggs and vanilla essence. Slowly pour on the cream, beating constantly to give a thick, creamy consistency. Pour the mix over the sponge base in the cake tin. Sit the tin in a baking tray filled with 2–3 mm (⅛ in) of warm water to help create steam during cooking. Place into the pre-heated oven and bake for 45–50 minutes until the top is golden. Remove from the oven and leave to cool completely and set before removing from the tin. If you find that after 50 minutes the cheesecake has not become golden, don't worry. Simply remove it from the oven and cool. It can be browned later under the grill or with a gas gun. Even without browning, it eats just as well.

Straight from the oven, creamy American Cheesecake.

Carrot Cake

Carrot cake is a rich, moist cake that is packed with flavours. I like just to eat it as it is, but many bought carrot cakes are finished with a lemon or orange butter cream. So with this recipe I'm going to give you a recipe for a flavoured butter cream to top the cake with, giving you a choice.

MAKES 2 × 900 g (2 lb) loaf cakes

300 ml (10 fl oz) sunflower oil	2 teaspoons crushed cloves
225 g (8 oz) soft brown sugar	1 teaspoon ground ginger
4 eggs	1 teaspoon bicarbonate of soda
175 g (6 oz) golden syrup	225 g (8 oz) carrots, grated
350 g (12 oz) self-raising flour	50 g (2 oz) desiccated coconut
2 teaspoons ground cinnamon	1 tablespoon chopped walnuts (optional)

For the Butter Cream

Finely grated zest and juice of 1 lemon or orange	100 g (4 oz) unsalted butter
	100 g (4 oz) icing sugar, sifted

Pre-heat the oven to 180°C/350°F/gas 4. Butter 2 × 900 g (2 lb) loaf tins.

Process or whisk together the oil, sugar, eggs and golden syrup. Beat in the flour, spices and bicarbonate of soda. Add the carrots, coconut and the chopped walnuts, if using. Pour the mix into the prepared tins and bake in the pre-heated oven for 40 minutes. To test, stick a skewer into the middle of a cake at an angle. If it comes out clean, the cake is cooked. If not, return it to the oven for another 5 minutes, then test again. Once cooked, leave to rest for 10 minutes before turning out of the tins. The cake is now ready to eat.

To make the butter cream, place the orange or lemon zest and juice in a pan and bring to the boil. Boil until reduced by three-quarters. This process will only take 1–2 minutes. Leave to cool.

Beat the butter until pale and creamy. Add the icing sugar and the orange or lemon reduction. Beat the mix well to spread the citrus flavour. Once the carrot cakes are cold this can be spread on top. You will have about 225 g (8 oz) of butter cream.

Cheesecake Cream or Marmalade Cheesecake Cream

You can make this as a straightforward cream or include the marmalade. The quantity of marmalade you use is really up to you, but I find this quantity makes the cream really tasty. It will keep in the fridge for up to three days. The beauty of this dish is that you can simply sit this mix on to a classic biscuit base for a good alternative cheesecake.

MAKES about 450 ml (15 fl oz)

100 g (4 oz) full-fat soft cream cheese
15 g (½ oz) caster sugar
100 g (4 oz) marmalade (optional)

150 ml (5 fl oz) double cream, lightly whipped

Beat together the cream cheese and sugar until the sugar has dissolved and creamed. Mix in the marmalade, if using. Once the marmalade has been completely mixed in, lightly fold in the whipped cream. Spoon the mix into a bowl and chill until set. Once set, the cream can be served as a separate dish from the bowl or spoon on to plates by curling with a warm tablespoon.

Caramel Cream Pots

These pots are almost like a caramel crème brûlée without the sugar topping. Having the caramel mixed into the brûlée mix gives you a bitter-sweet taste all the way through. I like to serve this with home-made biscuits: the Maple Syrup and Walnut Biscuits (see p.242) work well, giving a good nutty flavour and texture.

SERVES 8–10

For the Caramel

150 ml (5 fl oz) water   225 g (8 oz) caster sugar

For the Cream

450 ml (15 fl oz) milk   10 egg yolks
900 ml (1½ pints) double cream

Pre-heat the oven to 160°C/325°F/gas 3.

To make the caramel, bring the water and sugar to the boil gently, using a pastry brush dipped in cold water to brush away any crystallization around the sides of the pan. Heat gently until the sugar has dissolved completely, then boil fast for 10–15 minutes until a good, dark golden colour has been reached. Remove from the heat.

Bring the milk and cream to the boil, then whisk into the hot caramel. Lightly whisk the egg yolks and pour the caramel mix on top. Strain the mix through a sieve. Pour the mix into 150 ml (5 fl oz) ramekin moulds (size 1) and stand the moulds in a roasting tin half-filled with warm water. Cook in the pre-heated oven for approximately 45–50 minutes until just setting. Remove from the bath and leave to cool.

These can be served at room temperature, or chilled and served as a cold cream.

Sponge Base without Flour

Here's also another recipe for a sponge base without any flour. Instead it's got chocolate!

MAKES 1 × 28 × 20 cm (11 × 8 in) swiss roll or 1 × 20 cm (8 in) cake

100 g (4 oz) good quality plain chocolate
2 tablespoons coffee granules mixed
   with 1 tablespoon water

3 eggs, separated
75 g (3 oz) caster sugar
A pinch of salt

Pre-heat the oven to 180°C/350°F/gas 4.

Melt the chocolate with the coffee and then leave to cool. Beat the egg yolks, then add the sugar and beat until the mixture is pale and trails off the whisk in ribbons. Stir in the chocolate mix. Beat the egg whites and salt until they hold stiff peaks. Carefully fold the beaten whites into the rest of the mix and spread on the Swiss roll mould or cake tin. This can now be cooked in the pre-heated oven for 15–20 minutes.

Note

This sponge can be used as the base for the Chocolate Truffle Cake (page 196) or with the White and Dark Chocolate Cream/Mousse overleaf.

White and Dark Chocolate Cream/Mousse

I wasn't quite sure what title to give this recipe. It's really a recipe from many years ago that was called Chocolate Marquise. It is a good chocolate recipe to try as it simply can't go wrong. Another plus is how well it works with plain, milk or white chocolate. It can also be used for so many different puddings, from a basic marquise terrine to cold mousse soufflés or a good mixed chocolate slice. The choice is yours.

SERVES 8–10

For the Chocolate Swiss Roll Sponge

100 g (4 oz) caster sugar	25 g (1 oz) cocoa
2 eggs, separated	25 g (1 oz) plain flour

For the Chocolate Cream/Mousse

1 × 11 g sachet of gelatine	50 ml (2 fl oz) water
600 ml (1 pint) double cream	2 tablespoons liquid glucose
275 g (10 oz) chocolate (plain,	2 egg yolks (optional)
milk or white)	

Pre-heat the oven to 160°C/325°F/gas 3. Grease and lightly flour a 28 × 20 cm (11 × 8 in) Swiss roll tin for the sponge. If you are making a chocolate terrine, line a Le Creuset 25 cm (10 in) terrine mould or a 23 cm (9 in) loose-bottomed cake tin with greaseproof paper.

To make the sponge, whisk half of the caster sugar with the egg yolks until thick and pale. Whisk the egg whites to a soft peak, add the remaining caster sugar and whisk to a stiff meringue. Sift the cocoa and flour on to the egg yolk mix and fold in. Add a third of the meringue and whisk in. Carefully fold in the remaining meringue. Pour and spread the mix into the prepared tin about 1–2 cm ($\frac{1}{2}$–$\frac{3}{4}$ in) deep and bake for 20–25 minutes. Leave to cool.

To make the mousse, first soak the gelatine in cold water. Whip the cream to a soft peak. Break or grate the chocolate into small pieces. Bring the water and glucose to the boil and add the gelatine and chocolate. Remove from the heat and beat until the chocolate has become smooth. When cool, add the egg yolks, if using. The yolks simply enrich the flavour and give a silky texture. Fold in the whipped cream and the mix is ready to pour into the prepared mould. A slice of the sponge can be placed on top, cutting it to make it fit, so when you turn out the terrine the mousse is sitting on a sponge base.

Variations

The mousse mix could also be split in half using plain chocolate and white chocolate. If so, it's best to make them separately. Make the plain first so this can be setting in the fridge while you make and then pour in the white on top. This is also then topped with the sponge to finish.

The mix could even be split into three, starting with plain, then milk and finishing with white for a chocolate Neapolitan terrine.

I also like to use 15 cm (6 in) round or square flan cases or rings about 5–7.5 cm (2–3 in) deep. The sponge base can then be placed in the base and the mix poured on top. When making this variety, I normally make a dark and white mousse. A slice of this dusted with cocoa or chocolate shavings eats very well.

Also, a sort of Black Forest dessert can be made this way. For this, I make a full recipe using only dark plain chocolate. Using a round flan or cake tin, line with sponge and sprinkle with kirsch syrup. This is made by boiling 75 ml (3 fl oz) of water with 50 g (2 oz) of caster sugar and 1–3 measures of kirsch or rum (to taste!). Now the sponge can be spread with a home-made (see p.249) or bought cherry jam. The next stage is to cover the base with cherries. Griottine (steeped in alcohol) or tinned cherries can both be used. Fresh cherries also eat very well with this recipe. Take 225 g (8 oz) of fresh, stoned cherries, melt a knob of butter in a pan and, once sizzling, add the cherries with 25 g (1 oz) of caster or demerara sugar. These should now be cooked for a few minutes until tender. If you're going to use fresh cherries then a separate syrup will not be needed. Simply add a measure or two of kirsch or rum to the cherries at the last moment; this will create an instant syrup. These can now be spooned on to the sponge while still warm and then left to cool before topping with the dark chocolate mousse. This can now be simply finished with a dusting of cocoa or shavings of fresh chocolate.

This Black Forest variety can also be made into individual soufflés. Simply stick a strip of silicone or greaseproof paper around a ramekin dish, making sure it's at least 4 cm (1 $\frac{1}{2}$ in) above the mould. Follow the method above, cutting 4–6 discs of chocolate sponge and placing them in the ramekins, then finishing them in the same fashion with syrup, jam, cherries and mousse. Cold Black Forest soufflé is made.

There are plenty of alternatives already, but that's not all – there are many more. Why not add chopped hazelnuts and raisins for a fruit and nut terrine? Or perhaps use blackcurrants instead of cherries or maybe all summer fruits set in a soufflé. Oranges also go very well on marmalade-spread sponge with a sprinkle of Cointreau or Grand Marnier.

With all these combinations – and I'm sure you'll think of more – it almost creates a headache! But remember, this also eats so well on its own, without the sponge: just set in a terrine mould or bowl and spoon or slice on to a plate and enjoy.

Apple and Raisin and Honey and Rhubarb Brûlées

Crème brûlée is one of those puddings that we all enjoy but don't make often enough (if ever!) at home. It's basically just a fresh custard mix in ramekins, cooked in a water bath in the oven. The beauty of making these and serving them is that you really don't need to worry about presentation; they always speak for themselves.

SERVES 8

For the Apple and Raisin Brûlée

50 g (2 oz) raisins
8 egg yolks
50 g (2 oz) caster sugar

600 ml (1 pint) double cream
1 vanilla pod or a few drops of
vanilla essence

For the Stock Syrup

75 g (3 oz) caster sugar
150 ml (5 fl oz) water

1 measure Calvados or brandy
(optional)

To Garnish

2 Golden Delicious or
Granny Smiths apples

Icing sugar

For the Honey and Rhubarb Brûlée

50 g (2 oz) clear honey
225 g (8 oz) rhubarb
25 g (1 oz) caster or demerara sugar

Icing sugar (optional)
A knob of butter

The apple and raisin recipe needs to be started with a few hours' notice, giving the raisins time to soften. You will need 8 × 150 ml (5 fl oz) ramekins.

Pre-heat the oven to 180°C/350°F/gas 4.

Make the stock syrup by simply adding the sugar to the measured water and bringing it to the boil. This is now going to be used both for the raisins and apples. Take 2–3 tablespoons of the syrup and add the Calvados or brandy, if using. Add the raisins to the syrup, bring them to a simmer, then leave to stand for 2 hours. This will soften them giving a more tender texture.

Now make the crème brûlée mix. Mix together the egg yolks and sugar. Bring the cream to the boil with the vanilla pod or essence. Once boiled, remove the vanilla pod, if using, and split and scrape the insides into the cream. Now whisk the cream into the egg yolks and sugar.

Place the raisins in the ramekins. You now have two methods of finishing. The mix can be simply divided into the ramekins and placed in a roasting tin filled with hot water to come three-quarters up the sides of the moulds and cooked in the pre-heated oven for about 30 minutes until almost set.

Another method, which can give the brûlées a slightly lighter and creamier finish, is to sit the bowl with the mix over a pan of hot water and stir until the custard begins to thicken. This can now be finished as above, cooking for only about 15–20 minutes.

To test, remove one of the moulds from the water after 20 minutes and shake gently. There should still be slight movement in the centre of the custard. If it is still runny, put it back in the oven and check after another 5 minutes. Once ready, remove from the oven and water bath and allow to cool to room temperature. This is the temperature and consistency that I believe is the best to eat them at. Brûlées can be chilled, which will obviously give you a firmer texture.

While the brûlées are cooking and cooling, the apples can be prepared. It will take a quarter of an apple per portion. These should be peeled, quartered and then the core removed from each piece. Now slice the quarters thinly lengthways. Bring the remaining stock syrup to the boil and add the slices. As soon as it returns to the boil, remove the pan from the heat and allow to cool. The slices can now be taken from the stock and lightly dried before overlapping and covering the brûlées.

Pre-heat the grill.

Now it's time for the crispy sugar topping. Dust the apples heavily with icing sugar. The moulds can now be placed under a grill until the sugar begins to caramelize. To give a fine but crisp finish, the same process will need to be repeated at least once or twice more. For a more controlled glaze, a gas gun can be used. The brûlée is now ready and eats so well, cutting through the crispy apples, through the thick vanilla custard and then finding the rich raisins.

For the honey and rhubarb version, there's very little change to the basic recipe. Simply replace the caster sugar with 50 g (2 oz) of honey. The mix can now be cooked in ramekins as for the basic recipe. All you need now is the rhubarb topping.

Peel the rhubarb and cut into 1 cm ($\frac{1}{2}$ in) pieces. Melt the butter and, once bubbling, add the diced rhubarb with the caster or demerara sugar. The rhubarb, once slightly simmering, will only take 1–2 minutes before becoming tender. Turn the fruit carefully for even cooking and to avoid breaking it up.

Once cooked, the rhubarb can be placed immediately on top of the brûlée with some of its own syrup and served. Or allow to cool, then spoon on top, heavily dust with icing sugar and finish under the grill or with a gas gun, as for the apple recipe.

Soufflés

I think we are all a little afraid of serving a soufflé or, for that matter, even having a go at one at home. But they are not so difficult; there are a few golden rules we must all stick to for success: clean whisks and bowls, the soufflé dishes well buttered and sugared, and the oven temperatures right.

The classic sweet soufflé is made from a pastry cream, which is what I'm going to give you here, but I also have a quick and simple alternative. It doesn't have quite the same depth and texture but still eats very well and can be turned into a soufflé so quickly.

First we'll start with the traditional recipe. This one is going to be for a lemon soufflé. There are so many other flavours that can be made using the same recipe. So this is not a recipe just for lemon.

SERVES 4–6

For the Pastry Cream Base

300 ml (10 fl oz) milk	2 egg yolks
1 vanilla pod or a few drops of vanilla essence (optional)	Finely grated zest of 1–2 lemons, limes or oranges (optional)
50 g (2 oz) caster sugar	Icing sugar for dusting
40 g (1 ½ oz) plain flour	

For the Soufflés

8 tablespoons Pastry Cream (see above)	25 g (1 oz) caster sugar
Juice of 2 lemons	Butter and caster sugar for lining the moulds
2 egg yolks (optional)	
8 egg whites	

To make the pastry cream, bring the milk to the boil with the vanilla pod or essence, if using. Mix the caster sugar, flour and egg yolks together to a paste. If you are making this base for lemon, lime or orange soufflés, then add the finely grated zest of 1 or 2 fruits to the mix to increase the basic flavour. Remove the vanilla pod from the milk and pour the milk on to the flour mix, whisking as you pour. This mix must now be brought back to boiling point and cooked for 1–2 minutes, stirring. Transfer to a bowl and cover with clingfilm to prevent any skin forming. Cool at room temperature. You will have 400 g (14 oz).

Pre-heat the oven to 220°C/425°F/gas 7. You will need 4 size 2 soufflé dishes or 6 size 1 ramekins. The dishes should first be well buttered and then caster sugar should be added and rolled around the dish until it is well and completely coated.

Mix the 8 tablespoons of pastry cream with the lemon juice and the extra egg yolks, if using. These are optional but will give you an extra rich base. Whisk the egg whites to soft peaks and then add the caster sugar. Continue to whisk until slightly thicker. Add a quarter of the egg whites to the soufflé mix and whisk in until completely bound. The remaining whisked whites must now be very carefully folded in. Divide the soufflé mix between the soufflé dishes, smoothing the top with a palette knife. It is best now carefully to release the mix from the edge of the soufflé dish with the point of a knife. Place the soufflés on the bottom shelf of the oven for 12–15 minutes, to prevent the tops from becoming over coloured. Once well risen and cooked, remove from the oven and dust with icing sugar before serving.

These can now be served as they are or with a sauce. To make a lemon sauce simply follow the recipe suggestion from the Anglaise (Fresh Custard) Sauce (see p.246). Another alternative, or even both, is to serve the hot soufflé with iced lemon sorbet.

So there's the recipe for a completely home-made soufflé. Now for the quick and easy option. It will make the same quantity as before.

Quick Lemon Soufflé

200 ml (7 fl oz) tinned custard sauce	6 egg whites
Juice of 2 lemons	50 g (2 oz) caster sugar
2 egg yolks (optional)	

Simply follow the previous method of putting this together (see opposite), using 8 tablespoons of the tinned custard sauce. The advantage is not having to make the pastry cream. Release the mix from the edge of the soufflé dishes with the point of a knife. Cook the soufflés on the bottom shelf of the oven at the same temperature. I find that these take no more than 12–13 minutes to cook.

Loosen the remaining custard, with some milk or single cream to a better sauce consistency and flavour with lemon juice. You may also like to sweeten it with caster sugar.

Variations

Probably one of the most classic of all is Grand Marnier Soufflé. This recipe will work replacing the lemon juice with strongly reduced orange juice mixed with Grand Marnier and perhaps some finely grated orange zest. You can serve the soufflé with a rich Grand Marnier Sauce. Make this by first boiling 100 g (4 oz) sugar in 150 ml (5 fl oz) water to give a stock syrup. Roughly chop a whole orange (including pith and peel) and place in a pan with 150 ml (5 fl oz) orange juice, the stock syrup and 2–3 measures Grand Marnier. Simmer for 30 minutes until completely tender. Blitz in a liquidizer and push through a fine sieve. The sauce should have a coating consistency. If it is a little too thin, thicken with 1–2 teaspoons of arrowroot.

Fruit Sorbets

This fruit sorbet recipe appeared in More Rhodes Around Britain. *The basic recipe hasn't really changed, well not for most fruits. However, the reason that I am including it in this book is that I have found that when making pear or apple sorbets the fruit really does need to be doubled. The original recipe is for 225 g (8 oz) of fruit, so for apples or pears 450 g (1 lb) will be needed. The flavour and texture is immensely good.*

MAKES ABOUT 300 ml (10 fl oz) FRUIT SORBET OR
450 ml (15 fl oz) APPLE OR PEAR SORBET

225 g (8 oz) fruit or 450 g (1 lb) apples or pears, peeled and chopped

150 ml (5 fl oz) Stock Syrup (see p.218)
Juice of ½ lemon

For most fruits, simply mix the fruits with the syrup and lemon juice and blitz in a food processor or liquidizer, then push through a sieve.

For apples and pears, bring the fruits to a simmer with the syrup and lemon juice. Simmer for a few minutes until the fruit turns soft. The mix can now be blitzed in a food processor or liquidizer, then pushed through a sieve.

Whatever fruit you use, you can now churn the mix in an ice-cream machine for 20–30 minutes to a creamy sorbet consistency. If you don't have an ice-cream machine, then simply place the mix in the freezer, whisking every 10–15 minutes to break up the ice crystals as the mix freezes. The sorbet is now ready to use.

Ice-creams

I always use the same basic recipe for vanilla ice-cream, but the alternative flavours just keep coming! For most of these recipes the vanilla pod can be left out because the other flavours need to predominate.

If it is vanilla ice-cream you wish to make but you are finding it hard to get hold of fresh vanilla, then simply substitute a few drops of vanilla essence. The total basic recipe can also be replaced with tins of custard mixed with single cream, then add the flavour of your choice and churn in the machine. If you don't have an ice-cream machine, then put the mix into a bowl and freeze, turning with a whisk every 15 minutes until frozen.

If you are really stuck for time, then why not just buy a good quality vanilla ice-cream and add the flavour of your choice? It will still almost be home-made!

Fruit based ice-creams are best made with a Fruit Coulis (see p.183), then loosened with 150 ml (5 fl oz) of Stock Syrup (see p.218) and creamed with 3 heaped tablespoons of Crème Fraîche (see p.275). They're very quick and easy to make. All you have to do now is put them through the ice-cream machine.

*Clockwise from left: Mango (in the background),
Pear, Peach, and Cherry Sorbet.*

Vanilla Ice-cream

This is the base ice-cream, which you can vary in an infinite number of ways!

SERVES 4–8

300 ml (10 fl oz) double cream
300 ml (10 fl oz) milk
1 vanilla pod or a few drops of
    vanilla essence

6 egg yolks
175 g (6 oz) caster sugar

Mix together the cream and milk in a pan. Add the vanilla essence or split the vanilla pod, if using, lengthways and scrape the insides into the milk and cream, then add the scraped pod. Bring to the boil.

While this is heating, beat the egg yolks and sugar together until pale and light. This can be done in a food mixer. Pour on the milk and cream, stirring all the time until well blended. Stir from time to time until the ice-cream mix has cooled. Remove the vanilla pod.

Once cooled, churn the mix in the ice-cream maker. If you have made the full recipe, you'll need to churn it in two batches. Pour the mix into the machine and begin to turn. The ice-cream will take about 20–30 minutes and will have thickened and increased in volume. Don't leave the mix turning until completely frozen and set or it will be over-churned and slightly grainy in texture. Take out when thick and only just starting to freeze, then finish in the freezer. This will give you a lovely, silky-smooth texture.

If you don't have an ice-cream machine, simply turn the mixture into a freezer tray or bowl and freeze, turning regularly until set.

Liquorice Ripple Ice-cream

SERVES 4–8

Melt down 100 g (4 oz) of Pontrefract liquorice cakes in a small pan with 150 ml (5 fl oz) water, stirring occasionally until smooth. Leave to cool a little, then pour into one quantity of Vanilla Ice-cream (see above) at the last turn or two. This will give you white ice-cream with lines of black liquorice running through, perfect for serving with Black Treacle Pudding (p.167).

White Chocolate Ice-cream

The same quantity of plain or milk chocolate can be used with this recipe to make the flavour of your choice.

MAKES 1.25 litres ($2\frac{1}{4}$ pints)

1 quantity Vanilla Ice-cream (see opposite), made with 100 g (4 oz) caster sugar and without the vanilla pod

175–225 g (6–8 oz) white chocolate, grated

Follow the vanilla ice-cream recipe, using just 100 g (4 oz) of caster sugar instead of the 175 g (6 oz). Once the milk and cream are at boiling point, add 175 g (6 oz) of the grated chocolate. This should now be tasted for strength. If more is needed, then add the remaining 50 g (2 oz) and continue as for the vanilla recipe.

Variations

This recipe also works very well with 50 g (2 oz) of desiccated coconut added at the same time to give a rich white chocolate and coconut ice-cream. To make it even richer, serve it with the Chocolate Sabayon (see p.244). With or without the coconut, this ice-cream also goes very well with the Chocolate Scotch Pancakes (see p.233).

Another great chocolate ice-cream – whether it be dark, milk or white – is with Turkish Delight added. The Turkish Delight recipe (see p.220) can be followed or simply buy some to dice and add to the mix at the end of the recipe.

This recipe can also be made into Chocolate Ripple Ice-cream by simply pouring in the Rich Chocolate Sauce (see p.248) at the last turn or two. This will give you white chocolate creamy ice-cream with lines of dark chocolate running through.

To make Chocolate and Marshmallow Ice-cream, make the chocolate ice-cream with milk, plain or white chocolate. Cut some marshmallows into small pieces. To keep it separate, spoon some cold ice-cream mix on to the marshmallow. Churn the chocolate ice-cream, adding the marshmallow pieces at the end, not allowing the pieces to break down but instead keeping their texture mixed into the ice-cream. Once frozen and set, the chocolate ice-cream has small white toffee-like marshmallow pieces to make it even more exciting.

And here's just one more variation: add a few tablespoons of the Cherry Jam (see p.249) to give a rich chocolate ice-cream with a cherry jam ripple.

Milk or Plain Chocolate Fruit and Nut Ice-cream

As it is one of my old favourite chocolate bars, it seemed a great idea to turn fruit and nut into an ice-cream. I've simply made a chocolate ice-cream using 175–225 g (6–8 oz) of plain or milk chocolate. The nuts are a mix of hazelnuts and almonds, both lightly toasted to improve and release more flavour.

SERVES 4–8

1 quantity Vanilla Ice-cream (see p.216), made with 100 g (4 oz) caster sugar and without the vanilla pod	Brandy (optional)
175–225 g (6–8 oz) milk or plain chocolate, grated	50 g (2 oz) hazelnuts, toasted and chopped
100 g (4 oz) raisins	50 g (2 oz) almonds, toasted and chopped

For the Stock Syrup (optional)

100 g (4 oz) caster sugar	Brandy or liqueur (optional)
150 ml (5 fl oz) water	

The raisins can be left as they are or soaked in just enough neat brandy to cover, or in a stock syrup made by boiling the sugar and water until thickened. The stock syrup can, of course, be flavoured to taste with brandy or another liqueur.

To make the ice-cream, follow the White Chocolate Ice-cream recipe (see p.217). Once the milk and cream have come to the boil, add the grated chocolate to melt. Now complete the recipe as for vanilla ice-cream. Towards the last 2–3 minutes, the raisins and nuts can be added. This obviously changes the texture and taste of the ice-cream. It will become even richer if topped with the Rich Chocolate Sauce (see p.248).

Tutti-frutti Ice-cream

This is a really fun ice-cream to make. I simply add a selection of glacé fruits, raisins, cherries and angelica to the vanilla ice-cream, keeping in the vanilla for extra flavour.

You can buy a mixed tub of glacé fruits, or buy them loose to choose your own. This really isn't over important, although I'm amazed at the variety of fruits that can be bought crystallized; strawberries, melon, plums, damsons, greengages are just a few examples.

SERVES 4–8

1 quantity Vanilla Ice-cream (see p.216)   175–225 g (6–8 oz) glacé fruits
including raisins and angelica

The fruits should first be cut into pieces. To maximize the taste, all the fruits can be added once the ice-cream mix is cold. They can then be churned with the mix, which will help flavour the complete custard.

Variation

This recipe also works very well mixed with Lemon Curd Ice-cream. Make some by mixing 1 × 350 g (12 oz) jar of lemon curd with 2 tablespoons of Crème Fraîche (see p.275) and 1 tablespoon of natural yoghurt. All you need to do now is add the fruits and churn into ice-cream. You will have about 400 ml (14 fl oz) of ice-cream.

Turkish Delight

Turkish Delight has become an annual treat for me. Every Christmas a box of it seems to come my way and, I have to admit, I eat the lot!

I have included a recipe for Turkish Delight Ice-cream (see opposite) which, you can imagine, eats very well especially with a Rich Chocolate Sauce (see p.248) or Chocolate Sabayon (see p.244). It's really taking the famous chocolate bar idea and turning it into a fun pudding. You can make the ice-cream with a bought Turkish Delight, but if you fancy having a go yourself, here's the recipe.

The quantity of gelatine leaves will give you a softer texture than a bought version; 25 g (1 oz) of powdered gelatine or 8–9 leaves will match that texture. I personally prefer the softer sweet but it's really up to you. The red food colouring is optional but a pale pink colour works well in the ice-cream recipe.

MAKES about 675 g (1½ lb)

675 g (1½ lb) caster sugar
300 ml (10 fl oz) water
50 g (2 oz) glucose syrup
About 2 tablespoons rose water

A few drops of red food colouring
(optional)
100 g (4 oz) cornflour
2 × 11 g sachets of powdered gelatine
25 g (1 oz) icing sugar

Line a 20 cm (8 in) square tin or mould at least 2.5 cm (1 in) deep with clingfilm.

Boil together the caster sugar, water and glucose syrup with the rose water and food colouring, if using. Once up to the boil, cook for 8–10 minutes. Add a drop of water to 75 g (3 oz) of the cornflour to loosen. Soften the gelatine in water according to the instructions on the packet.

Remove the boiling syrup from the stove and add the gelatine. Once dissolved, whisk in the cornflour, cook for 2–3 minutes, then pour into the prepared tin or mould to about 2.5 cm (1 in) deep. Allow to cool, then chill for 2–3 hours until completely set.

To finish, mix together the remaining cornflour with the icing sugar. Turn the mix out of the mould and with a warm wet knife, cut into cubes and roll through the icing sugar/cornflour to coat lightly. Now all you have to do is eat it!

Turkish Delight Ice-cream

This recipe is for a basic vanilla ice-cream, replacing the vanilla with rose water to create that familiar Turkish Delight flavour. Of course, you're still going to need some diced Turkish Delight to finish the recipe and give the right texture to the dish. You can either make it (follow my recipe opposite)or buy some, dice it and add it at the last moment.

SERVES 4–8

300 ml (10 fl oz) milk
300 ml (10 fl oz) double cream
1–2 tablespoons rose water
6 egg yolks

175 g (6 oz) caster sugar
175–225 g (6–8 oz) Turkish Delight
   (see opposite) or bought

Mix together the milk and cream and flavour with the rose water. It's best to add 1 tablespoon, then taste before adding more, to give you the full depth of flavour. Bring to the boil. While the cream mix is coming to the boil, beat together the egg yolks and sugar until pale. Pour the boiled cream on to the egg yolks and sugar, whisking until well blended. Leave to cool. Once cold, this can be churned in an ice-cream machine, or frozen in a freezer tray, whisking every 30 minutes or so until set.

Dice the Turkish Delight and add to the ice-cream at the last 2–3 turns. The Turkish Delight Ice-cream is now ready to freeze and eat.

Variations

This recipe works very well with Rich Chocolate Sauce (see p.248) added, also at the end and not completely mixed in. This will give you a Turkish Delight and Chocolate Ripple Ice-cream. Or simply serve with warm or cold sauce poured over.

ABOVE *Ovaltine Ice-cream (see p.224) – the best mug of Ovaltine you'll ever have!*

LEFT *Turkish Delight (see p.220) and Rich Chocolate Sauce (see p.248)*

Ovaltine Ice-cream

This is a very rich ice-cream that doesn't really need anything to go with it – perhaps a shortbread or Maple and Walnut Biscuit (p.242) will be enough. I've also added some milk chocolate to enrich it even more, giving a fuller consistency to the finished dish. You will notice there is no sugar in this recipe. This is due to the sweetness of the Ovaltine and milk chocolate.

MAKES 900 ml (1½ pints)

300 ml (10 fl oz) milk
300 ml (10 fl oz) double cream
100 g (4 oz) Ovaltine powder
175 g (6 oz) milk chocolate, grated

6 egg yolks
2–3 measures Irish whiskey, 50–120 ml
   (2–4 fl oz) (optional)

Bring the milk and cream to the boil and whisk on to the Ovaltine. Add the milk chocolate and stir until melted. This mix can now be whisked on to the egg yolks and allowed to cool before finishing in the ice-cream machine. The Irish whiskey can be added before churning to give a richer flavour to the ice-cream.

I like to serve this ice-cream in a large mug with biscuits on the side, just as you would the drink.

Lemon Curd and Prune Ripple Ice-cream

I like to serve this with my Steamed Lemon Sponge with Prunes (see p.176). I have included my lemon curd recipe from More Rhodes Around Britain *here, or you can use a basic jar of curd.*

This recipe for lemon curd is very rich with a high butter content. If you prefer, you can cut the butter down to 50 g (2 oz) and also cut down by 1 egg yolk. The lemon curd will still work without being over-rich and will have a slightly more fluid consistency. There are two alternative methods.

SERVES 4–8

For the Lemon Curd

100 g (4 oz) caster sugar
100 g (4 oz) unsalted butter

Fintely grated zest and juice of
  1–2 lemons
3 egg yolks

For the Prune Ripple Ice-cream

4 tablespoons Crème Fraîche (see p.275)
2 tablespoons plain yoghurt
75 ml (3 fl oz) water

40 g (1½) oz caster sugar
75 g (3 oz) ready-to-eat prunes, stoned
  and chopped

For the first method for lemon curd, sit the sugar, butter, lemon juice and zest in a bowl and stir over a pan of simmering water. Once the butter has melted, beat vigorously until well combined. Beat in the egg yolks and continue to cook and stir for 15–20 minutes until the curd has thickened. Pour into a clean jar and cover with waxed paper or clingfilm. Once cooled, seal tightly and keep in the fridge. This should keep for at least two weeks.

For method 2, whisk the sugar and egg yolks together until light and creamy. Melt the butter with the lemon zest and juice and add to the mix. Cook, stirring, in a bowl over a pan of simmering water until thickened; this will also take about 15–20 minutes.

Mix the lemon curd with the crème fraîche and yoghurt. This can now be placed in the ice-cream machine and churned, or frozen in a freezer tray, whisking regularly until it begins to set.

Boil the water with the caster sugar and add the chopped prunes. Simmer for 1–2 minutes, then blitz to a purée. Leave to cool and chill.

When the ice-cream is ready, slowly add the prune purée. This will only need a few turns to leave the purée running through. Return to the freezer to set.

ABOVE *Iced Neopolitan Parfait (see p.228)*
RIGHT *George gives the seal of approval while Samuel and Gavin tuck in.*

Iced Neapolitan Parfait

Neapolitan Ice-cream was always a favourite of mine. Knowing that you had chocolate, strawberry and vanilla ice-creams all in one slice, it had to be a favourite! The recipes for all those flavoured ice-creams are featured in More Rhodes Around Britain, *so the classic ice-cream terrine can easily be made by following those. This recipe is going to give you a much lighter finish.*

Sweet parfaits are using more or less the same ingredients as ice-creams – egg yolks, cream and flavouring – but instead of heating the cream or milk and adding it to the egg yolk mix, the eggs and sugar are whipped to a light sabayon before adding those flavourings (chocolate, strawberry, etc.) and then folding in the whipped cream.

This dish may also look hard work with three separate recipes, but each layer has to begin freezing before topping with the next layer, so really there's no choice, each has to be made individually. I like to make Neapolitan with the strawberry on top followed by the vanilla and then the chocolate, so if you are making this in a terrine mould or loaf tin the strawberry will have to be made first. So when you turn out the parfait, that's sitting on the top.

SERVES 8–10

For the Strawberry Parfait

100 g (4 oz) strawberries, chopped	2 egg yolks
2 tablespoons strawberry jam	25 g (1 oz) caster sugar
2 tablespoons water	150 ml (5 fl oz) double cream

For the Vanilla Parfait Mix

50 g (2 oz) caster sugar	1 vanilla pod or 2–3 drops of
2 egg yolks	vanilla essence
	150 ml (5 fl oz) double cream

For the Chocolate Parfait Mix

50 g (2 oz) plain chocolate	25 g (1 oz) caster sugar
2 egg yolks	150 ml (5 fl oz) double cream

Line a 1.2 litre (2 pint) terrine mould or loaf tin with clingfilm or greaseproof paper.

To make a strawberry coulis, mix the strawberry jam with the water and strawberries. Warm to break down the strawberries, then purée. Alternatively, you can simply purée 225 g (8 oz) of fresh, frozen or tinned strawberries with 2 teaspoons of icing sugar.

Whisk the egg yolks and sugar in a bowl over a pan of hot water until doubled in volume, then remove from the heat and whisk in the cold strawberry purée. This will immediately reduce the temperature. The cream can now be either whipped and folded in or added and re-whisked until the mix trails off the whisk in ribbons. The strawberry parfait mix can now be spooned into the terrine and set to freeze for at least 1 hour.

To make the vanilla parfait, cut and scrape the vanilla pod and mix with the sugar and egg yolks, or add the essence to the sugar and egg yolks. Whisk in a bowl over a pan of hot water until doubled in volume, continue to whisk until cool, then whisk in the cream as for the strawberry recipe. Spoon into the terrine on top of the strawberry parfait and return to the freezer for at least a further 1 hour.

To make the chocolate parfait, whisk together the caster sugar and egg yolks in a bowl over a pan of warm water until at least doubled in volume. While whisking, the chocolate can be carefully melted in a separate bowl over a pan of hot water.

Once the sabayon is made, remove the pan from the warm water and whisk in the chocolate. This can now be either continually whisked by hand or machine, adding the double cream. This will cool the sabayon. Simply continue to whisk until the cream begins to thicken. Once the mix has reached a lightly whipped cream stage, it's ready to set and freeze in the terrine. Any excess mix can be frozen in ramekins, glasses or moulds.

Another method to finish the sabayon mix is to simply whip the cream separately, then fold in to the cooled sabayon. Pour into the terrine. To complete a total freezing of the parfait it's best left for a minimum 2–3 hours before serving.

Once set and frozen, the terrine can be turned out on to a small board (this may need to be lightly warmed under hot water) and the clingfilm or greaseproof removed. The presentation of the dish speaks for itself, a good slice showing the three very distinctive flavours doesn't need any help at all.

Variations

This parfait mix can be even lighter. Simply whisk the egg whites from the egg yolks in each recipe to a peak stage and fold into the mix after the cream has been added. The finished flavour will not be quite as rich, but the texture will be lighter.

For an instant strawberry coulis, simply purée 100–225 g (4–8 oz) of fresh, frozen or tinned strawberries with 2 teaspoons of icing sugar. Of course, to save all of that some shops and supermarkets sell good quality frozen purées that work very well. A few drops of strawberry liqueur also helps. Of course, raspberries can also be used.

Mincemeat Doughnuts

These have to be the easiest doughnuts you can possibly imagine. Whenever I've asked anybody whether they fancy making some home-made doughnuts, the reaction usually is, 'no thanks, I haven't got the yeast to make the dough'. Well, with this recipe you don't need yeast, but what you will have is the finished texture and taste. The important thing to remember is the thick white sliced bread must be fresh to give a light spongy texture.

You can eat the doughnuts as they are, or leave them without the sugar and serve them as a pudding with ice-cream, clotted cream or maybe an Anglaise (Fresh Custard) Sauce flavoured with rum (see p.246). They make a great alternative to traditional Christmas pudding. When you come to using these as a dinner party pudding, it's great fun to tell your guests they're having a deep-fried sandwich for pudding! They'll love it – have a go.

Serves 4

8 thick slices of white bread	100 g (4 oz) self-raising flour
50 g (2 oz) unsalted butter	25 g (1 oz) caster sugar
100 g (4 oz) mincemeat	150 ml (5 fl oz) strong dry cider
Oil for deep-frying	Caster sugar or icing sugar, sifted

Butter the slices of bread and place 4 slices butter-side up on the work surface. Divide the mincemeat between the slices of bread, placing a spoonful into the centre of each slice. Top with the remaining slices, pushing the bread gently around the dome of mincemeat. Using a 7.5 cm (3 in) round cutter, cut sandwiches from the bread, giving domed discs.

Heat a deep pan of oil to 180°C/350°F.

To make the batter, mix the flour and sugar, then add the cider, whisking and adding until a thick batter is achieved. It's important you have a thick batter. All you do next is dip the mincemeat sandwiches into the batter and carefully place them into the hot fat, a few at a time so that the pan is not crowded. The doughnuts will cook on one side only, so after 1–2 minutes turn them over with a slotted spoon, making sure it's golden on the cooked side. Continue to cook for another minute or so until completely golden brown. Remove from the pan with a slotted spoon and drain on kitchen paper. Continue with the remaining doughnuts. Dust the doughnuts with caster or icing sugar and serve.

Variations

Of course, how could I forget the classic jam doughnut? Well, this recipe suits just about any flavour you want. Just follow the same method, first making a jam, marmalade, lemon curd, apple, plum, raspberry, apricot – the flavours can just go on and on – domed sandwich and fry in the same way.

Mincemeat Doughnuts.

Christmas Pudding Parfait

This recipe has been designed to help you use up that half pudding we all have left after Christmas lunch – making it the perfect dish for New Year's Eve. As an extra advantage if you have guests, the pudding can, of course, be made a day or two in advance. The parfait can be made and moulded in a terrine mould or poured into individual ramekins – either looks really good. Serve the individual soufflés, or a couple of slices from the larger parfait on a plate. Dust around the outside with icing sugar and cinnamon and maybe decorate with a sprig of holly or some chocolate shavings to finish. You could even trickle a little maple syrup over the top – how does that sound? I'm also giving you a recipe for Rum or Cognac Sabayon, which goes very well with both versions. This needs to be made and served at the last minute.

SERVES 6–8

6 egg yolks	450 ml (15 fl oz) double cream
175 g (6 oz) caster sugar	4 egg whites
350 g (12 oz) Christmas Pudding	
(see p.179), chopped into small dice	

For the Rum or Cognac Sabayon

2–3 egg yolks	2–3 tablespoons rum or cognac
50–75 g (2–3 oz) caster sugar	

Line a 900 g (2 lb) terrine mould or loaf tin with greaseproof paper to make the parfait easier to turn out. Alternatively, tie a collar of greaseproof paper around the outside of 8 × 150 ml (5 fl oz) ramekin dishes with string or elastic bands.

To make the parfait, whisk together the egg yolks and sugar over a pan of warm water until the mix trails off the whisk in thick ribbons. Lightly whisk in the Christmas pudding, then leave to cool. Lightly whip the cream and fold into the cold Christmas pudding mix. Whisk the egg whites until they form stiff peaks, then fold into the mix. The parfait can now be poured into the prepared mould or ramekins and set in the freezer. The parfait will take a few hours to freeze.

To make the sabayon, mix all the ingredients together in a bowl sitting on a pan of hot water until the mix trails off the whisk in thick, light ribbons. The sabayon should almost hold a peak.

Now all you have to do is spoon some on to plates with the parfait, or serve it separately with the soufflés.

Chocolate Scotch Pancakes

These are really easy to make and cook. If you're not sure about the chocolate (after all, there are plenty of chocolate puds in this book!) the cocoa can simply be replaced with 50 g (2 oz) of self-raising flour. The beauty of sweet scotch pancakes is how much scope you have with them. From afternoon teas to a full dessert. The choice is yours! A good warm Coffee Anglaise (Fresh Custard) Sauce (see p.246) can be served with them or perhaps some clotted cream.

SERVES 6

175 g (6 oz) self-raising flour	2 eggs
50 g (2 oz) cocoa	100 g (4 oz) caster sugar
25 g (1 oz) unsalted butter	A pinch of salt
150 ml (5 fl oz) milk	Butter or oil for frying

Sift together the flour and cocoa. Melt the butter and whisk into the milk with the eggs, sugar and pinch of salt. You now have 750 ml ($1\frac{1}{4}$ pints) of chocolate scotch pancake batter.

To cook the pancakes, heat a thick-bottomed pan or griddle and brush with butter or oil. The batter can now be spooned, using a tablespoon, into the pan allowing one spoon per pancake. These will only take approximately 2–3 minutes before turning over. To help the timing for turning, small bubbles will appear on the surface. This tells you they are ready to turn. Once turned, cook for 2 minutes before removing from the pan. In a large pan, 4–6 pancakes can be cooked at the same time. To keep them warm while you are cooking the rest of the batter, simply wrap in a warm tea towel. You should have about 18 in all. The pancakes are now ready to eat.

Variation

For a dessert, I like to slice bananas and totally cover each pancake. These can now be heavily dusted with icing sugar and then caramelized under a grill or with a gas gun. You now have crunchy bananas on top of chocolate pancakes. Finish them with clotted cream and they are a treat!

Fruit Shortcake Biscuits

These biscuits have always been a favourite of mine, so I thought why not make some of my own? These can be used just as a basic biscuit or served with a pudding or ice-cream. There are also many combinations with this recipe: for example, chocolate chips can be added for some delicious chocolate and fruit cookies. The mix can also be made into small or large biscuits and even into small petits fours. *Of course by leaving out the currants and zest you'll have just a good shortcake biscuit.*

MAKES about 16 biscuits

50 g (2 oz) caster or icing sugar, sifted	1 egg yolk (optional)
100 g (4 oz) unsalted butter, diced	175 g (6 oz) plain flour, sifted
50 g (2 oz) currants	Caster sugar or icing sugar for dusting

If using caster sugar, beat it with the butter until soft and creamy. If using icing sugar, this can simply be creamed in by hand. The currants or any other flavour (such as the grated zest of a lemon or orange, see below) can now be added to the butter. An egg yolk can also be added to enrich the mix. If using, add the egg to the butter. Gently work in the flour. Any overworking will spoil the light crumbly texture. Shape the dough into a cylinder about 6 cm (2½ in) in diameter and 9 cm (3½ in) long, wrap in clingfilm and chill for 1 hour.

Pre-heat the oven to 200°C/400°F/gas 6. Lightly grease a baking sheet.

Cut the chilled dough into 15–20 discs about 2 mm thick, or roll out 2 mm thick and cut out with fluted rings. Lay the dough on the baking sheet and bake in the pre-heated oven for about 4 minutes until golden. If you are dusting with caster sugar, remove the biscuits from the oven after 4 minutes, sprinkle with caster sugar and cook for a further 1 minute. If you are using icing sugar, simply dust the cooked biscuits with icing sugar.

Variations

If you have creamed the mixture and it has become quite soft, this can be piped on to a greased baking tray with a fluted piping tube. These biscuits will obviously be thicker and fewer in quantity. They will take twice as long to cook. If it's small piped *petit four* biscuits, they will only need 5–6 minutes cooking time.

This recipe will also work with many other flavours. The finely grated zest of 1 lemon or orange (or even both!) or lime added to this mix will give you lovely shortbread biscuits with rich citrus flavours.

I also like to make poppy seed biscuits. These can be made by toasting a tablespoon of poppy seeds to release their flavour and adding them to the flour when mixing the biscuits together.

Clockwise from top: Lemon Shortcakes and Fruit Shortcakes (see opposite), Hazlenut Meringue Biscuits (p.236), thin Shortcakes (see opposite), Maple and Walnut Biscuits (p. 242), (centre) Poppy Seed Shortcakes (see above).

Hazelnut Meringue Biscuits

These biscuits eat very well with ice-creams. They are also very quick and easy to make. The mix is basically a meringue mix with the addition of flour, butter and hazelnuts. Once the biscuits have been piped on to the silicone paper, chopped hazelnuts or raisins/currants can be sprinkled on before cooking. Also, finely grated orange zest can be added to the mix before piping to give another flavour. All of these are optional extras, so here's the basic recipe.

MAKES about 24 biscuits

4 egg whites
100 g (4 oz) caster sugar
25 g (1 oz) plain flour, sifted

75 g (3 oz) ground hazelnuts
15 g ($\frac{1}{2}$ oz) unsalted butter, melted

Pre-heat the oven to 150°C/300°F/gas 2. Line a baking tray with silicone paper or lightly greased greaseproof paper.

Whisk the egg whites and sugar together until stiff. Gently fold in the flour. Add the ground hazelnuts and melted butter and mix carefully. This mix can now be piped on to silicone paper using a plain 1 cm ($\frac{1}{2}$ in) tube, into fingers approximately 7.5 cm (3 in) long. These can now be gently smoothed over and baked in the pre-heated oven for 30 minutes. Once cooked, leave to cool a little, carefully lift from the tray with a palette knife and leave to cool completely before storing in an airtight container.

Oatmeal and Parmesan Biscuits

These biscuits eat very well with cheese. I like to cut them no bigger than 2.5 cm (1 in).
This makes them just the right size for cheese bites. Herbs can also be added to this
recipe, a teaspoon of chopped parsley, sage or both work very well.

MAKES about 40 large or 80 small biscuits

275 g (10 oz) plain flour
A pinch of baking powder
25 g (1 oz) oatmeal
50 g (2 oz) porridge oats
A good pinch of salt

5 tablespoons freshly grated Parmesan
100 g (4 oz) unsalted butter
1 egg
5 tablespoons milk

Pre-heat the oven to 200°C/400°F/gas 6. Grease a baking tray or line with silicone paper.

Work together all the dry ingredients, using 1 tablespoon of Parmesan, with the butter. Beat the egg into the milk and mix with the rest of the dough. Roll out the dough thinly and cut with a 2.5–5 cm (1–2 in) cutter. Lay the discs on the baking tray. Sprinkle each biscuit with a little more Parmesan. Bake in the oven for about 10 minutes until golden brown. Leave to cool and the biscuits are ready to serve.

LEFT *Raisin Focaccia (see p.240) with Home-made Cherry Jam (see p.249)*
BELOW *Oatmeal and Parmesan Biscuits (see p.237)*

Raisin Focaccia

This recipe is really a basic focaccia bread with the addition of raisins that have been previously soaked in brandy. Focaccia is an olive bread that can be sweetened or eaten savoury. This recipe can have the raisins left out and simply be finished with sea salt or fresh herbs or both! I like to serve this as toast made on an open grill or barbecue with a pâté or maybe sautéed foie gras (that's a real treat!).

It really does make a good and interesting alternative to serve this with a pâté as a starter with home-made chutney. The sweet flavour of raisins that have been soaked in brandy takes away the raw alcohol flavour and, in fact, the brandy just lifts the raisin taste.

For this recipe I am using fresh yeast, but soaked dried yeast can be used, simply making up the quantity required. It's worth making two loaves as the bread freezes so well.

The first thing to do is soak the raisins. I like to make sure plenty are added, so that every slice has enough to capture the flavour. You don't have to soak them; or you can choose other liqueurs or spirits. Calvados works very well with the addition of grated apple to the recipe, or grated orange zest and Grand Marnier. The loaf can then be sliced, dusted with icing sugar and grilled to be used as a base for a pudding: perhaps hot crispy orange focaccia served with home-made orange ice-cream or chocolate mousse. Here's the recipe, before I get carried away with more ideas!

MAKES 2 × 675 g (1½ lb) loaves

For the Raisins

225 g (8 oz) raisins   250 ml (8 fl oz) brandy or liqueur

For Stage 1

2 teaspoons fresh yeast   2 eggs
2 tablespoons caster sugar   200 g (7 oz) strong plain flour, plus
200 ml (7 fl oz) lukewarm water   extra for kneading

For Stage 2

425 g (15 oz) strong plain flour   1 ½–2 tablespoons olive oil
2 teaspoons salt   Beaten egg to glaze
50 g (2 oz) unsalted butter, softened

Pour enough brandy or liqueur over the raisins just to cover them. These should now be left to soak for 24 hours. To speed up the process, put both ingredients into a pan and bring to a simmer. Once up to a simmer, remove from the heat and allow to cool before using. This will swell the raisins and help them take on the brandy.

For stage 1, bind together the yeast and sugar. Mix with the water and eggs. Add the mix to the flour and beat to a smooth batter. Cover the bowl with clingfilm and leave the batter to ferment for about 30 minutes.

The second stage is best done with an electric mixer, but you can work by hand. Place the batter in the mixing bowl and add the flour and salt from stage 2. Mix for 3 minutes on a low speed or 6 minutes by hand. Now add the butter and olive oil and mix for a further 4 minutes on medium speed or 8 minutes by hand. Now it's time to add the soaked raisins (including any excess brandy) and simply mix for a further 1 minute or 5 minutes by hand. Now the mix is complete and should be covered and left to prove in a warm place for 30–40 minutes.

Once proved, knock the mix back by hand and either separate into greased loaf tins or roll into oval shapes (cooking as free loaves), then re-prove for another 30–40 minutes.

Pre-heat the oven to 200°C/400°F/gas 6.

Bake the loaves in the pre-heated oven for 20 minutes. Brush with beaten egg and return to the oven for a further 5 minutes or so to give a shiny glazed finish. The bread can now be left to cool before serving. As you can see (p.238) there are plenty of shapes to choose from, and you can finish by serving with Home-made Cherry Jam (p.249).

Maple Syrup and Walnut Biscuits

These biscuits have a wonderful texture and nutty flavour. They eat well on their own or with dessert dishes such as the Caramel Cream Pots (see p.206).

MAKES 40–50 biscuits

225 g (8 oz) unsalted butter, softened
75 g (3 oz) caster sugar
1 egg yolk
1 tablespoon maple syrup

250 g (9 oz) plain flour plus extra
    for dusting
75 g (3 oz) walnuts, chopped

Cream together the butter and sugar. Add the egg yolk and maple syrup. Fold in the flour, binding to a dough. Add the chopped walnuts. Using a little more flour, mould the mixture and roll it into cylinder-shaped logs about 18 cm (7 in) long and 5 cm (2 in) diameter. Wrap in clingfilm and put in the fridge. The mix can now be left to chill and will last for several days in the fridge.

Pre-heat the oven to 180°C/350°F/gas 4.

To cook, simply cut the log into 5 mm ($\frac{1}{4}$ in) round or oval slices and bake the biscuits on a greaseproof papered tray in the pre-heated oven for 10–12 minutes until the biscuits become slightly golden around the edges. Once cooked, the biscuits can be either dusted with caster sugar or left as they are.

Quick Home-made Lemonade

This simple recipe goes well with the Maple Syrup and Walnut Biscuits (above), Griddled Scones (opposite) with summer fruits and cream, or any other home-made biscuits.

MAKES 1 pint

2 whole lemons (includiing pith and
    peel), chopped

4 tablespoons caster sugar
1 pint water

Blitz all the ingredients in a blender until the lemon is puréed and then push through a sieve. To serve, simply pour on ice.

Griddled Scones

These are great to eat at Sunday teatime with butter, jam and cream. They take no time to make and very little to cook, and we all seem to have these ingredients sitting in our cupboards. This recipe will give you about 20 scones – of course, you can halve the recipe, but I'm sure you'll eat 20! The other plus is the great variety of scones you can make by adding other flavours. I like to make them with the finely grated zest of lemon, but orange or lime can also be used. Chopped apple can be added with a pinch of cinnamon, or you can even make them Christmassy with glacé fruits. They can also be eaten as a pudding with fresh fruits and creamy sabayons. Just imagine lightly warmed raspberries tossed in butter and sugar sitting on the scones with a sweet White Wine Sabayon (see p.245) or griddled strawberries that have thick whipped cream spooned over the top. What do you think? Delicious, I hope! And one last tip – eat them as quickly as possible!

MAKES 20 scones

450 g (1 lb) self-raising flour plus extra for dusting
A pinch of salt
50 g (2 oz) unsalted butter plus extra for frying
50 g (2 oz) lard

175 g (6 oz) currants or sultanas
Grated zest of 1 lemon
100 g (4 oz) caster sugar
2 eggs
2–4 tablespoons milk

Sift and mix the flour with the salt, then rub in the butter and lard. Fold in the currants or sultanas, lemon zest and sugar. Make a well in the centre and add the eggs and milk, mixing in the flour to form a soft dough. The dough can now be rolled out to 1 cm ($\frac{1}{2}$ in) thick and cut into 6 cm ($2\frac{1}{2}$ in) rounds, or moulded by hand into 1 cm ($\frac{1}{2}$ in) thick individual scones.

Heat a frying-pan or griddle and cook over a medium heat in a little butter for 4–5 minutes on each side until golden brown. The scones are now ready to eat.

Variation

The scones eat very well with Griddled Strawberries. These are simply strawberries cooked on a grill plate, giving a slightly bitter, burnt tinge that is then balanced with a dusting of icing sugar. I like to eat these with Crème Fraîche (p.275) to finish the dish.

For a richer scone, use 100 g (4 oz) unsalted butter instead of 50 g (2 oz) lard.

Chocolate Sabayon – and Others

This is a rich sauce but much lighter than many basic chocolate sauces. The sabayon is very tasty and goes with so many dishes: the Pear and Hazelnut 'Pasties' (see p.188) is a great example. It also eats well as a topping for home-made ice-cream or sorbet served in a glass. The other option is to treat the sabayons as zabaglione and serve any of the flavours with a home-made biscuit or two.

For the chocolate recipe, I am using some whole eggs to hold the mix together and prevent the quantity from breaking down. Adding the melted chocolate to a basic sabayon recipe will always reduce the volume. So the addition of whole eggs will obviously help hold the complete volume. I also like to add rum, coffee liqueur or Cointreau to the mix for extra flavour.

MAKES about 450 ml (15 fl oz)

2 egg yolks	3–4 tablespoons chocolate liqueur,
2 eggs	Cointreau, coffee or rum (or water)
50 g (2 oz) caster sugar	100 g (4 oz) good quality plain
	chocolate, melted

This can be made by two methods. Both need a pan of simmering water to help thicken the eggs and hold their volume.

The first method is to mix the egg yolks, whole eggs, sugar and liquid together and add the melted chocolate. This can now be whisked over the pan of water until at least doubled in volume.

The second method is to simply whisk the egg yolks, whole eggs, sugar and liquid over the pan to a sabayon stage (at least doubled), and then slowly pour in the melted chocolate while still whisking. After 1–2 minutes of continual whisking the warm sabayon is ready.

Both methods will give you the same result: a thick light chocolate creamy sabayon.

The sabayon can be continually whisked until it reaches room temperature. If you do this, the sabayon will keep for a little longer, although if it gets too cold, the chocolate will become thicker and lose that lovely soft, light texture, so the sabayon is really at its best when made and served immediately.

Note

It is important that the bowl does not come into contact with the simmering water.

Sabayon

Sabayons go particularly well with ice-creams or can be spooned over tarts or flans and then made into a golden brown glaze under the grill. This recipe is different from the original; you can add almost any flavours and tastes to suit the dessert of your choice.

MAKES 900 ml (1½ pints)

4 egg yolks	6 tablespoons liqueur, such as
50 g (2 oz) caster sugar	Champagne, white wine, brandy,
	Irish whiskey, Marsala, fruit liqueurs
	(pear, apple, raspberry, etc.), coffee

All these flavours can be made using the same method, whisking together the yolks with the sugar and the flavour of your choice over a pan of simmering water, which will at least double the volume.

Note

The sabayon can also be made in an electric mixer. To help it along, simply warm the bowl first.

Variations

There are many other flavours that can be added to a sabayon. To this quantity, the grated zest of 1–2 lemons, oranges or limes can be added, replacing half the Champagne or white wine with the juice of the fruit. This will give you a very strong citrus fruit sabayon that will eat well with a steamed sponge or maybe ice-cream of the same flavour. Of course, all of the flavours can be mixed. A good home-made or bought raspberry ice-cream or sorbet with a lemon sabayon is delicious. Or perhaps chocolate ice-cream or steamed sponge with orange sabayon or a good white chocolate ice-cream with lime sabayon.

To add even more taste to these, three-quarters of the liquid, wine or flavouring can be replaced with lemon curd or good orange marmalade to make it even more flavoursome.

Reducing the sugar content to 25 g (1 oz) and adding 3–4 tablespoons of golden syrup with 1–2 tablespoons of water gives you an amazing golden syrup sabayon. Eating that spooned over a golden syrup steamed sponge instead or as well as custard is wonderful.

Another variation is to make an Irish whiskey sabayon to go with the Rich Stout Cake on page 198 to make a unique Stout Cake Pudding (see Variation on p.200).

Anglaise (Fresh Custard) Sauces

This recipe can act as a base for so many different flavours. You must only ever serve it warm, not boiled, as that would scramble the egg yolks in the cream mix. The fresh vanilla is optional and can be omitted when using other flavours.

MAKES 750 ml (1½ pints)

8 egg yolks	300 ml (10 fl oz) milk
75 g (3 oz) caster sugar	300 ml (10 fl oz) double cream
1 vanilla pod, split (optional)	

Beat the egg yolks and sugar together in a bowl until well blended. Split and scrape the insides of the vanilla pod, if using, into the milk and cream and bring to the boil. Sit the bowl over a pan of hot water and whisk the cream into the egg mix. As the egg yolks warm, the cream will thicken to create a custard. Keep stirring until it coats the back of a spoon. Remove the bowl from the heat. The custard can now be served warm or stirred occasionally until it cools.

Variations

For Lemon Custard Sauce, add the pared rind of 2 lemons, not the pith, to the milk and cream when heating, then leave it in the mix throughout the cooking process. Once the custard has thickened, add the juice of a lemon and taste. If the lemon flavour is not strong enough, simply add more lemon juice to taste. Strain the custard through a sieve.

For Orange Custard Sauce, add the pared rind of 2 oranges to the milk and cream when heating, then cook as for the basic recipe. Orange juice will not be used in this recipe. To lift the flavour of the sauce, try adding a few drops of Cointreau or Grand Marnier.

For Rum Custard Sauce, add some rum to taste at the end of cooking the vanilla custard. A few spoonfuls of desiccated coconut could also be added to the milk to make a Rum and Coconut Custard Sauce.

Coffee Custard Sauce can be made by replacing the vanilla pod with 2 teaspoons of good freshly ground coffee and cooking as for the vanilla recipe. Once the coffee custard has completely cooled, just strain through a sieve to remove any excess granules.

Chocolate Custard

This is a must for chocolate fans – well, in fact, everybody. It eats so well with a steamed sponge, or you can even use this recipe to make a chocolate bread and butter pudding. Leave out the currants or raisins and replace them with cherries and what do you have, Black Forest bread and butter pudding. Just imagine finishing that with lots of grated chocolate melted over the top. So there you are, another recipe in this introduction – that's the fun of cooking, it's just non-stop with endless combinations.

If you do decide to have a go at the chocolate bread and butter pudding, then you will not need to cook out the custard as I am with this recipe. Simply pour the custard mix over the bread and leave to soak for 20–30 minutes before cooking in a water bath in a pre-heated oven at 180°C/350°F/gas 4 for 20–30 minutes until thickened and just set. If you're not keen on cherries, then simply spread orange marmalade on the bread and have a chocolate, orange bread and butter pudding.

MAKES 750 ml (1¼ pints)

300 ml (10 fl oz) milk
300 ml (10 fl oz) double cream
50 g (2 oz) good quality plain chocolate,
    grated (or 100g (4 oz) for real
    chocolate lovers), grated

8 egg yolks
75 g (3 oz) caster sugar

Heat the milk and cream together, then pour a quarter over the grated chocolate. Once the chocolate has melted, add the remaining cream. Beat together the egg yolks and sugar and pour the warm chocolate cream over, stirring as it's poured. This can now be strained through a sieve and then cooked in a bowl over a pan of hot water until thickened, stirring all the time. The custard is now ready to serve. Or you can chill and set it to be used for a dark chocolate trifle.

Rich Chocolate Sauce

Chocolate sauce is very easy to make. However, when using chocolate, it's important never to overheat it as this will leave you with a grainy texture. Instead, what we are after is a rich thick glossy sauce. Here are a couple to choose from. The first has been taken from More Rhodes Around Britain *and the second, well, this must be the ultimate thick chocolate sauce. It's very rich and tasty. It can be thinned out with the addition of more cream or milk.*

EACH recipe makes about 450 ml (15 fl oz)

For the Chocolate Sauce

225 g (8 oz) good quality plain chocolate   40 g ($1\frac{1}{2}$ oz) caster sugar
150 ml (5 fl oz) milk   25 g (1 oz) unsalted butter (optional)
75 ml (3 fl oz) double cream

For Ultimate Chocolate Sauce

225 g (8 oz) good quality plain chocolate   25 g (1 oz) unsalted butter
250 ml (8 fl oz) double cream

To make the first sauce, melt the chocolate in a bowl over a pan of hot water. Boil the milk and cream with the sugar and stir into the chocolate. Stir in the butter, if using, while the sauce is warm to enrich the flavour and texture. Allow the sauce to cool.

To make the ultimate chocolate sauce, melt the chocolate with the cream in a bowl over a pan of hot water and once warm, add the butter. You now have a thick rich chocolate sauce. This is best eaten cold or just warm. Trying to serve this as a hot sauce will simply separate the butter.

Home-made Cherry Jam or Sauce

This recipe is almost the same process as for the Home-made Blackberry Jam in More Rhodes Around Britain. *This cooks and stays slightly softer, making it into a thick cherry sauce with all the texture left in the cherries. I like to add the finely grated zest of an orange to give a slightly bitter taste against the cherries. The recipe is lovely to eat as a jam or can be used to accompany many puddings: the American Cheesecake (see p.202) is one and why not just spoon it over ice-cream?*

If you intend to eat the jam within a month, simply allow the jam to cool a little then spoon into warmed jam jars, leave to cool, then chill. The sugar and pectin are both natural preservatives so the jam will keep perfectly fresh.

If you want to store the jam for longer, you'll need to sterilize the jars. To do this, place them in a large pan, cover them with cold water, then bring the water to the boil and boil for 10–15 minutes. Carefully remove and dry the jars. Once the jars are filled, covered and sealed, you can sterilize them further by sitting the jars on a wire rack or cloth in a large pan and almost covering with water. Bring the water to the boil, then boil again for 10–15 minutes. Remove from the pan, dry and cool. Stored in a cool, dark place, the jam will last almost indefinitely until opened.

MAKES about 675 g (1½ lb)

900 g (2 lb) cherries, stoned	Juice of 1 lemon or orange
450 g (1 lb) sugar with pectin	Finely grated zest of 1 orange (optional)

Warm and sterilize, if necessary, 2 or 3 jam jars. The glass should be warm before adding the hot jam to prevent the jars from shattering.

Place the stoned cherries, sugar, citrus juice and zest, if using, into a preserving pan or large pan and bring to a simmer. Increase the heat to a rolling boil and skim off any impurities rising to the top. Keep the jam boiling for 4–5 minutes, then remove from the heat, again skimming any impurities. You will now have a rich, deep, red shiny jam with the cherries still holding some shape and texture. Leave the jam to cool slightly, then spoon it into the warm jars, seal and label.

Puff Pastry

This recipe is useful for all kinds of desserts and for savoury pies as well. It's very satisfying to make your own pastry, but you can resort to the chill cabinet of your supermarket if you are short of time.

MAKES about 450 g (1 lb)

225 g (8 oz) unsalted butter
225 g (8 oz) strong plain flour
A pinch of salt

150 ml (5 fl oz) cold water
A few drops of lemon juice

Cut off 50 g (2 oz) of the butter, melt it then leave it to cool. The remaining block should be left out to soften. Sift the flour and salt together into a large bowl and make a well in the centre. Pour the water, lemon juice and cooled, melted butter into the well in the flour and gently fold in the flour to make a pliable dough. Wrap in clingfilm and allow to rest in the fridge for 20 minutes.

On a lightly floured board, roll out the pastry from four sides, leaving a lump in the centre. The dough should look like a crossroads. The remaining block of butter should have softened to a similar texture to the dough; it should be easy to roll without melting but not so hard that it will break the pastry.

Sit the butter on the centre lump of the dough (A) and fold over each pastry flap (B). Pat the pastry into a 30 × 15 cm (12 × 6 in) rectangle and leave to rest in the fridge for 10–15 minutes.

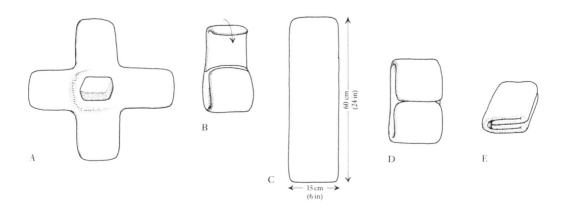

Roll out the pastry lengthways to make it double in length to about 60 cm (24 in) but the same width (C). Fold in both ends to the centre (D) and then fold once more (E). This is called a double turn and should be completed a further three times, each time rolling out the same length and then finishing with a double turn. Always roll with the folded edge on the left, and always leave to rest for 20–30 minutes in the fridge before each turn. The pastry should now be rested for at least 30 minutes in the fridge before using.

To make pastry cases, butter and flour your chosen moulds. This quantity is more than enough to line a 25 cm (10 in) ring or 6×10 cm (4 in) rings. Roll out the pastry thinly and line the moulds, leaving any excess turned over the sides of the rings. Sit the cases on a baking sheet and rest in the fridge for 10–15 minutes. Line with greaseproof paper and baking beans or rice. Bake in a pre-heated oven at 200°C/400°F/gas 6 for 15–20 minutes until the pastry is baked and golden. Remove the paper and beans, then use a sharp knife to trim off any excess pastry around the tart cases, leaving the cases in the pastry rings.

Shortcrust Pastry

This recipe really is short – in ingredients and in texture! This quantity is really the minimum amount to make for a good texture. The beauty of this pastry is that it freezes so well to be used later.

MAKES about 400 g (14 oz)

175 g (6 oz) unsalted butter, chopped   4 tablespoons cold water
240 g ($8\frac{1}{2}$ oz) plain flour

Rub the butter into the flour until a crumble effect is achieved. Add the water and fold in very lightly until the pastry is only just beginning to form and bind. Press the pastry between two sheets of clingfilm. The pastry will have a marbled look; this indicates just how short the pastry is going to be. Leave the pastry to rest for 20 minutes before rolling and using.

Sweet Shortcrust Pastry

To make a sweet pastry, simply add 50 g (2 oz) of sifted icing sugar to the flour.

Frangipane (Almond Paste)

Some recipes are absolute classics that can be used in so many dishes. Well, this is certainly one of them. One thing I have found with this recipe is just how versatile it is. It's the mix that's used in Bakewell Tart. I'm using it in a few recipes in this book; Plum and Almond Slice (see p.190), Cherry and Almond Tart (see p.184) and Pear and Hazelnut 'Pasties' (see p.188). If you want smaller quantities, simply halve or quarter the recipe.

MAKES ABOUT 900 g (2 lb)

225 g (8 oz) unsalted butter   50 g (2 oz) plain flour
225 g (8 oz) caster sugar   4 eggs
175 g (6 oz) ground almonds

Cream together the butter and sugar until almost white. Mix together the ground almonds and flour. Add an egg at a time to the butter and sugar mixture, sprinkling in a handful of the almond and flour at the same time. This helps the butter and sugar cream to accept the eggs. Once all the eggs have been added, just continue to fold in the remaining almond and flour mix. The frangipane is now ready to use.

Variations

Here are some alternatives for many different dishes.

The first alternative is to replace the ground almonds with ground hazelnuts. The mix cooks and tastes just as moist but with a definite hazelnut flavour.

To lift this or the almond mix, chopped hazelnuts, almonds or walnuts can be added (about 50 g (2 oz) to this recipe). This gives you a completely different texture. It's also good, sometimes, to add a mix of two or even all three nuts. The variations are just unlimited: raisins, currants or sultanas can also be added. I like to soak them in brandy or a liqueur before adding them to the mix for extra taste. This, of course, can become a fruit and nut bakewell tart, pasty or flan by using some of each.

As I have mentioned in the Pear and Hazelnut 'Pasties' recipe, chocolate chips can be used, giving yet another texture. Why not have a fruit, nut and chocolate chip tart topped with Chocolate Ganache (see p.168). Of course, the frangipane can be made into a chocolate almond/hazelnut frangipane quite simply by omitting 25 g (1 oz) of the flour and replacing it with 25 g (1 oz) of cocoa. Also, to make it even richer 25–50 g (1–2 oz) of fresh grated plain chocolate can be added.

So now you'll have a chocolate frangipane mix that can also have all of those other flavours added, the nuts, chocolate chips, currants, etc., or all together. That would make a very rich and tasty chocolate fruit and nut tart!

Another – yes there's more! – combination is to add the finely grated zest of 2 oranges to the chocolate frangipane mix and bake this in a tart case and then completely cover the top with orange segments. These can now be heavily dusted with icing sugar and glazed under the grill or with a gas gun for a brûlée-style topping. Whichever way you glaze the tart, cover the pastry edge with thin foil all the way round to prevent it catching and burning.

The grated orange zest can also be used in the basic frangipane mix (orange and hazelnut works particularly well) so if you fancy having a go at this recipe why not spread the pastry base with orange marmalade first (that will go very well with the chocolate and orange mix) and then top with the orange mix and bake. This can now be finished with the Chocolate Ganache (p.168), already mentioned, on top or with the brûléed orange segments and served with Chocolate Sabayon (see p.244) or Rich Chocolate Sauce (see p.248). Prunes or Medjool dates also go very well in a plain frangipane or with chocolate orange or lemon.

Now about the lemon, here's yet another combination. Use the finely grated zest of 2–3 lemons, and you can also add the juice of one lemon to the mix. The lemon will also work with the chocolate frangipane; it's surprising how well lemon goes with chocolate.

I feel that an almond or hazelnut lemon frangipane tart eats very well when completely topped with berries. Fresh raspberries, blackcurrants or summer fruits make a good topping and also a fruit jam or lemon curd can be spread in the pastry first for extra taste. Brush the fruits with a jam syrup (1 tablespoon of jam to 2 tablespoons of water, boiled together) or perhaps top the whole tart with a meringue or lemon-flavoured meringue and glaze in a hot oven. Also the fruits, raspberries for example, can be placed in the tart sitting on top of the jam or lemon curd and then topped with the sponge and baked. This gives you a nice surprise when you cut into the flan. Remember, all of these can be made into individual tarts. A nice chocolate frangipane tart filled with chopped nuts and raisins, topped with mint and chocolate chip sorbet. How does that sound?

I think that's enough combinations for now …

Stocks, Sauces and Pickles

The stocks and sauces here include some of my classic recipes, but Vegetable Stock (see p.259) is new and gives a full, almost aromatic flavour.

ABOVE *There's always time for a joke in the kitchen – so long as it's not on a plate!*
LEFT *Dressings give any dish a great depth of flavour.*

There are plenty of recipes for dressings, which I have used both in starters and some main courses. A good dressing can give a lighter finish to a dish than a sauce, still with a great depth of flavour. The Mustard Dressing (see p.271) and the Red Wine Dressing (see p.274) are probably used the most. They have a loose mayonnaise consistency and a taste that lends itself to so many of the other flavours.

There are relishes here too, a chutney and even a recipe for Home-made Tomato Ketchup (see p.266)! And with that one you may not have 57 varieties but you'll make it at least 57 times!

Gary creating a recipe; you can see the finished result on p.29.

Apple and Mustard Seed Relish

This recipe came from chatting with two of my chefs, Stuart and Wayne. We were looking for a relish that would eat well hot or cold with the Pork and Black Pudding Patties (see p.90). Basically, we had left a patty to go cold and then tasted and realized it eats like a coarse pork pâté or terrine. Hence we needed a relish to go with it. Apples must be the most classic accompaniment to pork and mustard also works very well. The relish was born. And if you try the relish with the Pork and Black Pudding Patties and the Irish Potato Cakes (see p.151), you'll have the perfect combination for a main course. This is one of the beauties of cooking, finding recipes almost by accident. We've since found that the relish eats well warm with the hot patties as well. So we have a double bonus! The relish keeps very well refrigerated for up to one month.

MAKES about 1 kg (2 lb)

8 dessert apples, peeled, cored and cut into 5 mm (¼ in) dice
175 g (6 oz) caster sugar
200 ml (7 fl oz) white wine vinegar
3 tablespoons white mustard seeds,
plunged in boiling water and soaked for 2 hours
Finely grated zest of ½ lemon
2 onions, finely chopped
Salt and freshly ground black pepper

Place the sugar, vinegar, drained mustard seeds and lemon zest in a pan and bring to the boil, then boil until reduced by half. Add the chopped onions and simmer for 3–4 minutes until softened. Add the diced apple and cook for 4–5 minutes until soft but just holding its shape. Drain off the liquid, leaving the apples and onions to one side, then continue to boil and reduce by half again. Once reduced, remove from the heat and return the apple mix to the syrup. Season with salt and pepper and leave to cool. The relish is now ready to use or can be served warm.

Chicken Stock

Chicken stock is one of our most important bases. It's used for most soups and many cream sauces. It's also very simple to make. I'm sure your local butcher will help you out with some chicken bones. If not, then cook a boiling fowl with vegetables in water and you will have a tasty stock and the bird to eat as well. You'll need a large stock pot, about 8.5 litre (15 pint) capacity, but if you don't have one you can easily reduce the quantities. (For information on ready-made alternatives, see p.262.)

MAKES 2.25 litres (4 pints)

2 onions, chopped
2 celery sticks, chopped
2 leeks, chopped
25 g (1 oz) unsalted butter
1 garlic clove, crushed

1 bay leaf
1 sprig of fresh thyme
A few black peppercorns
1.8 kg (4 lb) chicken carcasses, chopped
3–4 litres (6 pints) water

In a large stock pot, lightly soften the vegetables in the butter without colouring. Add the garlic, bay leaf, thyme, peppercorns and chopped carcasses. Cover with the cold water and bring to a simmer, skimming all the time. Allow the stock to simmer for 2–3 hours. Strain through a sieve. The stock is now ready to use and will keep well chilled or frozen.

Vegetable Stock

I have included a basic recipe for vegetable stock in my last two books. However, the joys of cooking are the endless variations that recipes can have and this one is no exception. I think this gives you a fuller vegetable flavour, helped by the acidity of the lemon and bite from the pink peppercorns. It can be made without the carrots to give you a whiter stock, but the carrots do tend to give a sweetness to the finished flavour. I like to use this stock for vegetarian risottos and other braised dishes.

Makes 1.2 litres (2 pints)

225 g (8 oz) carrots (optional)	1 sprig of fresh thyme
2 onions	1 teaspoon coriander seeds
4 celery sticks	1 teaspoon pink peppercorns
2 leeks, white part only	$\frac{1}{2}$ lemon, sliced
1 fennel bulb	1.5 litres (2 $\frac{1}{2}$ pints) water
1–2 courgettes	A pinch of salt
1 bay leaf	Vegetable oil

All the vegetables should first be cut into 1 cm ($\frac{1}{2}$ in) dice.

Warm the vegetable oil in a pan, then add all the diced vegetables along with the herbs, coriander, peppercorns and lemon. Cook without colour for 8–10 minutes, allowing them to soften slightly. Add the water with a good pinch of salt and bring to a simmer. Once at simmering point, cook for 30 minutes without a lid. During this time the stock should have reduced, increasing the flavour and depth. The stock can now be strained through a sieve, leaving you with about 1.2 litres (2 pints). If you find there is more than this quantity, then simply boil to reduce. You can also reduce if you find that the flavour is not full enough.

Fish Stock

To make a good fish stock, you'll need a friendly fishmonger. Turbot and sole bones produce the best stock, giving a good, full taste and clear jelly-like finish. The stock is good for poaching fish and for making fish soups and sauces. (For information on ready-made alternatives, see p.262).

MAKES about 2 litres (3½ pints)

1 large onion, sliced	1 bay leaf
1 leek, sliced	6 black peppercorns
2 celery sticks, sliced	900 g (2 lb) turbot or sole bones, washed
50 g (2 oz) unsalted butter	300 ml (10 fl oz) dry white wine
A few fresh parsley stalks	2.25 litres (4 pints) water

Sweat the vegetables in the butter without colouring. Add the parsley stalks, bay leaf and peppercorns. Chop the fish bones, making sure there are no blood clots left on them. Add them to the vegetables and continue to cook for a few minutes. Add the wine and boil to reduce until almost dry. Add the water and bring to a simmer. Allow to simmer for 20 minutes, then strain through a sieve. The stock is now ready to use, or to store for a few days in the fridge.

Veal or Beef Stock or *Jus*

This stock does take a long time to make, but it really is worth making and so satisfying. It will give you great sauces and, of course, will store well in the freezer. It is best started in the morning, which will allow the stock to cook throughout the day. Ask your butcher for a few beef or veal trimmings to make the stock. (For information on ready-made alternatives, see p.262).

MAKES about 5 litres (9 pints) of stock or
900 ml (1½ pints) *jus*

3 onions, halved
2–3 tablespoons water
2.25 kg (5 lb) veal or beef bones
225 g (8 oz) veal or beef trimmings
225 g (8 oz) carrots, coarsely chopped
3 celery sticks, coarsely chopped

1 leek, chopped
3–4 tomatoes, chopped
1 garlic clove, halved
1 bay leaf
1 sprig of fresh thyme

Pre-heat the oven to 120°C/250°F/gas ½.

Lay the onion halves flat in a roasting tray with the water. Place in the pre-heated oven and allow to caramelize slowly until they have totally softened and coloured. This process will take 1–2 hours. The sugars in the onions will slowly cook and give a wonderful taste. Put the onions on one side.

Increase the oven temperature to 200°C/400°F/gas 6.

Place all the bones and trimmings in a roasting tray and roast for about 30 minutes until well coloured. Roast the chopped carrots and celery in another roasting tray for about 20 minutes until lightly coloured.

When ready, add the bones, trimmings and vegetables to the onions in a large stock pan along with the leek, tomatoes, garlic, bay leaf and thyme. Fill the pan with cold water – you'll need about 5 litres (9 pints). Bring the stock to a simmer and skim off any impurities. Allow to cook for 6–8 hours, and with this you will achieve the maximum taste.

When ready, drain and discard the bones and vegetables. This is now your veal stock and you can cool it and freeze it in convenient quantities.

Alternatively, you can make a *jus* from the stock. Allow the liquid to boil and reduce down to about 900 ml (1½ pints), skimming occasionally. The stock should be thick and of a sauce consistency. Make sure that you taste all the time during reduction. If the sauce tastes right but is not thick enough, thicken it lightly with cornflour mixed in water. (Of course, I do hope that won't be necessary!) You now have a veal *jus*, a classic sauce.

Alternative Stocks and Sauces

Making fresh stocks at home is not always possible, so here are a few good commercial alternatives I have tried, which make some of my recipes a little easier.

Fish and Chicken Stocks

Alternatives to these can be found in the chill cabinet of most quality supermarkets. They are sold in plastic tubs each containing about 284 ml (9–10 fl oz). The beauty of these is they taste great, they have good colour and jelly texture, and they are sold as stocks ready to use. They really are the best I've found, but if you can't get hold of them there are also some good quality stock cubes.

Beef and Veal *Jus*

In the basic recipe, these start out as stocks and then for use in other recipes they are reduced to a sauce consistency. I've found a sauce which will cut out all of this, and is an instant *jus* to use as a base sauce in many of the recipes asking for veal or beef *jus*. Madeira Wine Gravy or White Wine Gravy are both made by Crosse & Blackwell in their Bonne Cuisine range, and should be available in just about every supermarket or good grocery shop. The Madeira flavour gives good body and, when made, it has a lovely glossy finish. My only advice is to mix them with 600 ml (1 pint) of water instead of 300 ml (10 fl oz). This way, when slow-braising or stewing, there's room for reduction and they won't become too thick.

Other Sauces and Ingredients

Another sauce I found, also in the Bonne Cuisine range, is their Hollandaise Sauce. If you are unsure about making hollandaise, give this version a try; it's so easy.

There's only one other small suggestion. If you don't have any chillies, use the chilli sauce made by Maggi. It's sold in bottles and can be added slowly to taste.

As for dried pastas and ready-made pastry, all varieties can easily be found in local shops. If you're lucky enough to have a good delicatessen nearby, then perhaps buy your pasta there; it's often made on the premises.

Tomato Stock

This must be one of the easiest stocks to make — it doesn't even have any cooking time! I use this recipe for a vegetarian tomato and spinach risotto. The tomato stock on its own is very strong due to the acidity of the tomatoes. I normally mix half tomato with half vegetable stock to gives you a good balance between the two.

For the best results and maximum quantity, it's best to use overripe tomatoes. These can be bought from the local greengrocer at a very good price and also have a lot more flavour. I often have tomatoes sitting in my fridge for far too long, so this is a great way of using them up. You can just make some from a few tomatoes and freeze it until you have enough to make the risotto (see p.120).

MAKES 450 ml (15 fl oz)

1.5–1.75 kg (3–4 lb) overripe tomatoes   600 ml (1 pint) Vegetable Stock
(see p.259)

Quarter the tomatoes and blitz in a food processor or liquidizer with the stock. Now just leave to drain in a sieve or muslin cloth. Do not push through a sieve or you will be left with a tomato coulis. It's only the water that we want to use. This is best left overnight in the fridge or in a cool place. In the morning, the natural waters will have completely drained off, giving you a good strong tomato stock.

Note

For totally natural tomato stock, simply blitz them on their own and leave to drain in the sieve or cloth. This will give you pure tomato water that can be mixed with the vegetable stock.

Cranberry Sauce with Orange

Cranberries are not always available fresh, but the frozen ones are equally good for this recipe. The shallots and port add extra flavour to this sauce but it can be made just with the fruit, juice and sugar. If you don't include them, add a little more orange juice.

MAKES ABOUT 450 g (1 lb)

1 teaspoon chopped shallots (optional)	Juice of 2 oranges
1 glass of port, about 50 ml (2 fl oz) (optional)	450 g (1 lb) fresh or frozen cranberries
	100 g (4 oz) caster sugar

Place the shallots and port, if using, in a pan and boil until reduced by half. Add the orange juice and again boil to reduce by half. Add the cranberries and sugar and simmer for 10–15 minutes, until the cranberries have softened. The sauce is now ready. It can be made up to 2 weeks in advance, kept chilled, then served hot or cold as needed. I use this sauce with the Turkey Saltimbocca recipe on p.86.

Lemon Butter Sauce

This is one of the simplest sauces. It has a silky texture and perfectly complements cod and salmon dishes in particular.

SERVES 4–6

225 g (8 oz) unsalted butter	50 ml (2 fl oz) Chicken Stock (see p.258)
Juice of 1 lemon	or Vegetable Stock (see p.259)
	Salt and freshly ground white pepper

Chop the butter into 1 cm ($\frac{1}{2}$ in) pieces and put it into a pan with the lemon juice and stock. Bring to a simmer, whisking all the time. Do not allow the sauce to boil or the butter will separate. If it is too thick, add more stock. If you like a sharper taste, add more lemon juice. Season with salt and pepper and serve immediately. To give a creamier texture, simply blitz the sauce with an electric hand blender.

Garam Masala

Garam Masala was a mixture of spices put together originally to 'spice' people up! This lifted the body and prepared you for a hard winter and work. It was quite a hot spice and helped set people's appetites in India for hot dishes. It has since become a very varied mixture of spices for different dishes, some hotter than others.

The spice mixture does not have to be used just in Indian curry dishes, it will liven up vegetarian risottos, pancakes, ratatouille, lentils and most tomato-based dishes, as well as cream and yoghurt sauces. This recipe is a combination that should suit all of these. Once made, keep in an airtight container and use when wanted. Of course, you can buy garam masala already made, but the aromatic smell and flavour when you've made it yourself is wonderful.

MAKES about 50 g (2 oz)

2 tablespoons coriander seeds	1 tablespoon black peppercorns
2 tablespoons cumin seeds	2 teaspoons cloves
1 teaspoon cardamom seeds	$\frac{1}{2}$ teaspoon freshly grated nutmeg
1 cinnamon stick	$\frac{1}{4}$ teaspoon ground mace
2 bay leaves	$\frac{1}{4}$ teaspoon ground ginger

Dry roast all the ingredients, except the nutmeg, mace and ginger, in a dry pan over a medium heat until they colour and become aromatic. Leave to cool, then add the remaining spices and grind to a powder in a coffee grinder or blender. Store in an airtight jar.

Home-made Tomato Ketchup

Tomato ketchup is a sauce we've all grown up with and will, I'm sure, continue to be popular for many years to come. For me there's one 'real' tomato ketchup and that's Heinz. However, you know me by now, I love to have a go at recipes, so this is a home-made version. If you use demerara rather than caster sugar, it will give a stronger taste. In the ingredients, a choice of three vinegars is listed. The first choice is, of course, cider, followed by white wine or the malt. One thing I'm definitely not trying to do is go into any sort of competition with that famous company but we should all try – at least once!

MAKES 600 ml (1 pint)

1 clove
1 bay leaf
½ teaspoon ground coriander
½ teaspoon ground cinnamon or 5 mm (¼ in) cinnamon stick
250 ml (8 fl oz) cider, white wine or malt vinegar
8 tablespoons demerara or caster sugar

1.5 kg (3 lb) net weight of ripe tomatoes after quartering and seeding
½ teaspoon sea salt
½ tablespoon English mustard powder
1 garlic clove, crushed
A dash of Tabasco sauce
1 tablespoon tomato purée

Tie the clove, bay leaf, coriander and cinnamon stick, if using, in a piece of muslin. Place the vinegar and sugar in a heavy-based pan and bring to a simmer. Add the tomatoes and all other ingredients and bring to the boil, stirring to prevent any sticking. Once up to the boil, reduce the temperature and simmer, stirring occasionally, for 40 minutes. Be careful the mix doesn't stick to the base of the pan. Discard the muslin bag, blitz in a food processor or liquidizer and then push the sauce through a sieve.

If you find the sauce to be loose and thin once cold, then simply re-boil and thicken with a little cornflour or arrowroot mixed to a paste with a little water, being careful not to make it too starchy. This will prevent the tomato water separating from the sauce.

Home-made Tomato Ketchup.

Tomato Dressing or Sauce

Here's another recipe I picked up in New York. It's really tasty to eat and has so many uses. Fish or meat work well with it, so anything from grilled sea bass, pan-fried or deep-fried cod to sausages, pork chops, chicken, liver, or steaks, the dressing goes with all. This is a last minute sauce that will not keep well if made too far in advance. If you haven't got the capers, then just leave them out, and if you don't have sherry vinegar just replace with half malt vinegar.

MAKES about 150 ml (5 fl oz)

2 tablespoons unsalted butter	1 tablespoon diced tomato, flesh only
1 tablespoon tomato ketchup	1 tablespoon chopped capers
3 tablespoons sherry vinegar	Freshly ground black pepper
1 tablespoon diced apple	

Melt the butter to a golden nut-brown stage. Add all the other ingredients and bring to the boil. Add a twist of black pepper and serve.

Variations

Chopped fresh herbs can be added to the sauce: parsley, tarragon and basil will all work together or on their own.

Spicy Tomato Dressing

This is a really quick and easy dressing to make. I use this recipe for salad dressings and also sometimes to add to the Sweet Pepper and Chilli Relish (see p.280). It's also a great dressing to mix with warm pasta as a vegetarian dish or to serve with grilled fish or meat. You will get the best flavour if you use half extra virgin olive oil and the other half a cheaper oil.

MAKES 500 ml (14 fl oz)

9 tablespoons tomato ketchup
120 ml (4 fl oz) white wine vinegar
3 tablespoons Worcestershire sauce
A few drops of Tabasco sauce

150 ml (5 fl oz) extra virgin olive oil
150 ml (5 fl oz) olive oil
Salt and freshly ground black pepper

Mix together the tomato ketchup, white wine vinegar, Worcestershire sauce and Tabasco sauce. Now gradually whisk in the olive oil, by hand or in a processor or liquidizer, until completely mixed. Taste and season with salt and pepper.

Variations

Extra garnishes can also be added to give a chunkier texture. Finely chopped shallots, diced tomato flesh and chopped fresh basil or tarragon all work very well.

Watercress and Herb Dressing

This is really a variation of pesto sauce, made by the same method but with a different finished taste. It is used in the recipe for Grilled Sea Trout with Soured New Potatoes and Watercress Dressing (see p.58).

MAKES about 600 ml (1 pint)

50 g (2 oz) pine nuts
150 ml (5 fl oz) olive oil (more can be
    added for a looser consistency)
1 large garlic clove, crushed
2 large bunches of watercress,
    about 175 g (6 oz)

1 bunch of fresh chervil
1 bunch of fresh tarragon
½ bunch of fresh flatleaf parsley
1 bunch of fresh coriander
1 bunch of fresh basil
Salt and freshly ground black pepper

Heat the pine nuts in the olive oil until lightly coloured. Leave to cool. It's very important to keep an eye and always stir the pine nuts while they are cooking as they over-colour and burn easily. Once cold, blitz in a food processor or liquidizer with the garlic, watercress and all the herbs until fine. Season with salt and pepper. This recipe is a cross between a dressing and a paste, so the mix must be quite thick.

Stuart's still telling that joke!

Mustard Dressing

This is a basic recipe for a simple dressing that I have used in many recipes. It's so versatile and has a creamy texture. If you have a favourite mustard – such as English, French or grain – then simply use the one of your choice.

MAKES 300 ml (10 fl oz)

4 teaspoons Dijon mustard
2 tablespoons white wine vinegar
8 tablespoons walnut oil

8 tablespoons groundnut oil
Salt and freshly ground black pepper

Whisk the mustard with the vinegar. Mix together the two oils and gradually add to the mustard, whisking all the time as you would if making mayonnaise. Once everything is thoroughly mixed, taste for seasoning with salt and pepper.

Variations

This can also be made into a herb dressing by adding a choice of chopped mixed fresh herbs, or perhaps just chopped fresh tarragon to give you a mustard and tarragon dressing that will go so well with fish or poultry.

The addition of 1–2 egg yolks mixed with the mustard and white wine vinegar will guarantee a creamy texture, almost like mayonnaise.

Hazelnut Dressing

This is a good dressing for basic salads or vegetarian dishes. It's full of flavour with the hazelnut taste that's sparked with the addition of shallots, leek and, of course, the sherry vinegar. The strength of the vinegar you use will determine the quantity you need – use just 2 tablespoons and add a little more if the flavour demands. The dressing goes very well with the Mushroom Pancake Gâteau (see p.132) as an alternative to the mushroom sauce given in the recipe.

MAKES 250 ml (8 fl oz)

4 tablespoons hazelnut oil
4 tablespoons groundnut oil
2–3 tablespoons sherry vinegar
3 teaspoons water

2 shallots, finely chopped
1 leek, finely chopped
Salt and freshly ground black pepper

Mix the oils and vinegar together and blitz in a food processor or liquidizer. Add the water and continue to blitz. Mix together the shallots and leek and add to the vinaigrette. Season with salt and pepper. The dressing is now ready to use.

Note

The leeks can be blanched very quickly in boiling water to give a richer taste and colour.

Poivre Vert Dressing

This recipe is an extra I wanted to include because it can have so many uses with many recipes, even though I haven't featured it specially anywhere in the book. It goes particularly well with the Peppered Roast Beef (see p.104) along with a good mixed salad. Or just use it as a dressing for a mixed salad.

MAKES about 200 ml (7 fl oz)

4 large shallots or 1 onion,
   finely chopped
1 tablespoon green peppercorns,
   lightly crushed
4 tablespoons brandy

6–8 tablespoons Basic Vinaigrette
   (see p.276) or Mustard Dressing
   (see p.271)
Salt

Mix the shallots with the peppercorns in a small pan and add the brandy. Bring to the boil, then boil to reduce until almost dry. Add the basic vinaigrette or mustard dressing and season with salt if needed. This can now be used as a warm or cold dressing.

Variations

When you have some roast beef, pork or lamb left over from Sunday lunch and you're having it sliced for supper, then try this dressing with it. It lifts a basic dish and makes it very special.

Red Wine Dressing

This recipe is very similar to the Mustard Dressing (see p.271). The difference is, of course, the vinegar. In this dressing, the wine vinegar is the predominant taste. It's best to use a good quality, thick, red wine vinegar, possibly aged. If you manage to find a Cabernet Sauvignon vinegar it really will be the best. Failing that, simply use a standard red wine vinegar; the dressing will still work but not have quite the strength. It may be a good idea to take a quantity of the vinegar and boil it to reduce it by half in order to strengthen the taste. Anyway, just like the Mustard Dressing, this can be used for many dishes and salads.

MAKES 175 ml (6 fl oz)

3 teaspoons Dijon mustard	6 tablespoons walnut oil
3 tablespoons red wine vinegar	6 tablespoons groundnut oil
(preferably Cabernet Sauvignon)	Salt and freshly ground black pepper

Whisk together the mustard and red wine vinegar. Mix the two oils together and gradually whisk into the mustard and vinegar a drop at a time, as you do when making mayonnaise. Once the ingredients are well blended, season with salt and pepper. The dressing is now ready.

Mayonnaise

Home-made mayonnaise is so easy to make and much tastier than bought alternatives.

MAKES about 600 ml (1 pint)

3 egg yolks	Salt and freshly ground white pepper
1 tablespoon malt, white wine or	300 ml (10 fl oz) olive oil
balsamic vinegar	1 teaspoon hot water
A pinch of English or Dijon mustard	A few drops of lemon juice (optional)

Whisk the egg yolks, vinegar, mustard and seasonings together, then slowly add the olive oil, whisking continuously. When all the oil has been added, finish with the hot water and correct the seasoning. A few drops of lemon juice can be added to enhance the taste.

Crème Fraîche

What is crème fraîche and how does it taste? These are questions that we have all asked at some point. Crème fraîche is a cream product that has been brought to Britain by the French. Most French chefs, and now British ones too, use crème fraîche to finish sauces, savoury and sweet.

Crème fraîche has many qualities and advantages that we shouldn't ignore. Firstly, any double or clotted creams have an average fat content of 48 per cent, whereas crème fraîche has just 30 per cent. In fact, a new, light crème fraîche has just 15 per cent fat.

Classic cream is made by standing fresh milk for hours until thick cream forms on the surface. Crème fraîche is made by pasteurizing the milk before the cream has formed. This then separates to cream and skimmed milk. The cream is pasteurized again to give it extra life on the shelf. Selected lactic cultures are then added which give it acidity. The crème fraîche is now ready to use.

It's great to add to sauces at the last moment, giving them a silky, sharp finish. It also works well as an alternative salad dressing just mixed with a squeeze of fresh lemon juice. And next time you make a curry, finish it at the last moment with a couple of spoons of crème fraîche – you'll love it!

As for puddings, either just eat it as it is or add some icing sugar and spoon on to your strawberries. It also works very well when mixed with fruit sauces or coulis to give you a sweet/sharp sauce. Maybe try one to go with my Mincemeat Doughnuts (see p.230).

Here's a recipe for how to make your own crème fraîche.

MAKES 450 ml (15 fl oz)

150 ml (5 fl oz) buttermilk	300 ml (10 fl oz) double cream

Mix the two together, cover and leave at room temperature for 8–10 hours until thick. This home-made version is thinner than the one you will find on the supermarket shelves. The crème fraîche should be chilled immediately. It will keep for 5–6 days.

Soured Cream, Lime and Mint Yoghurt

This recipe is an extra flavour that suits many different dishes. In this book it's used in Steamed Halibut on Spinach (see p.64) and also the Grilled Calves' Liver Steak with Spiced Potatoes (see p.106). It also works very well in a cucumber salad accompanying a curry or mixed into mashed or forked potatoes to go with grilled fish or perhaps roast lamb against its mint flavour. Of course, one of the beauties is just how easy it is to make.

MAKES 350 ml (12 fl oz)

150 ml (5 fl oz) soured cream
150 ml (5 fl oz) natural yoghurt
Juice of 1 lime

1 heaped teaspoon chopped fresh mint
Salt and freshly ground black pepper

Whisk all the ingredients together and season with salt and pepper. The flavour of mint will increase the longer it is kept. I told you it's easy!

Basic Vinaigrette

Once made, this basic dressing can sit in your fridge and be used at any time and for any dish you might fancy. The vinegar just gives a slight sweetness to the taste.

MAKES 600 ml (1 pint)

300 ml (10 fl oz) extra virgin olive oil
   (French or Italian)
300 ml (10 fl oz) ground-nut oil
25 ml (1 fl oz) balsamic vinegar
1 bunch of fresh basil
$\frac{1}{2}$ bunch of fresh tarragon

3–4 sprigs of fresh thyme
12 black peppercorns, lightly crushed
3 shallots, finely chopped
2 garlic cloves, crushed
1 bay leaf
1 teaspoon coarse sea salt

Warm the olive and ground-nut oils together. Place all the remaining ingredients into a 750 ml (1$\frac{1}{4}$ pint) bottle. Pour the oil into the bottle and close with a cork or screw top. For best results, leave to marinate for a week, which will allow the flavours to enhance the oils. To help the dressing along, shake the bottle once a day. Taste for seasoning, drain and use.

Home-made Mint Sauce/Reduction

This is probably the easiest recipe in the book. The quantity here will probably last for at least three meals to go with lamb. Of course, whenever vinegar is being used it preserves, so just keep this in a jar chilled and it will last indefinitely. Apart from just using this as a straight mint sauce I use it as an enhancer for gravies and other sauces. If you are making a lamb stew, just a teaspoon of this will lift all the flavours. Or, as in the gravy for the loins of lamb (see p.96), I've used 5 teaspoons to create a mint gravy flavour. So the next time you have roast lamb for lunch why not just make a rich mint gravy to go with it.

MAKES 120 ml (4 fl oz)

150 ml (5 fl oz) malt vinegar
½ bunch of fresh mint

1½–2 heaped tablespoons demerara sugar

The mint for the sauce needn't be picked or chopped, just left as it is.

Pour the vinegar on to the mint in a small pan. Add the demerara sugar. Using 2 tablespoons will make the sauce sweeter, which some tastebuds prefer. Simply bring to the boil and cook for a few minutes until the sugar has dissolved. Leave to cool. Once cool, it's best to leave all the mint leaves in and simply bottle or jar. This will then increase the mint flavour. In time the mint will completely discolour; this is only due to the acidity of the vinegar.

To make into mint sauce, strain some of the vinegar through a tea strainer and add chopped fresh mint.

Gremolata

Gremolata is an Italian recipe that is normally used to serve with a veal osso bucco. Basically it's a mix of crushed garlic, zest of lemon and chopped flatleaf parsley. This is then sprinkled over the finished dish.

With this recipe you can do exactly that, or just sprinkle it over a chicken noodle dish to give it some extra zing. However, I'm turning this into a gremolata butter. This keeps well chilled or frozen. It can be used to toss with new potatoes or vegetables, or to melt over grilled fish or meat. You can leave out the parsley, if you prefer, and simply add it to any finished dish. I also use the gremolata in a recipe with cod (see p.59), worked into mashed potatoes.

MAKES ABOUT 250 g (9 oz)

2–3 garlic cloves, crushed
Juice and finely grated zest of 3 large
 lemons
225 g (8 oz) unsalted butter

Salt and freshly ground black pepper
$\frac{1}{2}$–1 bunch of fresh flatleaf parsley,
 chopped

Mix the crushed garlic with the chopped lemon zest and lemon juice either with a fork or in a food processor. Mix into the butter and season with salt and pepper. Add the parsley and stir well. The gremolata butter is now ready and the flavours work themselves into the butter.

Parsley and Tarragon Butter

If you're looking for something to excite a grilled or pan-fried fish dish, then try cooking it with this butter, or placing a tablespoonful on top and just melting it under the grill. It's packed with flavour and works a treat. It also eats very well with pasta dishes. The butter will keep for 1–2 weeks in the fridge and almost indefinitely if frozen.

MAKES 350 g (12 oz)

2 tablespoons very finely chopped onions
About 3 tablespoons dry white wine
225 g (8 oz) unsalted butter
1 teaspoon Dijon mustard

2 heaped tablespoons chopped fresh parsley
1½ heaped tablespoons chopped fresh tarragon
Freshly ground black pepper
Juice of 1 lemon

Place the chopped onions in a small pan and just cover with white wine. Boil to reduce until almost dry. Leave to cool. Soften the butter in a bowl, then add the mustard, parsley and tarragon. Season with a twist of pepper and the lemon juice. Mix in the now cold onions and the butter is made.

It's best to shape and roll the butter in clingfilm, giving you a cylinder shape. This can now be cut into rounds to garnish your fish, pasta or chicken dish.

Sweet Pepper and Chilli Relish

This dish is a variation of the piccalilli recipe from my first book, Rhodes Around Britain. *It has most of the basic flavours but a few changes to give it quite a different taste.*

I like to serve this relish with pork or chicken – its sort of sweet-and-sour flavour works well with either. One of the best pork dishes to serve it with is a Confit of Pork Belly (see p.92). To go with this relish, I cook the belly in small starter portions and just serve the relish warm, with the confit sitting on top. The pork is so tender it can be carved with a spoon and eaten with the lovely flavour of sweet peppers.

Makes approximately 3 × 600 ml (1 pint) kilner jars

300 ml (10 fl oz) white wine vinegar	2 large onions
150 ml (5 fl oz) malt vinegar	225 g (8 oz) caster sugar
A pinch of chopped dried chilli	15 g ($\frac{1}{2}$ oz) ground turmeric
4 red peppers	25 g (1 oz) English mustard powder
2 yellow peppers	2 tablespoons cornflour
2 fresh red chillies	2 tablespoons chilli oil

Boil the two vinegars with the chopped dried chilli. Leave to cool for 30 minutes. Strain through a sieve, discarding the chilli.

Cut the peppers in half lengthways and remove the core and seeds. Cut the pepper halves into 1 cm ($\frac{1}{2}$ in) strips. The red chillies must also be halved and have all core and seeds removed. Now chop the chillies very finely. Once the chillies have been chopped, always remember to wash the chopping board and your hands well. This is because the strong chilli flavour will linger, and the oil will irritate your lips or eyes if you have any on your hands.

The onions should be halved and cut into 1 cm ($\frac{1}{2}$ in) thick slices. Make sure the onions are broken down from thick pieces into individual strips. Mix the sugar with the dry ingredients and moisten with a little of the cold boiled vinegars. Boil the remaining vinegar and whisk on to the mix. Now return to the heat and bring to the boil and cook for 3 minutes.

While this is cooking, warm the chilli oil in a frying-pan. Fry the peppers and onions very quickly in the hot pan, allowing them to colour around the edges. They must not be allowed to stew as this will make them soft. Add the chopped red chillies to the onions at the last moment.

The next stage is to simply pour the hot thick sauce over the peppers, onions and chillies in a bowl and leave to cool. The relish is now ready and should be ladled into sterilized jars and kept chilled for up to 1 month. This eats very well cold or served warm.

Variations

A basic salad dressing or olive oil can be added to loosen the sauce into a dressing. It also eats very well when mixed with Spicy Tomato Dressing (see p.269) or for a quicker alternative just add 2–3 tablespoons of tomato ketchup to the recipe for a sweeter, richer taste.

Pesto Sauce

Pesto can be bought in supermarkets, but here is a simple version to make yourself.

SERVES 4

50 g (2 oz) pine nuts
150 ml (5 fl oz) olive oil
1 small garlic clove, crushed

1 large bunch of fresh basil (2 bunches
will give you a richer taste)
Salt and freshly ground black pepper

Simply colour the nuts lightly in the olive oil, then allow to cool. Add the crushed garlic, basil and a pinch of salt and pepper and blend to a purée. This is now ready and can be kept for 2–3 days in the fridge.

Note

In this recipe I am not using Parmesan, which is normally found in pesto sauce. If you prefer the Parmesan version, simply add 25–50 g (1–2 oz) freshly grated cheese to the ingredients.

Plum Chutney

This chutney eats very well with hot or cold meats, especially roast duck with vegetables, as well as pâtés and terrines.

MAKES 2 × 600 ml (1 pint) kilner jars

900 g (2 lb) plums, stoned and quartered
900 g (2 lb) cooking apples, peeled, cored and roughly chopped
2 onions, sliced
2 garlic cloves, crushed
600 ml (1 pint) malt vinegar

175 g (6 oz) golden syrup
175 g (6 oz) demerara sugar
2 teaspoons salt
2 tablespoons pickling spices in a muslin bag

Simmer the plums, apples, onions and garlic in the malt vinegar for 20 minutes. Add the syrup, sugar, salt and the muslin bag of spices and continue to simmer for $1\frac{1}{2}$ hours, stirring occasionally. The mixture should be quite thick.

Should the chutney seem to be a little liquid, then taste the liquor and check for seasoning. It may taste perfectly seasoned. If this is the case then it cannot be reduced any further as it will become too strong. If there is still room for reduction, then increase the heat and cook for another 30 minutes or so until thicker. If the flavour is too strong to reduce further, simply pour off some of the excess liquor. This can then be mixed with a *jus* or gravy to make a rich plum sauce. Once cooked, store in the jars and keep refrigerated.

Piccalilli Sauce

By the way, here's a great way of making piccalilli into a sauce. This has been taken from the basic recipe in my first book, Rhodes Around Britain, *but I'm giving it to you again just in case you haven't got that one yet!*

The ingredients have been halved and this will still give you at least 1.2 litres (2 pints) of sauce.

It keeps very well in the fridge for up to 1 month and eats well as a salad dressing or mixed with mayonnaise as an alternative prawn or crab cocktail sauce. I also use it as a straight piccalilli sauce to go with smoked fish such as trout, mackerel or eel; and salad; or hot fish or shellfish kebabs.

MAKES 1.2 litres (2 pints)

1 small or $\frac{1}{2}$ large cauliflower, cut into 1 cm ($\frac{1}{2}$ in) pieces
1 large onion, cut into 1 cm ($\frac{1}{2}$ in) dice
50 g (2 oz) salt
300 ml (10 fl oz) white wine vinegar
150 ml (5 fl oz) malt vinegar
A pinch of chopped dried chilli

175 g (6 oz) caster sugar
25 g (1 oz) English mustard powder
15 g ($\frac{1}{2}$ oz) ground turmeric
2 tablespoons cornflour
$\frac{1}{2}$ cucumber, peeled, seeded and cut into rough 1 cm ($\frac{1}{2}$ in) dice

Mix the cauliflower with the onion and sprinkle with the salt, then leave in a sieve or colander to stand for 24 hours.

Boil the two vinegars together with the chilli, then leave to cool and stand for 20 minutes before draining and discarding the chillies. Mix the sugar with the remaining dry ingredients. Pour a quarter of the vinegars on to the dry ingredients and mix. Re-boil the remaining vinegar and pour and whisk on to the sugar mix. Bring back to a simmer and cook for 3 minutes.

Mix the salted cauliflower and onions with the cucumber and pour the hot sauce over the vegetables. Leave to cool. Once cool, blitz in a food processor or liquidizer until fine, then push through a sieve to leave you with a smooth, rich piccalilli sauce. Store in airtight jars.

Note

If you don't want the sauce, then just leave it as a pickle.

Index

Page numbers in *italic* refer to the illustrations